God's Ambassadors

Studies on the Westminster Assembly

Series Editors
John R. Bower and Chad Van Dixhoorn

VOLUMES IN SERIES:

❖ *Covenanted Uniformity in Religion: The Influence of the Scottish Commissioners on the Ecclesiology of the Westminster Assembly*
Wayne R. Spear

❖ *Divine Rule Maintained: Anthony Burgess, Covenant Theology, and the Place of the Law in Reformed Scholasticism*
Stephen J. Casselli

THE WESTMINSTER
ASSEMBLY PROJECT

God's Ambassadors

THE WESTMINSTER ASSEMBLY
AND THE REFORMATION OF THE
ENGLISH PULPIT, 1643–1653

Chad Van Dixhoorn

Reformation Heritage Books
Grand Rapids, Michigan

God's Ambassadors
© 2017 by Chad Van Dixhoorn

All rights reserved. No part of this book may be used or reproduced in any manner whatsoever without written permission except in the case of brief quotations embodied in critical articles and reviews. Direct your requests to the publisher at the following addresses:

Reformation Heritage Books
2965 Leonard St. NE
Grand Rapids, MI 49525
616-977-0889 / Fax 616-285-3246
orders@heritagebooks.org
www.heritagebooks.org

Printed in the United States of America
17 18 19 20 21 22/10 9 8 7 6 5 4 3 2 1

Names: Van Dixhoorn, Chad B., author.
Title: God's ambassadors : the Westminster Assembly and the reformation of the English pulpit, 1643-1653 / Chad Van Dixhoorn.
Description: Grand Rapids, Michigan : Reformation Heritage Books, 2017. | Series: Studies on the Westminster Assembly | Includes bibliographical references and index.
Identifiers: LCCN 2017008708 (print) | LCCN 2017010591 (ebook) | ISBN 9781601785343 (hardcover : alk. paper) | ISBN 9781601785350 (epub)
Subjects: LCSH: Westminster Assembly (1643-1652) | Preaching—England—History—17th century. | Church renewal—England—History—17th century. | England—Church history—17th century.
Classification: LCC BX9053 .V36 2017 (print) | LCC BX9053 (ebook) | DDC 262/.552—dc23
LC record available at https://lccn.loc.gov/2017008708

For additional Reformed literature, request a free book list from Reformation Heritage Books at the above regular or e-mail address.

For my parents,
because they made me listen to sermons.

Sumus inter homines angeli; inter illos qui regi regum inserviunt.
—Oliver Bowles, assembly member

Albeit thy preacher bee a man of no very extraordinary gifts, yet in regard he is an Ambassadour sent from God unto thee if he faithfully (though perhaps not so eloquently) deliver his message unto thee thou oughtst to heare it; and honour him for his Masters sake. His feete cannot but seeme beautifull to thee if they be shod with the Preparation of the Gospell of Peace.
—Daniel Featley, assembly member

The mayne errand of the ambassadour of the gospel, is that sinners would be converted to God; the guilty sinner that knowes he deserves nothing but wrath, when he heares of an ambassador, he expects to heare something from an angry God.... [but] the gospel is called the gospel of peace.
—A student's notes on a sermon preached by Anthony Tuckney, assembly member

Contents

Foreword xi
Series Preface xiii
Preface xv
Acknowledgments xix
Abbreviations xxiii
Note on Dating xxv

Part I: Blind Guides and Scandalous Ministers
1. The Call for Reform 3
2. The Road to Reform 17
3. "Democratick Annarchie" 31

Part II: A Reforming Assembly
4. Purifying Pulpits: Assembly Examinations 41
5. The Pastor's Office: Assembly Debates 63
6. Ordaining Preachers: The Directory for Ordination 73
7. Directions for Preaching: The Directory for Public Worship 89

Part III: In Theory
8. On Preachers: Godly, Trained, and Ordained 105
9. On Preaching: The Word of God as the Ordinary
   Means of Grace 121
10. On Preaching: Audible and Visible Words 129
11. On Preaching: Christ-Centered Sermons 143
12. On Preaching: Christ-Centered Exegesis 151
13. On Study and Style: "The Spirit's Working" 163
14. Conclusions 171

CONTENTS

Epilogue.. 179

Appendix 1: The Duties of a Minister....................... 181
Appendix 2: The Directory for Ordination.................. 185
Appendix 3: The Subdirectory for Preaching 193

Bibliography... 197
Index.. 211

Foreword

It is a rare privilege to introduce a book by saying with a fair degree of confidence that its author is a leading world authority on his subject and that its theme fits into a larger area in which he is almost certainly *the* leading world authority. But in the case of *God's Ambassadors* this is simply the fact of the matter. Dr. Chad Van Dixhoorn has already put both scholarship and the church in his debt through his groundbreaking researches into the discussions, debates, and writings of the divines of the Westminster Assembly. Now he puts us further in his debt with this absorbing exploration of their views on preaching—a subject very close to his own heart.

Anything that Dr. Van Dixhoorn writes in this area commands our attention. But this book carries a special attraction because it combines a double interest of the author—the assembly proceedings on the one hand, and the topic of preaching on the other. It should, therefore, engage the interest not only of scholars but also of those who make the most use the documents of the assembly (or should!), namely ministers and preachers. Not only those who trace their theological and ecclesiastical roots back through the Westminster Assembly, but all who have an interest in and concern for preaching should find in *God's Ambassadors* much to inform, stimulate, and cause reflection.

There are at least three particular reasons for commending this book. The first is that it combines scholarly excellence with practical relevance. Students of the Westminster Assembly are always eager for further insight into the thinking of the divines. Preachers worth their salt always want to grow in their calling to "preach the word" (2 Tim. 4:2). Indeed, if Paul's exhortation to Timothy is anything to go by, such growth is not only a great desideratum but also an apostolic command (1 Tim. 4:15)!

A second reason is the sheer fascination of the narrative itself. Here we read the hair-raising, eye-popping descriptions of scandalous ministers given by John White, a member of both Parliament and the assembly. Here too, we are given indications of the corruption of a pastoral system, reminding us why Milton's *Lycidas* described some ministers in acidic terms: "Blind Mouths, The hungry sheep look up and are not fed." We are left in little doubt about the impoverished levels to which much preaching had sunk in seventeenth-century England. It is in this context that we are introduced to the deeply serious discussions of men whose chief goal in life was to communicate the gospel of Christ. And in passing we are given occasional glimpses of the idiosyncratic—such as the inclusion of the autopsy report in the published version of Simeon Ashe's funeral sermon for Jeremiah Whitaker!

A third reason is that this new study should help to highlight what must rank as one of the most stimulating two-page summaries of preaching thus far published in the English language—namely, the Directory on Preaching set within the larger Directory for the Public Worship of God. It would be rash to suggest that its counsels should be followed in the twenty-first-century church *au pied de la letter*. Nevertheless, it provides a series of extremely valuable and thought-provoking principles for modern preachers to take into account and make contemporary as they address congregations and audiences 350-plus years further on in the church's life.

There is so much else here. To improve the level of preaching in the country was only one of the assembly's multifaceted concerns. But it gave rise to many sessions of discussion and doubtless much private conversation (how fascinating it would be if every assembly member had followed the Scots commissioner Robert Baillie's example and left behind volumes of *Letters and Journals*!). In addition, a group of men who conducted five thousand ministerial examinations must have something to say to the modern church about the prerequisites for and principles governing gospel ministry. All this and more *God's Ambassadors* brings before the reader, along with a veritable cornucopia of quotations that both interest and instruct. All in all, *God's Ambassadors* provides stimulation on every page.

Authors as well as actors sometimes find themselves "typecast." I can imagine that Dr. Van Dixhoorn might well want to be set free from our hopes and expectation that he will continue to publish on the Westminster Assembly and its work. But if he were to move on to pastures new, in common with many others for whom the assembly and its productions have long been of interest, I for one would be glad that in this work he has chosen to write on the much overlooked theme of the divines' discussions of preaching. So in addition to the rare privilege of introducing a book by a world authority, it is also a pleasure to be able to suggest to readers that the pages that follow contain a feast of good things.

Sinclair B. Ferguson

SERIES PREFACE

Studies on the Westminster Assembly

The Westminster Assembly (1643–1653) met at a watershed moment in British history, at a time that left its mark on the English state, the Puritan movement, and the churches of England, Scotland, and Ireland. The Assembly also proved to be a powerful force in the methodization and articulation of Reformed theology. Certainly the writings of the gathering created and popularized doctrinal distinctions and definitions that—to an astonishing degree and with surprising rapidity—entered the consciousness and vocabulary of mainstream Protestantism.

The primary aim of this series is to produce accessible scholarly monographs on the Westminster Assembly, its members, and the ideas that the Assembly promoted. Some years ago, Richard Muller challenged post-Reformation historians to focus on identifying "the major figures and… the major issues in debate—and then sufficiently [raise] the profile of the figures or issues in order to bring about an alteration of the broader surveys of the era." This is precisely the remit of these Studies on the Westminster Assembly, and students of post-Reformation history in particular will be treated to a corpus of material on the Westminster Assembly that will enable comparative studies in church practice, creedal formulation, and doctrinal development among Protestants.

This series will also occasionally include editions of classic Assembly studies, works that have enjoyed a shaping influence in Assembly studies, are difficult to obtain at the present time, and pose questions that students of the Assembly need to answer. It is our hope that this series—in both its new and reprinted monographs—will both exemplify and encourage a newly invigorated field of study and create essential reference works for scholars in multiple disciplines.

John R. Bower
Chad Van Dixhoorn

Preface

Ordered, That the Committee for plundered Ministers shall nominate none to any Parsonage or Benefice, but such as shall first be examined by the Assembly of Divines, or any Five of them, and approved of by Certificate under their Hands: And the Assembly is desired to appoint a Committee to this Purpose.
—House of Commons, July 27, 1643

This day the Assembly of Divines sate at Westmin. for the trial of severall persons which are to be admitted into the Ministry.
—*The Moderate Publisher of Every Daies Intelligence,*
March 24, 1653

Of all the tasks assigned to the Westminster Assembly, only one persisted from 1643 to 1653: the examination of preachers.[1] Every other endeavor of the assembly was either completed or abandoned as the years dragged on. But from its first weeks to its final days, apprehensive preachers waited in the antechamber next to the Jerusalem Chamber for their turn to be interviewed and assessed by the "Assembly of Divines," as the last great Protestant synod was known in the seventeenth century. These ministers and ministerial candidates hoped to leave the abbey with a certificate of approval to enter a new pastoral charge. And they knew that it would be granted only if they approximated the kind of preacher that could play a part in the assembly's attempted reformation of the English church.

The Westminster Assembly, summoned by the Long Parliament (1640–1653) in an attempt to reform the Church of England, was obsessed with pulpit reform. The gathering not only conducted thousands of examinations

---

1. See *Journal of the House of Commons, 1643–1644* (London: His Majesty's Stationery Office, 1802), 3:183 (July 27, 1643); and *The Moderate Publisher of Every Daies Intelligence,* Num. 90, Friday, March 18 to Friday, March 25, 1652 (London, 1652), 771. The inclusive term "preachers" is employed because it encompasses both candidates for the ministry and ordained ministers.

of preachers (expending more sessions scrutinizing men than drafting documents!) but it also had a lot to say about preaching and the importance of the pulpit in the texts that it eventually produced.

In the hope of properly tuning expectations, it needs to be said at the outset that this book is not a history of the assembly. The assembly and its work have recently attracted interest from ecclesiastical, historical, theological, and literary quarters, and there have been efforts in the past few decades to highlight one or another aspect of the gathering's work or to produce materials and tools for a do-it-yourself history.[2] Nonetheless, my "life" of the assembly as a whole is still in progress, and it will require more pages than this volume provides.

Nor is this an account of the personalities impacted by the assembly. The stories of those who were examined by the assembly are not told here. The parliamentary archives in Westminster Palace and accounts of clergy by John Walker and Edmund Calamy (1600–1666) are the proper starting places for such biographical or metabiographical pursuits.[3]

---

2. Recent publications on the Westminster Assembly have focused on the synod's members, its theology, texts, or some aspect of its work; these will complement and enrich a new history of the Westminster Assembly but offer no direct competition to it. For studies of assembly members, see J. Coffey, *Politics, Religion and the British Revolutions: The Mind of Samuel Rutherford* (Cambridge: Cambridge University Press, 1997); and Y. Cho, *Anthony Tuckney (1599–1670): Theologian of the Westminster Assembly* (Grand Rapids: Reformation Heritage Books, forthcoming). For recent theological studies, see R. Letham, *The Westminster Assembly: Reading Its Theology in Historical Context* (Phillipsburg, N.J.: P&R, 2009); J. V. Fesko, *The Theology of the Westminster Standards: Historical Context and Theological Insights* (Wheaton, Ill.: Crossway, 2014); and C. B. Van Dixhoorn, *Confessing the Faith: A Reader's Guide to the Westminster Confession of Faith* (Edinburgh: Banner of Truth, 2014). For a textual study, see John Bower, *The Larger Catechism: A Critical Text and Introduction* (Grand Rapids: Reformation Heritage Books, 2010). For recent studies of the assembly, see H. Powell, *The Crisis of British Protestantism: Church Power in the Puritan Revolution, 1638–44* (n.p.: Manchester University Press, 2015); C. B. Van Dixhoorn, "Politics and Religion in the Westminster Assembly and the 'Grand Debate,'" in *Alternative Establishments in Early Modern Britain and Ireland: Catholic and Protestant*, ed. R. Armstrong and T. O'hAnnrachain (Manchester: Manchester University Press, 2013), 129–48; and C. B. Van Dixhoorn, "The Westminster Assembly and the Reformation of the 1640s," in *The Oxford History of Anglicanism*, vol. 1, *Reformation and Identity c.1520–1662*, ed. A. Milton (Oxford: Oxford University Press, 2017). Even the account available in the first volume of C. B. Van Dixhoorn, ed., *The Minutes and Papers of the Westminster Assembly, 1643–1652* (Oxford: Oxford University Press, 2012) serves more as a narrative map for the assembly's minutes and a key to the gathering's papers than a proper history. It is a guide for those who are able to construct parts of the assembly's history for themselves.

3. A. G. Matthews, ed., *Walker Revised: Being a Revision of John Walker's "Sufferings of the Clergy during the Grand Rebellion, 1642–1660"* (Oxford: Oxford University Press, 1948); A. G. Matthews, ed., *Calamy Revised: Being a Revision of Edmund Calamy's Account of the Ministers and Others Ejected and Silenced, 1600–1662* (Oxford: Oxford University Press, 1934); T. Richards, *A History of the Puritan Movement in Wales from the Inception of the Church at Llanfaches in 1639 to the Expiry of the Propagation Act in 1653* (London: The National Eisteddfod Association,

PREFACE   xvii

This book is also not a study of sermons—another topic that has not been ignored in recent years. The most comprehensive study of sermons is no doubt Hughes Oliphant Old's magisterial survey *The Reading and Preaching of the Scriptures in the Worship of the Christian Church*.[4] The most creative study may be Arnold Hunt's, who thought to ask how people heard sermons; his book also offers one of the best surveys of the study of early modern preaching.[5] Work on early modern sermons themselves continues apace with coordinated seminars drawing together experts in English literature, divinity, and history. Although the weight of recent studies may tilt toward those preachers best recognized and promoted by the Church of England's establishment, there is hardly any real imbalance in the past century of sermonic study. The preaching of puritans has been plundered for every historical and theological purpose and has been the subject of innumerable learned essays, monographs, and theses. Admittedly, even treatments of so narrow a subject have often been too wide-ranging, without clearly defined subject samples or controlled chronological boundaries; still other studies have exalted individual preachers or single sermons as representatives of their contemporaries or as exemplars for present preachers to imitate with minimal modification. I mention this not because I am suiting up for a battle nor because *God's Ambassadors* is posturing to supplant these prior descriptions of preaching. I am simply noting the currents of scholarship characteristic especially in theological seminaries and flagging the fact that this study will take a different tack.

On a positive note, I happily admit that this book can afford to be concise precisely because of the huge amount of work already accomplished by other historians of preaching. It is also brief because of my own insistence that this be first and foremost a focused study of the Westminster Assembly and its members. It is only secondarily, and hypothetically, a sampling or particular instance of a larger movement of reinvigorated puritan preaching during the English civil wars and interregnum.

So what is this book? I have often asked that question myself, for it offers neither a straightforward narrative nor a thematically organized collection of essays. The best that I can offer by way of answer is that it is a three-legged treatment of the Westminster Assembly's endeavor to reform the pulpit in England from 1643 to 1653. It first tells the story of the puritan

---

1920); C. E. Surman, ed., *The Register-Booke of the Fourth Classis in the Province of London, 1646–1659* (London, 1953); Parliamentary Archives, Main Papers of the House of Lords.

4. Seven volumes have appeared under the general title of *The Reading and Preaching of the Scriptures in the Worship of the Christian Church* (Grand Rapids: Eerdmans, 1998–2010).

5. A. Hunt, *The Art of Hearing: English Preachers and Their Audiences, 1590–1640* (Cambridge: Cambridge University Press, 2010); see esp. his masterful introduction.

quest for a reformation in preachers and preaching and how the Westminster Assembly tried to play a part in that movement. The second part of the book looks at the assembly's own reform efforts, tracing its debates and exploring key documents on the subject of preaching. These chapters both highlight disagreements within the assembly's ranks and showcase the gathering's collective plan for the church going forward. The final cluster of chapters seeks to set forth the rationale behind the assembly's writings and reforms, both in terms of biblical exegesis and practical theology. It is there that I infer why the assembly did what it did; I attempt to illustrate what its members were looking for as they probed men's lives and listened to men preach.

Hopefully these three legs will together strike readers as something like a well-supported step stool for future research. I recognize that some will conclude that this study is still lacking something, that it looks more like a maimed quadruped missing an appendage. All I can offer in response are a few appendices at the conclusion of the book along with my sense that a fuller study has always been just out of my reach, given other projects also in progress, and my hope that a limited study is better than none at all. While I hope that readers will brave their way through all the chapters of the book, it may be worth noting that the first two parts of *God's Ambassadors* may be most interesting to historians, the last part to practitioners of preaching. The work as a whole is intended chiefly for pastors, seminary students, and theologians, although the subject of preaching—and the attempt to find good preaching—is of perennial interest to people who listen to sermons.

Acknowledgments

The subject of the Westminster Assembly and preaching was my oldest academic love, and a thesis on the topic was the first child of my research, taking the form of a graduate thesis at Westminster Theological Seminary in Philadelphia. Although no pages from that study survive intact in *God's Ambassadors*, a few paragraphs do. Where this book finds its real continuity with that thesis is in the revival of my twin interests in synods and sermons.

Since the completion of that master's thesis sixteen years ago (an endeavor that felt more like the beginning of something than the end) I have spent most of my time considering the Westminster Assembly, preaching on a regular basis, training preachers, and occasionally thinking about how these three things relate. While working as a fellow of Wolfson College, Cambridge, and then during a British Academy post-doctoral fellowship in the history faculty at the University of Cambridge, I put together some lectures on the Westminster Assembly and preaching. Subsequently, I was invited to share my thoughts in a variety of stimulating contexts. Evangelical Anglicans first encouraged the study when I was asked to deliver the 2005 St. Antholin lecture. Historians at the Dr. Williams's Centre for Dissenting Studies in London then heard some more developed lines of argument in 2006. And snippets were delivered to ministers at a Banner of Truth conference in Leicester in 2007.

In 2008 I began *God's Ambassadors* in earnest, focusing especially on the assembly's debates and members' writings. I wrote a full draft of the work before becoming convinced that I needed to spend more time pillaging the assembly's own texts on the subject. At that point I was called to serve as one of the pastors of a church near Washington, D.C., and so the book had to take a backseat, or back pew.

In 2013 I received another opportunity to complete the work: A generous fellowship was offered by the Folger Shakespeare Library in Washington, D.C., that wonderful resource for early modern history, literature, and theology, conveniently located next door to another unparalleled local institution, the Library of Congress. I rewrote most of the book that spring, but unfortunately, on the second-to-last day of the fellowship, I discovered what I considered to be a more compelling way to present my material. I asked the publisher to wait for a later installment, took some notes on how the book ought to look, and went back to preaching and teaching.

It was only in 2015, with a new appointment from Reformed Theological Seminary that graciously allowed me a first year of lightened teaching duties, that I was able to consider bringing this book to completion. Therefore, as I see it, I owe a debt to four institutions: Westminster Theological Seminary, where I came to appreciate the assembly and preaching in new ways; the University of Cambridge, where I began the book; the Folger, where most of the writing was done; and Reformed Theological Seminary, which enabled this study to be brought to completion.

During the long evolution of this book many people read drafts of one or more chapters, including Melanie Westerveld, Mark Burkill, Jason Rampelt, Alison Searle, Polly Ha, Douglas McCallum, Andy Young, Justen Ellis, John Morrill, John Bower, Stephen Tracey, and students both at Greenville Presbyterian Theological Seminary and at Reformed Theological Seminary. Polly's comments particularly shaped the 2008 embodiment of the book, John Bower's the final version, and John Morrill's both versions. The study was also advanced by the opportunity to consider the assembly and exegesis in an essay later published in a festschrift for Palmer Robertson.[1] Portions of that chapter and of the printed St. Antholin lecture have found their way into this study. I am thankful for all of these friends and their interest in this developing study, and for Sinclair Ferguson who found the time to write a foreword to this book. Additional thanks go to Andrew Buss of Collaborative Editorial Solutions for his expert copyediting and to Jay Collier and his staff at Reformation Heritage Books who guided *God's Ambassadors* from manuscript into print.

I hope it has been obvious through the years that I appreciate the people who have shaped my thinking or who have provided occasions for me to speak or write on this subject. Nonetheless, I wish to especially acknowledge my gratitude for my parents, Henry and Thea Van Dixhoorn, who took me to churches that understood the power of a good sermon and to whom this book is dedicated. Words cannot tell how thankful I am for my children and their support and for my wife, Emily, who is a source of

---

1. C. B. Van Dixhoorn, "Preaching Christ in Post-Reformation Britain," in *The Hope Fulfilled: Essays in Honor of O. Palmer Robertson*, ed. R. L. Penny (Phillipsburg, N.J.: P&R, 2008), 361–89.

joy, wisdom, and good advice. Among her most useful encouragements is the oft-repeated dictum that if I can't write something well I should at least write it poorly—and then try to fix it later. I believe that with this volume, I have followed Emily's advice at least three times.

Abbreviations

Add. MS	Additional manuscript
Baillie, *Letters*	Robert Baillie, *Letters and Journals*, ed. D. Laing (Edinburgh: for Robert Ogle, 1841–42), 3 vols.
BL	The British Library, London
Bodl.	Bodleian Library, Oxford
CUL	Cambridge University Library
CUL Dd XIV.28(4)	Cambridge University Library, manuscript notes of John Lightfoot on the proceedings of the assembly (not in Lightfoot's *Works*). Transcription in C. B. Van Dixhoorn, "Reforming the Reformation: Theological Debate at the Westminster Assembly, 1643–1652" (PhD diss., University of Cambridge, 2004), vol. 2.
EUL	Edinburgh University Library
FSL	Folger Shakespeare Library, Washington, D.C.
Lightfoot, *Journal*	J. Lightfoot, *The Whole Works of the Rev. John Lightfoot*, ed. J. R. Pitman (London: J. F. Dove, 1824), vol. 13.
MPWA	C. B. Van Dixhoorn, ed., *The Minutes and Papers of the Westminster Assembly, 1643–1652* (Oxford: Oxford University Press, 2012), vols. 1–5.
NLS	National Library of Scotland, Edinburgh
ODNB	*Oxford Dictionary of National Biography*
PA	Parliamentary Archives, Westminster

PRRD	R. Muller, *Post-Reformation Reformed Dogmatics* (Grand Rapids: Baker, 2003), 4 vols.
WCF	The Westminster Confession of Faith, in J. R. Bower, ed., *The Confession of Faith: A Critical Text and Introduction* (Grand Rapids: Reformation Heritage Books, forthcoming).
WLC	The Westminster Larger Catechism, in J. R. Bower, ed., *The Larger Catechism: A Critical Text and Introduction* (Grand Rapids: Reformation Heritage Books, 2010).
WSC	*The Humble Advice of the Assembly of Divines, Now by Authority of Parliament Sitting at Westminster, concerning a Shorter Catechism, with the Proofs thereof out of the Scriptures, Presented by Them Lately to Both Houses of Parliament. A Certain Number of Copies Are Ordered to Be Printed Onely for the Use of the Members of Both Houses and of the Assembly of Divines, to the End That They May Advise Thereupon* (London: J. F., [1648]).

Note on Dating

The English New Year in the 1640s, and in the centuries preceding, did not begin on January 1. Instead it began on Lady Day, March 25. This older form of dating the commencement of the year is now called Old Style, and our current form, with the year beginning January 1, is called New Style.

In Scotland, however, New Style dating was used beginning in the year 1600. As readers can imagine, this makes telling a story that involves both England and Scotland a little more challenging. For example, the Westminster Assembly (based in England) would date its finished review of its Psalms translation as February 1646 (Old Style). Both today and in seventeenth-century Scotland, that same event would be dated February 1647 (New Style).

This difference in dating, of course, affects dates between January 1 and March 24 only; for the remainder of the year, the two styles of dating are in agreement. Nonetheless, to minimize confusion for readers of *God's Ambassadors*, this study converts all dates in the historical narrative between January 1 and March 24 to New Style. The publication information provided in the footnotes for books, however, is left unchanged—thus, English books are dated in Old Style and Scottish books in New Style.

One more note on dating: where a person's life date is rendered, for example, "d. 1646/7," it indicates that the person died either in one year or the other, in this case 1646 or 1647. A similar scheme is used for birth dates when the precise year is unknown.

PART I
Blind Guides and Scandalous Ministers

The Westminster Assembly was appointed by Parliament to reform the Church of England since the majority of Parliament wanted change and did not think the church would reform itself. The assembly was charged to propose changes for Parliament's consideration—changes in worship, church government, and doctrine. In addition to this, the assembly established (with Parliament's blessing) a national system of examinations, a filter through which all preachers had to pass. It was an attempt to address perceived weaknesses in English preaching by means of sifting through England's preachers.

The assembly's own work is introduced in part 2, but first the assembly's reforms are put in various contexts. Chapter 1 places the assembly's statements and this study in its theological and historiographical contexts, introducing the assembly's perspectives on preaching and exploring the relationship between the assembly and puritanism. The following two chapters place the synod's work in its ecclesiological and political ecosystems, for the Westminster Assembly's commitment to preaching reforms had precedents in earlier puritan history, and this history of commitment and complaint is traced in chapter 2, "The Road to Reform."

The stage on which the events of the assembly were to be played out, however, was civil war London, or rather Westminster, as King Charles I and a rebel Parliament engaged in a high stakes battle for control of the political process, the economy, and the church. The massive unrest of the middle decades of the seventeenth century, discussed in chapter 3, "Democratick Annarchie"—a phrase borrowed from Robert Baillie (1602–1662), offering a Scotsman's perspective on England—provides a lively context for reading the assembly's texts and viewing its activities. Arguably, this political and religious turmoil makes the gathering's measured statements about preaching appear more interesting today and perhaps more relevant.

CHAPTER 1

The Call for Reform

This ensuing summary declaration, of the grounds and causes, whereupon this parliament hath proceeded against divers ministers, to sequester their benefices from them, and to place in their roomes, godly, learned, orthodox divines, diligent preachers of the Word of God, may serve thee for many excellent purposes.... Thou maiest hereby discerne one principall ground and cause of the general ignorance and debauchery of the gentry and people of this kingdome. Like priest, like people.

—John White, member of Parliament

"Like priest, like people."[1] In a nominally Christian society like England, as in all Constantinian church-state arrangements, the welfare of the *polis* was tethered to the well-being of the *ecclesia*. Or to put it the other way around, when a tide of ignorance or immorality affected the church, it invariably affected the state. This meant that the governments of both institutions felt an obligation to cooperate in reform, or at least to inform the other of its duties.

The intertwining of church and state gave ministers of church and state a degree of freedom to intermeddle with each other's affairs, but it did not mean that the two parties enjoyed an equal authority and influence. In England, at least since the Reformation, and for some centuries prior, the state was preeminent in power. In the 1640s this was evidenced by the fact that it was the English Parliament that summoned the Westminster Assembly and that required the synod to effect governmental and liturgical reforms, suggest doctrinal clarifications, and address various practical concerns related to the church. The shape and main tasks of the assembly were directed by the two houses of Parliament. In fact, the House of Lords and the House of Commons added thirty of their own number as observers to the gathering, and the assembly meeting at Westminster Abbey was

---

1. J. White, *The First Century of Scandalous, Malignant Priests, Made and Admitted into Benefices by the Prelates* (London, 1643), sig. A2.

required to submit all of its reports and discuss all of its substantial disagreements with the men meeting across the street at Westminster Palace.[2]

The assembly would attempt to shape the direction of reform obliquely—most often by way of petitions that were declared to be "humble" at the head of each document but that could be direct, even brash in the main body of a letter. A July 1643 petition by the assembly offers an excellent example of direct, almost impatient communication. Its tone was felt to be justifiable because the nation was in desperate trouble. Members thought their day was marked by a "bruitish ignorance" with a "palpable darknesse possessing the greatest part of the people in all places of the Kingdome." The gospel was in "great dishonour" and "poure soules" were in everlasting danger.[3]

One of the chief problems in the kingdom had to do with the ministry of the church, and thus it was of some encouragement that during the winter and spring of 1643 a parliamentary committee had begun ejecting scandalous clergymen from their churches.[4] John White, a parliamentary member of the Westminster Assembly, publicly catalogued the failings of a hundred ministers ejected from their pulpits from London and the surrounding area. His book had the (no doubt intended) effect of suggesting that all ministers thus ejected would be equally scandalous, which was surely not true. It also implied that bishops, had they received reports of the activities of these ministers, would have done nothing about it. This was not fair; it has been estimated that about a quarter of the ministers in England were under the oversight of bishops sympathetic to the concerns of the godly, and even those bishops who supported the anti-puritan policies of Archbishop William Laud had concern for morals.[5] But the book did highlight inefficiencies or lapses in episcopal oversight and perhaps the opportunity costs associated with the Laudian practice of hounding puritans, whereas the worst excesses persisted right under their noses.

White's tawdry tale begins with John Wilson of Arlington, accused of buggery and attempted bestiality, and drifts into accounts of drunken ministers and "popishly affected" pastors (perhaps the two most common complaints) as well as accounts of clergy who were womanizers, rapists, thieves, gamblers, Sabbath-breakers, and outspoken critics of Parliament. The pamphlet offers accounts of battery, sexual assault, verbal abuse in

---

2. See C. B. Van Dixhoorn, "Scottish Influence on the Westminster Assembly: A Study of the Synod's Summoning Ordinance and the Solemn League and Covenant," *The Records of the Scottish Church History Society*, 37 (2007): 55–88.

3. *MPWA*, 5:10 (Doc. 1).

4. *MPWA*, 1:217.

5. For the estimate of sympathetic bishops, see J. T. Cliffe, *The Puritan Gentry: The Great Puritan Families of Early Stuart England* (London: Routledge, 1984), 171.

the home (one minister threatening to burn his wife and children alive), bribery, neglect of the pulpit, flirting from the pulpit, misogynist jokes from the pulpit, making a business venture out of burials, begging for money during Communion, and bad-tempered behavior: throwing Communion elements on the ground, name-calling from the pulpit, public cursing, even excommunicating a lame man who did not kneel at Communion. The credibility of these accounts is enhanced by the enumeration of places and names (including, unfortunately, the names of victims), by the fact that these all constituted cases tried publicly (at least by Parliament, if not in the regular courts), and by the fact that the book was printed with parliamentary authority.[6]

White's booklet focused on ministers near the metropolis, but of course problematic pastors were scattered all across the nation and so the assembly would continue to petition Parliament to rid the land of inept pastors, sectarian pastors, popish pastors, and all lay preachers.[7] But as the assembly saw it, their "Wisedomes" across the street (a compliment, not a snide comment) also needed to "find out some way to admit into the Ministery such godly and hopefull men as have prepared themselves and are willing thereunto." Without this positive effort, "there will suddenly be such a scarcity of able and faithfull Ministers, that it will be to little purpose to cast out such as are unable, idle or scandalous."[8] In addressing the matter of ministers, the assembly was making a point about preachers, and they were doing so in words that members of Parliament would easily understand: The "unable" and "idle" men to be removed from churches were non-preaching ministers—mere "blinde guides." Those "prepared" and "willing" to take their places, on the other hand, would be able to proclaim the Word itself rather than read the printed sermons of others or, worse, administer sacraments without preaching at all.

The Assembly and Preaching

Members of the Westminster Assembly believed that a ministry designed by God "for the gathering and perfecting of the saints" is above all else to be a preaching ministry. In the assembly's 1646 Confession and in its 1647 Larger Catechism there are frequent references to the minister—who for them, would also always be a preacher.[9] Ministers, along with magistrates,

---

6. White, *First Century of Scandalous, Malignant*.

7. *MPWA*, 5:11 (Doc. 1; inept preachers); *MPWA*, 5:22–23 (Doc. 4; antinomian preachers); *MPWA*, 5:36 (Doc. 14; popish preachers); *MPWA*, 5:87 (Doc. 31; lay preachers).

8. *MPWA*, 5:11 (Doc. 1); see also *MPWA*, 5:177 (Doc. 61).

9. WCF, 25:3. Robert Godfrey also notes a greater emphasis on the ministry in the Larger Catechism than the Shorter in his essay "The Westminster Larger Catechism" in *To Glorify*

are the people the church is particularly to pray for.[10] Ministers are the sole persons able to administer or dispense the sacraments[11] and, with other church officers, administer discipline.[12] Ministers are the ones who are to assemble in synods and, "If magistrates be open enemies to the church, the ministers of Christ, of themselves, by virtue of their office,...may meet together in such assemblies."[13]

Yet while the minister had all of these duties (and many more), his chief task appears to be preaching. At the head of the list is the fact that "under the gospel...Christ the substance [is] exhibited, [and] the ordinances in which this covenant is dispensed are the preaching of the Word, and the administration of the sacraments." While Christ is preached both in sermon and sacrament, "repentance unto life" and "faith in Christ" is "preached by every minister of the Gospel," particularly in the sermon.[14] The majority in the assembly held that it is not only by overt censures, particularly those related to the sacrament of the Supper, but also by the regular "ministry of the Gospel" that "the keys of the kingdom of heaven are" exercised in the church "to retain, and remit sins; to shut that kingdom against the impenitent,...and to open it unto penitent sinners."[15] For this reason, the Larger Catechism offers parishioners a how-to manual for listening to sermons, and explains that among "the duties required in the second commandment" are "the receiving, observing, and keeping pure and entire, all such religious worship and ordinances as God hath instituted in his word"—such as "the reading, preaching, and hearing of the word."[16]

The hope that preaching offers the spiritually destitute is a recurring theme in the assembly's writings. Preaching is one way in which the

---

and *Enjoy God: A Commemoration of the Westminster Assembly*, ed. J. L. Carson and D. W. Hall (Edinburgh: Banner of Truth, 1994), 138.

10. WLC, 183.

11. WLC, 169, 176; WCF, 27.4; 28.2; 29.3.

12. WCF, 30.2.

13. WCF, 31.2.

14. WCF, 15.1. In referring to the "gospel," in distinction from "the Gospels," the assembly has in view teaching about the person and work of Christ.

15. WCF, 30.2. The connection between preaching and the exercising of the keys of the kingdom is also present in the Heidelberg Catechism, Q&As 83–84. In addition to these two questions, the Heidelberg Catechism also states that "the Holy Ghost...works faith in our hearts by the preaching of the gospel, and confirms it by the use of the sacraments" (Q&A 65).

16. WLC, 160: "It is required of those that hear the word preached, that they attend upon it with diligence, preparation, and prayer; examine what they hear by the scriptures; receive the truth with faith, love, meekness, and readiness of mind, as the word of God; meditate, and confer of it; hide it in their hearts, and bring forth the fruit of it in their lives"; see also WLC, 63, 108. The Confession's chapter "Religious Worship and the Sabbath Day" also lists, in section five, "sound preaching, and conscionable hearing of the Word, in obedience unto God, with understanding, faith, and reverence" as one part of religious worship (WCF, 21:5).

covenant of grace is administered under the New Testament.[17] Through preaching the elect are called out of their sin and into a state of grace. True, not every hearer is saved.[18] What is more, some who are mentally unable to understand the preaching may still be saved,[19] but, as the chapter "Saving Faith" explains, "The grace of faith, whereby the elect are enabled to believe to the saving of their souls, is the work of the Spirit of Christ in their hearts, and is ordinarily wrought by the ministry of the Word: by which also [the Word preached], and by the administration of the sacraments, and prayer, it [i.e., faith] is increased and strengthened."[20]

The assembly did not offer a vision of preaching that was intended to compete with sacraments or prayer, but nonetheless it is the efficacy of preaching that is underlined repeatedly by the assembly. In one of its texts the assembly would argue for the importance of preaching, insisting that it is one of the duties of a faithful presbytery (a regional gathering of elders) to "admonish, or further to censure" ministers for "Affected lightnesse & vanity in preaching" or for the "willfull neglect of preaching, or slight performance of it."[21] In another, the assembly argued that an improperly guarded administration of the Lord's Supper undoes the good effects of a sermon.[22] As it happens, the assembly never put it the other way around, even though the gathering's members would believe the opposite to be true.

The assembly underlined the importance of preaching and preachers implicitly by mentioning ministers an astonishing thirty-two times in its confession and catechisms. It highlights the preacher's importance most unusually by giving preaching tips in the Directory for Public Worship. Nonetheless, while any number of citations demonstrate the significance of preaching in the minds of assembly members, nothing so puts into perspective their theory of preaching's preeminence than the Larger Catechism's 155th question and answer, "How is the word made effectual to salvation?" The response is clear: "The Spirit of God maketh the reading, but especially the preaching of the word an effectual means of enlightening, convincing, and humbling sinners; of driving them out of themselves, and drawing them unto Christ; of conforming them to his image, and subduing them to his will; of strengthening them against temptations and corruptions; of building them up in grace, and establishing their hearts in holiness and comfort through faith unto salvation."

---

17. WLC, 35.
18. WLC, 68; WCF, 10.4.
19. WCF, 10.3.
20. WCF, 14.1.
21. *MPWA*, 5:211 (Doc. 77).
22. *MPWA*, 5:233 (Doc. 83).

Preaching, by this analysis, is something of use to any person prior to and during the whole of the Christian life. It is not that Scripture is to be slighted. Supernaturally, Scripture and sermon are both effectual through the Spirit's work, for the same spiritual purposes. And yet, while the Larger Catechism's list states what preaching "especially" does, it implies that the reading of the Word is able to do the same. For the assembly Scripture is foundational, preaching derivative—only Scripture is "sufficient to give that knowledge of God and of His will, which is necessary unto salvation."[23] There is a reason why the assembly, like every other Reformed confessing body, has a chapter on Scripture in its confession and why it was not obliged to offer a chapter on preaching. And yet there can be no doubt that the Westminster Assembly gives preaching a pride of place as an "especially" powerful means of grace.

The prominence of preaching, so heavily underlined in the two catechisms of the assembly, must be kept in perspective not only when compared to the reading of the Word but also when set beside prayer. In describing special worship events such as days of thanksgiving or fasting (days that would always contain preaching), the Westminster Assembly insisted that the main emphasis of the occasion was to be found in the congregation's petitions or praises.[24] The fact that prayer is important to the assembly can be seen in other contexts too. Preaching and prayer, as duties of the minister, are usually paired together in enumerations of pastoral responsibilities. Notably, prayer is sometimes put first (and in one of the assembly's catalogues of divine ordinances given for the good of congregations, preaching appears not first, but fifth).[25]

And that is only the beginning. When the gathering came to write a preface for its Directory for Public Worship, including a history of episcopal abuses, the assembly complained not only about prior attacks on preaching, "justling it out as unnecessary, or, (at best) as farre inferior to the Reading of Common prayer," but also the way in which enforced use of the Book of Common Prayer had led to an "idle, and unedifying ministry" content with "sett forms made to their hands by others, without putting forth themselves to exercise the guift of praier, with which our Lord Jesus Christ pleaseth to furnish all his servants whom he calls to that office."[26] Concern to allow freedom for prayer was featured as much as the concern to promote proper preaching.

---

23. WCF, 1.1.
24. *MPWA*, 5:155–57 (Doc. 53).
25. *MPWA*, 5:56 (Doc. 19), p. 119 (Doc. 42), p. 129 (Doc. 45), pp. 205, 208 (Doc. 77).
26. *MPWA*, 5:119 (Doc. 42).

Nonetheless, most members of the assembly chose to accentuate that, for purposes of persuasion, the most effective weapon in the Spirit's arsenal is the Word of God preached. Coming from an assembly of preachers, this could be decoded as an elongated plea for job security. After all, as Robert Norris points out, there is something unsurprising about a group of preachers stressing preaching.[27] Yet the clearest reason for this insistence on preaching appears to be found in the assembly's instructions for hearers, where sermon attendees are told that "it is required of those that hear the word preached, that they…receive the truth with faith, love, meekness, and readiness of mind, as the word of God."[28] Preachers are delivering the Word of God.

And yet not everything preached is to be considered the "Word of God." Only when the Word is properly interpreted is it God's Word brought to the people. Nor was everyone supposed to preach that Word. While the assembly's Directory for Public Worship stressed that all should read their Bibles, the Larger Catechism stresses that "the word of God is to be preached only by such as are" both "duly approved and called to that office" and "sufficiently gifted."[29] The assemblymen believed the exalted Christ sits at the right hand of God, and "furnisheth ministers and people with gifts and graces, and maketh intercession for them."[30] Christ gives His people gifts—some the gift of preaching—and commissions the preacher and makes the preaching "a demonstration of the Spirit, and of power," effective by His Spirit and "not in the enticing words of man's wisdom."[31] Both the communications of the assembly intended only for Parliament and the public texts designed for a wider audience present an elevated and unified view of preaching as the most effective regular means of grace for the church that God has to offer. Together they make it clear that the concern to establish and maintain a faithful preaching ministry is uppermost in the assembly's reforming interests.

---

27. R. M. Norris, "The Preaching of the Assembly," in *To Glorify and Enjoy God: A Commemoration of the Westminster Assembly* (Edinburgh: Banner of Truth, 1994), 65. It should be noted that the divines themselves were hardly in a lucrative position: The Parliament was invariably behind in paying them their already small allowance for their enormous task.

28. WLC, 160.

29. *A Directory for the Publique Worship of God, throughout the Three Kingdoms of England, Scotland, and Ireland* (London: for Evan Tyler, Alexander Fifield, Ralph Smith, and John Field, 1644), 13–14; see also WLC, 158.

30. WLC, 54.

31. WLC, 53; WLC, 159, 155.

This Study

It is not the intention of this study to pretend that it was unique for the assembly to stress the importance of preaching or to announce that biblical preaching, with appropriate qualification, is the Word of God.[32] Indeed, as the following chapter will demonstrate, this emphasis and these claims were, in fact, part of the assembly's Reformed heritage. The Westminster Assembly's reformation of preaching had more to do with people than ideas. It is not impossible that the theology and practice of preaching took a new turn because of the assembly's writings, but the real story is not that people preached differently because of the Westminster Assembly but that different people were preaching. Preaching was reformed, in the main, by changing the preachers.

At the same time, this revolution in the personnel of the English church is both an important and a neglected story. Perhaps it has received scant attention because the assembly's efforts to reform English pulpits were undone at the Restoration and had no clear impact on Scottish, Irish, or later American history (the contexts in which the assembly's impact was felt most profoundly) and has therefore proved to be of little interest to historians. Only two historians have given it any attention: William Shaw, while discussing the reform of the pulpit from the perspective of Parliament, recognizes that "the approval and certification of ministers was a large part of the Assembly's work."[33] And the English historian S. W. Carruthers offers two chapters on the examination of ministers in his collection of essays on the assembly.[34] On the other hand, the assembly's work in pulpit reform may also have been neglected, because the minutes and papers of the assembly needed to be edited and collected before the assembly's debates, documents, and work related to the preaching ministry of England could be fully understood. As a component of this project, the *Minutes and Papers of the Westminster Assembly* also showcased the systematic archival and editorial labor of Inga Jones and especially Joel Halcomb, both of whom focused on the identification of persons examined by the assembly and the relationship between the Westminster Assembly and a key committee of the House of Commons.

---

32. See chapter 2; and Hunt, *Art of Hearing*, chapter one.

33. W. A. Shaw, *A History of the English Church during the Civil Wars and under the Commonwealth, 1640–1660* (London: Longman, Green, 1900), 2:197.

34. S. W. Carruthers, *The Everyday Work of the Westminster Assembly* (Philadelphia: Presbyterian Historical Society, 1943), ch. 13–17. Carruthers provides lively vignettes relating to the examination of ministers and the supply of ministers. His study is not systematic in its treatment of assembly sources but makes excellent use of the journals of the two houses of Parliament.

Nonetheless, as soon as that work was completed, it raised a pressing historical question: What was the assembly looking for in a preacher? The full story of the assembly's work cannot be told simply in terms of personal histories, assembly procedures, and assembly writings. It must also deal with theological ideas. Most assembly members were advocates of a particular kind of preacher and preaching ministry. They held and developed core commitments concerning ministerial godliness, training, and ordination as well as their convictions about the nature and form of the proclamation itself. This is why this study offers contextual chapters, concentrated reflections on the assembly and its writings, and chapters focused on the activities and writings of assembly members.

Puritanism and Preaching

In what follows, quotations and illustrations are drawn from the speeches and writings of the assemblymen, while narrative portions recount aspects of the assembly's work. For that reason, I ought to have perhaps contented myself with a study about the Westminster Assembly only, and its theology and practice of preaching, especially since the assembly and its members supply the entirety of my subject sampling. In point of fact, a much larger study would be required to demonstrate conclusively that the assembly's membership is a representative sample of puritan thinking on the topic of preachers and preaching.

But can a historian have his cake and eat it too? On the one hand, by focusing on the Westminster Assembly's reformation of preaching I am offering a study that has some strict demographic controls with a clearly defined subject group. On the other hand, I think this study does speak into conversations about puritanism. While there are frequent scuffles over the definition of "puritanism," whenever the dust settles, the members of the assembly are always left standing; no one seriously doubts that they are candidates for the puritan brotherhood. This narrowly defined subject group happens to have been particularly influential, and it would only promote artificial distinctions if we were to isolate the assembly from the wider phenomenon and historiography of puritanism. As later chapters will endeavor to show, the Westminster Assembly proved to be the answer to an almost century-old puritan dream for further reformation in the Church of England.

Of course, to link this study to "puritanism" is to face the nettlesome question of defining and employing the term itself. I remember reading a historian who noted that the definition of puritanism has been discussed to good effect and avoided with equally happy results. As John Coffey and Paul Lim point out, "Defining Puritanism has become a favorite parlour game for early modern historians."[35] At the same time, there is widespread diffidence among early modern theologians over the thing that is puritanism, the key problem being that the term originated, and was usually applied, as a term of abuse.[36]

Many readers will know that there is a thriving industry dedicated to defining puritanism in the most negative, most amusing way possible. The combination of dour strictness with which puritans are wont to be stereotyped is wonderfully captured by H. L. Mencken's suggestion that puritanism is "the haunting fear that someone, somewhere, may be happy," and by Garrison Keillor's comment that seventeenth-century puritans were the type of people who left for America "in the hope of finding greater restrictions than were permissible under English law at that time."[37]

In the sixteenth and seventeenth centuries the epithet "puritan" was reliably employed as a term of opprobrium, not of friendship. To define puritanism through the writings of opponents would be a bit like trying to understand communism by reading the collected writings of Joseph McCarthy, or the convictions of Senator McCarthy through the cartoons drawn at his expense.[38] In practice I, along with other recent historians, prefer to categorize assembly members and those like them with terms of approval, like "godly," over terms of abuse, like "puritan." As Tom Webster explains, the reason for this preference is that "godly" is the term these people preferred for themselves.[39] Puritans often called themselves "professors" because they professed faith in God. But they liked to provide adjectives for professors, and "godly" was the most common adjective, often used in a substantive form, "the godly."

---

35. J. Coffey and P. C. H. Lim, eds., *The Cambridge Companion to Puritanism* (Cambridge: Cambridge University Press, 2008), 1.

36. For reticence toward the exercise of defining puritanism by a leading scholar of the subject, see P. Lake, *Moderate Puritans and the Elizabethan Church* (Cambridge: Cambridge University Press, 2004), 10–11: "The difficulties in defining 'puritanism' are easier to identify than solve and I really have nothing original to say on that subject." For the best brief discussion of the term, see P. Collinson, "Puritans," *Oxford Encyclopedia of the Reformation*, ed. H. Hillerbrand (Oxford: Oxford University Press, 1996), 364–70. Cf. Randall Pederson, *Unity in Diversity: English Puritans and the Puritan Reformation, 1603–1689* (Leiden: Brill, 2014), for another recent work devoted to defining Puritanism.

37. V. Fitzpatrick, *H. L. Mencken* (Macon, Ga.: Mercer University Press, 2004), 37; "Garrison Keillor," in *The Yale Book of Quotations*, ed. F. R. Shapiro (New Haven: Yale University Press, 2006), 417.

38. I am only adding color to a similar analogy suggested by M. G. Finlayson in *Historians, Puritanism, and the English Revolution: The Religious Factor in English Politics before and after the Interregnum* (Toronto: University of Toronto Press, 1983), 47.

39. T. Webster, *Godly Clergy in Early Stuart England: The Caroline Puritan Movement, c. 1620–1643* (Cambridge: Cambridge University Press, 1997), 3.

And yet it cannot be denied that the term "puritan," although an insulting one, is a historical and a historiographical one with which we must reckon. It has been in use at least since 1575, and probably earlier, because in some sense the definition of a puritan was clear enough: Those who were puritans themselves (and not simply those who were their neighbors!) were usually sure about who was in and who was out of the inner circle of the godly.

Yet it is difficult to delineate the meaning of the term with true puritanical rigor. This is in part because puritans were uncertain when to take the term as an insult and when as a compliment. Take the Westminster divines themselves. On one occasion William Gouge (1575–1653) tried to distance himself from the label by giving it a historical referent: the term "puritan" properly referred to ancient separatists who thought themselves perfectly pure.[40] On another occasion Gouge mentioned that puritans were considered precisians, Sabbatarians, and Jews—a more knotty string of adjectives.[41] Gouge would not consider himself overly precise, nor would he relish being called a Jew. But he was comfortable being called a Sabbatarian. Since the label puritan could imply some positive associations for the godly, its acceptance or rejection must often have relied on the tone of voice in which it was uttered or the context in which it was applied or the person speaking. And so on a third occasion Gouge's colleagues at King's College spoke of him derisively as an arch-puritan. But Gouge was willing to pass the story on to his son Thomas, and Thomas was happy to relate the incident in a biographical essay, because both appreciated what it said of the elder Gouge's piety and attentive study of the Scriptures.[42]

Definitions of puritanism are further complicated because meanings shift over time. Historians of the late Elizabethan period have argued, plausibly, that the term puritan was used nearly synonymously with presbyterian, a meaning probably carried into the early years of James's reign.[43] Often it was restricted to clergy only, an unhappy descriptor for the "assiduous

---

40. W. Gouge, *A Guide to Goe to God* (London, 1636), 255.

41. W. Gouge, *The Sabbaths Sanctification* (London, 1641), 30.

42. T. Gouge, in "The Life and Death of Doctor Gouge," in W. Gouge, *A Learned and Very Useful Commentary on the Whole Epistle to the Hebrewes* (London, 1655), not paginated.

43. See, for example, M. Todd, *Christian Humanism and the Puritan Social Order* (Cambridge: Cambridge University Press, 1987), 10n25. Here and elsewhere this study deliberately avoids capitalization of terms such as *episcopalian*, *presbyterian*, and *congregationalist*. The capitalization of these words promotes the idea of unified movements, oversimplifying assembly history. After all, the gathering was characterized not only by a-tug-of-war between major ecclesiological options but also by intramural contests within these developing traditions. What is more, capitalization of these terms promotes categories that are anachronistic in the 1640s as all of the assembly's voting members were Church of England ministers, not ministers of discrete denominations.

preacher."[44] In later Jacobean and early Caroline years, annoyed English people used the word to refer to all who were strict in their life and perhaps Calvinist in their doctrine, and during the same time period Roman Catholic polemicists tried to use the epithet "puritan" to scare off Englishmen from all things Protestant.[45] By the 1640s, some among the godly actually began to approve of its use among themselves.[46] Others applied the term to their forebears with some affection: godly folk during the civil war spoke about the good old puritans of years gone past.[47]

At the same time, even as godly people were becoming comfortable with the appellation of puritanism, the term may have begun to lose its positive meaning entirely. A puritan was simply, for most people, something that no one in broader society wanted to be. In that case the term functioned as a key part of what Thomas Gataker (1574–1654) called a "negative divinity": one was acceptable if he was not a papist or schismatic or heretic or a puritan.[48] If this dual shift in usage is correct—finding acceptance among the godly and as a nondescript term to be avoided by everyone else—then it may explain why the term started to struggle to stand on its own. Like many words that are overworked and underpaid, the term puritan showed its age prematurely. As one reads the literature of the civil wars and interregnum, it becomes apparent that layers of adjectives were applied to make the term "puritan" more presentable in public. We begin to read of "doctrinal puritanism,"[49] of "judaizing puritanism,"[50] and of "novelizing puritans."[51] In England, at least, although the godly movement was still characterized by a spiritual vigor, the body of terms associated with it became laden with historical overtones. By the end of the 1640s it was past its prime as a serviceable descriptor, with other terms taking its place.[52] In fact, shortly after

---

44. C. Burges, *Two Sermons Preached to the Honorable House of Commons Assembled in Parliament at Their Publique Fast* (London, 1641), 73.

45. E. Calamy, *Gods Free Mercy to England Presented as a Pretious, and Powerful Motive to Humiliation* (London, 1642), 6; D. Featley, *A Second Parallel together with a Writ of Error Sued against the Appealer* (London, 1626), 97; W. Twisse, *Of the Morality of the Fourth Commandment* (London, 1641), 34.

46. E. Reynolds, *Eugenia's Teares for Great Brittaynes Distractions* (London, 1642), 20.

47. E. Calamy, *The Godly Mans Ark, or, City of Refuge in the Day of His Distress* (London, 1657), Epistle Dedicatory; S. Marshall, *The Power of the Civil Magistrate* (London, 1657), 24; and S. Marshall, "The Life of Christ," in *The Works of Mr Stephen Marshall, Late Minister of the Gospel at Finching-Field in Essex* (London, 1661), 77.

48. T. Gataker, *A Sparke toward the Kindling of Sorrow for Sion* (London, 1621), 10.

49. Calamy, *Gods Free Mercy*, 20; D. Featley, *A Parallel: Of New-Old Pelgiarminian Error* (London, 1626), To the Reader.

50. Burges, *Two Sermons*, 75.

51. Featley, *Second Parallel*, 45.

52. E. Corbet, *Gods Providence, a Sermon Preached Before the Honourable House of Commons at Their Late Solemne Fast* (London, 1642), 21; James tolerated papists and persecuted

the death of Charles I in 1649, a member of the Westminster Assembly noted that godly people were now derided as Huguenots—what we *used* to call puritans, he explains.⁵³

This last comment, by Francis Cheynell (bap. 1608, d. 1665), quite sensibly suggests that the use of a negative epithet like "puritan" tended to slide away once the godly were on top of the hill. It also reminds us that puritanism was not, in fact, merely an English phenomenon. During the 1580s and 1640s there were profound Scottish influences on puritanism. During the early decades of the seventeenth century, connections with pious people in the Netherlands were especially strong. During the 1620s and 1630s, American colonists presented a vision that inspired godly people in the mother country, and Irish puritans showed that godly men could lead a Reformed university or rise to the status of archbishop at the very time when the puritan cause in England looked increasingly desperate.⁵⁴ Mid and late century, as France became a painful place for Reformed people, a new strain of fervent Protestant piety entered England from across the Channel, once more altering the mix that was called puritanism. It is because of this international mix of influences, the development of the term over time, the varying reception of the term among the godly themselves, and the activities and associations of puritans themselves that this study contents itself with the simple but apt definition of a puritan cited by Patrick Collinson: the "hotter sort of Protestant."⁵⁵

The Westminster Assembly contained many hot Protestants, and the assembly itself arguably constitutes an important chapter in the history of the puritan movement. Many of its members spent time in prison for defying the establishment. Indeed, even to meet at the assembly was to defy the direct command of the king. It is also the case, however, that the assembly embodied the diversity that obtained among the godly, a diversity that is evident when considering puritan perspectives on preaching. The membership of the assembly, selected by both houses of Parliament, was also self-selecting in that men chose whether or not to attend. Nonetheless, the choice of the assembly's members was not dictated by a single parliamentary vision. In the first place, Parliament was made up of various parties. Second, the matters of the assembly and the nomination of its membership were entwined not only with political concerns but also personal

---

puritans, "as they then called men that were seriously and invicibly pious." F. Cheynell, *Divine Trinunity of the Father, Son, and Holy Spirit* (London, 1650), 470.

53. Cheynell, *Divine Trinunity*, 14. See M. G. Finlayson's questions in *Historians, Puritanism, and the English Revolution*, 42–76.

54. For the lesser-known case of Ireland, see A. Ford, *James Ussher: Theology, History, and Politics in Early-Modern Ireland and England* (Oxford: Oxford University Press, 2007).

55. P. Collinson, *The Elizabethan Puritan Movement* (1967; Oxford: Clarendon, 1990), 27.

interests—as with any other matter before the Long Parliament. The upside of the lack of a cohesive plan or demographic in choosing assembly members is that, considered individually, these men displayed enough diversity about the practice and theory of preaching that a student of their ministries can discover the essential and peripheral elements of their desired reformation. Considered collectively, the assembly's membership offers a century of working life from men of different temperaments and training and from across different localities, and thus captures the experience and wisdom of generations of godly ministers.

This study enlists a defined cohort of subjects; it also employs a coherent diversity of sources. Chief among them are the minutes of the assembly, revealing both premeditated and extempore comments by assembly members on the widest range of subjects; the papers of the assembly (both printed and manuscript), giving the views of the assembly as a whole; and the writings of individual members penned before, during, and after the event of the assembly. These not only outline the reforms of the assembly and the gathering's collective pulpit theology but also allow us to canvas the views of the assembly's members.

It remains to be said that in analyzing the writings of the assembly and its members on the subject of preaching, I am not restricting myself to a discussion of what might be called the distinguishing marks of puritan preaching, those emphases that set the self-consciously godly preacher apart from the man in the next parish. I think there is a danger of inadvertently underplaying the significance of rather more basic aspects of puritanism in a quest for the unique marks of the godly. The doctrine of Scripture, for example, is not the most obvious place to go if one wishes to hear the things that made puritans tick where others tock. Nonetheless, though the godly did not hold a monopoly on a high view of Scripture, it happens to be at the very heart of puritanism and puritan preaching. Indeed, many characteristics of a puritan preacher are similar to the characteristics of a garden-variety Protestant preacher. What is more, those characteristics that separate or distinguish puritans from other Protestants may not be the features that best explain puritans as people or puritan preachers as preachers. Thus, I seek to identify those aspects of the assembly's reforms that members considered most significant, even though some of those traits are not unique to the assembly. My hope is that this study of the assembly will further conversations about puritanism, post-Reformation theology, and the subject of preaching, and that further studies will in turn correct the faults of this one.

CHAPTER 2

The Road to Reform

If we look back to the beginnings of our troubles, and recall what it was the Professors of England would have had, let them speak: when you were fain to get into houses privately to keep Fasts together, afraid that any should see you, lest the Bishops should know it, why did you Fast, why did you utter such sad Complaints to God, why did your tears drop so, what was your burden?...why, that he would root up these persecuting Bishops, and all the rabble that belongs to them, that we may have none but Christs own Officers, & Ordinances pure without this mixture, no Railes, Surplice, Crosse, &c. this was the businesse why men thus prayed, and fasted; and for these things the old solid Puritan prayed many yeers since, though died before these times; well, what those deceased Christians prayed for, and these living, God hath given this generation.

—Stephen Marshall

The Westminster Assembly's first petition to Parliament included a call for "speedy proceeding" on the part of Parliament against "scandalous Ministers."[1] Nonetheless, the difficulty with ministers was not merely a matter of personal purity or even purity of worship, as Stephen Marshall and others complained.[2] The equally serious problem was that many ministers could not preach.

A Want of Preaching

The (very) godly presbyterian elder Nehemiah Wallington recalled how his father, coming to London in 1572, went eight years without hearing a sermon preached in his parish.[3] The clergymen that filled the pulpit could administer sacraments and read sermons, but as the godly were quick to

---

1. *MPWA*, 5:11 (Doc. 1).
2. S. Marshall, *The Power of the Civil Magistrate* (London, 1657), 23–24.
3. Hunt, *Art of Hearing*, 188.

point out, "reading is not feeding." Taking someone else's sermon and reading it was "as evil as playing upon a stage, and worse too," according to a bitter John Field.⁴ Another stalwart among the godly, Thomas Cartwright, put it more positively: Preaching the Word was like blowing on a fire—it produced more heat than mere reading.⁵ Without such preaching the Church of England had become lukewarm—in many places, cold. As one bold petition informed Queen Elizabeth in 1571, "an infinite number of your Majesty's subjects, for want of preaching of the word (the only ordinary means of salvation of souls)" are perishing.⁶

There was a "want of preaching." There was also a dearth of *good* preaching. Already in the sixteenth century, Protestant Reformers could be scathing in their criticisms of much popular preaching, and Englishmen who had visited the continent savored not only the meaty expository sermons of the Reformers but also the delicious critiques of Protestant humanists of what passed for preaching in their own day. John Calvin, for example, derided the traditional sermons to which he had been exposed. He recalled attempts at preaching that alternated between impressing the populace and keeping people awake: "What one sermon was there from which old wives might not carry off more whimsies than they could devise at their own fireside in a month? For as sermons then were usually divided, the first half was devoted to those misty questions of the schools which might astonish the rude populace, while the second contained sweet stories, or not unamusing speculations, by which the hearers might be kept on the alert."⁷

The Reformers responded with their own model and a clearly articulated theology of preaching. Both the practice and the theory impacted puritanism. This was especially true of John Calvin. Eager listeners aided the dissemination of Geneva's most prominent preacher, and his sermons were translated and widely distributed in England and elsewhere. Decades later his legacy would often be recalled by speakers in the Westminster Assembly.

Calvin's understanding of the preacher's tasks and privileges illustrated the commitments of his own generation of reformers and profoundly informed the next. He explained that the preacher has "climbed up into the pulpit…that God may speak to us by the mouth of a man. And he does us that favor of presenting himself here and wishes a mortal man to be

---

4. Collinson, *Elizabethan Puritan Movement*, 120.

5. H. Davies, *The Worship of the English Puritans* (Morgan, Pa.: Soli Deo Gloria, 1997), 186.

6. P. Collinson, *Archbishop Grindal, 1519–1583* (Berkeley: University of California Press, 1979), 18.

7. In J. Calvin and J. Sadoleto, *A Reformation Debate*, ed. J. C. Olin (Grand Rapids: Baker, 1976), 65.

his messenger."⁸ The metaphor of messenger is one of two dominant ones that historian T. H. L. Parker finds in Calvin's sermons. Calvin viewed preaching (so long as the Bible was properly understood and delivered) as delivering the Word of God. Just as a child can faithfully deliver the message of a father, or an ambassador the communication of a king, so a preacher can relay the message of God. None of these messages needed to be composed of verbatim quotations to be accurate. Relaying the message does not remove its authority. "It is the Word of God," summarizes Parker, "inasmuch as it delivers the Biblical message, which is God's message or Word."⁹ The other picture observed by Parker is Calvin's metaphor of the school of God, or school of Christ. The preacher is to learn from the master (God or Christ) at the school (the Bible) and teach what he has learned, and that only. If the preacher has first learned from the master, he may give "pure teaching" from the "pure Word." If the preacher faithfully passes on what he has learned, then the sovereign Master "presides" over the gathering; He is "'in the midst' of his people."¹⁰ The pulpit is, to change the metaphor, "the throne of God, from where he wills to govern our souls."¹¹

Parker's study of Calvin's pulpit theory insists that the Reformer did not "elevate preaching to an equality with Scripture. Scripture is definitive and sovereign; preaching must be derivative and subordinate. Obviously, Scripture does not have to conform to preaching; preaching must conform to Scripture."¹² All the same, "it is clear that Calvin is using the term, 'the Word' to refer primarily to any preaching, granted of course, that it is in accord with Holy Scripture."¹³ Just as baptism and the Lord's Supper are made effectual to the recipient by the Holy Spirit, so too is preaching. He concludes by noting that, for Calvin, preaching "is itself God's Word in a twofold sense: first, because the same message that was revealed to the

---

8. *Calvini Opera* in *Corpus Reformatorum* (*CO*), 53.266.15–30, cited in T. H. L. Parker, *Calvin's Preaching* (Louisville: Westminster John Knox Press, 1992), 24–25.

9. Parker, *Calvin's Preaching*, 23. Similar sentiments are expressed by Heinrich Bullinger in *The Decades of Henry Bullinger* (Cambridge: Cambridge University Press, 1849–52; reprint, New York: Johnson Reprint, 1968), 8:64, 67; and in the Second Helvetic Confession, 1.4.

10. *CO* 53.264.8 in Parker, *Calvin's Preaching*, 25.

11. *CO* 53.520.40 in Parker, *Calvin's Preaching*, 26.

12. Parker, *Calvin's Preaching*, 23. Parker's study of Calvin is useful; his treatment of Bullinger in the same text does not take into account the full scope of Bullinger's writing on preaching, and presents a skewed picture of the topic. For Bullinger, see *PRRD*, 2:83–84. It may also be worth noting that Calvin's 1536 edition of the *Institutes* says nothing of preaching, save for a reference to the need for all "successors of the Apostles" to be preachers: "Those [ministers] who do not devote themselves to the preaching of the gospel and the administration of the sacraments, wickedly impersonate the apostles" (Calvin, *Institutes of the Christian Religion: 1536 edition*, trans. and ed. F. L. Battles (Grand Rapids: Eerdmans, 1986), 5:55. For Calvin, one could not be a minister without preaching.

13. Parker, *Calvin's Preaching*, 30.

Biblical writers is delivered by the preaching Church, and that message is God's message or Word; secondly because the same Spirit of God who gave the message continues to ensure that that message shall accomplish in any generation what he had originally intended in giving it."[14]

In discussing preaching, Calvin's *Institutes of the Christian Religion* complements the message of his sermons. In the fourth book of the *Institutes* he argues that just as God graciously gave the Israelites not only the law but also priests as interpreters, "so today he not only desires us to be attentive to its reading, but also appoints instructors to help us by their effort."[15] Calvin then suggests that this is "doubly useful," for, "on the one hand, he proves our obedience by a very good test when we hear his ministers speaking just as if he himself spoke."[16] On the other hand, the human interpreters display God's kindness; lest His majesty overwhelm even the pious, He uses preachers to "draw us to himself."[17] But preaching is not always for the good of the hearers. Sometimes it is used for the hardening of unbelieving hearts. Whether its effects are positive or not, the medium is always important and powerful.[18]

Naturally, Calvin recognized that not everyone thought so highly of preachers or preaching—certainly not everyone in Geneva. To those who say, "The authority of the Word is dragged down by the baseness of the men called to teach it," Calvin explained that they only "disclose their own ungratefulness." Indeed, those who refuse to hold to this "ordinary manner of teaching" are "fanatical men" who will "entangle themselves in many deadly snares." Their motives can be inferred from their actions: "Many," he declared, "are led by pride, dislike, or rivalry to the conviction that they can profit enough from private reading and meditation." Yet to refuse in "stubbornness" the "yoke of being taught by human word and ministry" is "like blotting out the face of God which shines on us in teaching." The reason? "Believers were bidden of old to seek the face of God in the sanctuary (Ps. 105:4), as is oftentimes repeated in the law (Ps. 27:8; 100:2; 105:4; I Chron. 16:11; II Chron. 7:14) for no other reason than that for them the teaching of the law and the exhortation of the prophets were a living image

---

14. Parker, *Calvin's Preaching*, 30–31.

15. J. Calvin, *Institutes of the Christian Religion*, ed. J. T. McNeill, trans. F. L. Battles (Philadelphia: The Westminster Press, 1960), 4.1.5.

16. Calvin, *Institutes*, 4.1.5. The editor notes that in his homilies on 1 Samuel 42, Calvin says pastors and prophets are "the very mouth of God" (*Institutes*, 1018n11). Calvin carefully states elsewhere that although this is the case, post-apostolic preachers are to preach only what the Scripture says, and invent no new doctrines (*Institutes*, 4.8.9).

17. Calvin, *Institutes*, 4.8.9.

18. Calvin, *Institutes*, 3.24.13.

of God, just as Paul asserts that in his preaching the glory of God shines in the face of Christ (II Cor. 4:6)."[19]

Without lowering the place of preaching, Calvin was careful to qualify this discussion in two ways. First, he anticipated the objection of the parishioner who wants to know if God always and only uses the outward and ordinary means of preaching. In answer, Calvin argued that "although God's power is not bound to outward means, he has nonetheless bound us to this ordinary manner of teaching."[20] Second, he noted that in his day there is "great controversy over the efficacy of the ministry." Citing a variety of passages, Calvin argued that preaching is only and always effective when God changes hearts, sends His Spirit, and gives the growth.[21] But while God receives all the glory, Calvin also noted that "God often commended the dignity of the ministry by all possible marks of approval in order that it might be held by us in the highest honor and esteem, even as the most excellent of all things."[22] For,

> God testifies that, in raising up teachers for them, he bestows a singular benefit upon men when he bids the prophet exclaim, "Beautiful are the feet and blessed the coming of those who announce peace" (Isa. 52:7), and when he calls the apostles "the light of the world" and "the salt of the earth" (Matt. 5:13–14). And this office could not be more splendidly adorned than when he said, "He who hears you hears me, and he who rejects you rejects me" (Luke 10:16). But no passage is clearer than that of Paul in the second letter to the Corinthians, where he, as if purposely, discusses this question. He therefore contends that there is nothing more notable or glorious in the church than the ministry of the gospel, since it is the administration of the Spirit and of righteousness and of eternal life (II Cor. 4:6; 3:9).[23]

It is clear that for Calvin, the ordinary means of grace are not in any way mundane. To cite two additional examples, Calvin's comments on Luke 10:16 indicate that sermons are to be respected by the hearers;[24] Calvin's treatment of Romans 10:14–15, 17 illustrates that for the Genevan, preaching is God's ordinary means of grace and is a "pledge and proof of the

---

19. Calvin, *Institutes*, 4.1.5.
20. Calvin, *Institutes*, 4.1.5. Elsewhere, when speaking about other outward and ordinary means, Calvin notes that the Lord's Supper cannot be properly administered apart from the preached Word (*Institutes*, 4.17.39).
21. Calvin, *Institutes*, 4.1.6.
22. Calvin, *Institutes*, 4.3.3.
23. Calvin, *Institutes*, 4.3.3. See also 4.1.5 and 4.3.1.
24. J. Calvin, *Calvin's Commentaries: A Harmony of the Gospels, Matthew, Mark and Luke*, trans. T. H. L. Parker, ed. D. W. Torrance and T. F. Torrance (Grand Rapids: Eerdmans, 1972), 2:17–18.

divine love." In his conclusion he states that "this is a noteworthy passage on the efficacy of preaching, for Paul declares that faith is produced by preaching" whenever "the Lord is pleased to work."[25]

Preaching and the Episcopate

While Calvin's convictions about preaching were inspirational for Edward VI's church (and heretical for Mary's), they were not even aspirational for Elizabeth's. In fact, the increased reading of prefabricated homilies during Matthew Parker's time as Archbishop of Canterbury (1559–1575), combined with threats of ejection leveled at nonconformists, led to more vigorous assertions on the part of puritans regarding the cardinal place of preaching in the church even as godly preachers were gradually marginalized.[26] Only the death of Parker and the enthronement of Edmund Grindal as archbishop (r. 1576–1583) were able to stem the tide of puritan discontent.

In the brief season of his active rule, Grindal worked for the promotion of preaching and was eager to support means of educating or rehabilitating ill-prepared or lazy ministers. He was eager to bless not only "exercises" where one minister might preach or lecture but also the activity called "prophesying," an immensely popular event among the godly, imported from Zurich by returning Marian exiles, wherein a group of preachers team-preached a single sermon: one expounded a passage, the next explained its doctrine, another listed its uses or preached its applications. The prophesyings, as well as the extended meetings among ministers that usually followed, were useful for training preachers—for taking men who because of either indolence or lack of ability read only other people's sermons, and equipping them to construct and deliver their own sermons. Most bishops turned a benevolent blind eye to prophesyings since the majority of the episcopate could see their usefulness. As it happened, the prophesyings were not approved by the queen, but her desire to halt them could usually be evaded or incompletely enforced.

Grindal's well-known spirit of cooperation in promoting preaching made him a favorite among the godly. Men radicalized by Parker grew quiet under Grindal; puritans were happy to be mere Protestants. Unfortunately, soon after he was consecrated archbishop, rumors reached the queen about disorderly prophesyings. Elizabeth summoned Grindal to London

---

25. J. Calvin, *Calvin's Commentaries: The Epistle of Paul the Apostle to the Romans and to the Thessalonians*, trans. R. Mackenzie, ed. D. W. Torrance and T. F. Torrance (Grand Rapids: Eerdmans, 1991), 231–33. See also Calvin's comments on Isaiah 52:7 (*Commentary on the Book of the Prophet Isaiah*, trans. W. Pringle [Grand Rapids: Baker, 1993], 3:99–100).

26. P. Seaver, *The Puritan Lectureships: The Politics of Religious Dissent, 1560–1662* (Stanford: Stanford University Press, 1970), 17.

and informed him that she wanted prophesyings abolished. She reminded him of her view that it was enough for a given county to have a handful of preachers. No more than that were needed. Fatefully, Grindal informed the queen that she was wrong: the "public and continual preaching of God's word is the ordinary mean and instrument of the salvation of mankind. St. Paul calleth it the ministry of reconciliation of man unto God. By preaching of God's word the glory of God is enlarged, faith is nourished, and charity is increased. By it the ignorant is instructed, the negligent exhorted and incited, the stubborn rebuked, the weak conscience comforted."[27] Grindal also made an assertion about the relationship between monarchs and the church: "Bear with me, I beseech you Madam, if I choose rather to offend your earthly Majesty than to offend the heavenly Majesty of God." And, "Remember, Madam, that you are a mortal creature."[28] Prior to this point no one had thought it wise to inform the queen of these facts. Deeply angered, Elizabeth suspended Grindal from his archiepiscopal duties from 1577 until his death in 1583, permitting him to attend to administrative matters only and delegating his tasks to more pliable prelates, including John Whitgift, who helped to quench the prophesying movement in the southern province of the church and, after Grindal's death, took his place at Lambeth Palace (1583–1604).[29]

Whitgift was the implacable foe of puritanism, with a special gift for pushing people away from the middle of the church and toward the edges. He poured all of his energies into crushing presbyterianism (the form that puritanism tended to take in his day) as if there were no other enemy to England. He spied on them, arrested them, and endeavored to entrap them. He brought them before the High Commission and interrogated them. They were exiled and jailed. The extreme elements of the underground presbyterian press responded with pamphlets authored by the fictional Martin Marprelate, which discussed in public the doings of Canterbury's "Caiaphas." The pamphlets were witty, acidic, and widely read. But it was the undoing of Whitgift's more impatient opponents, for "Martin's" scurrilous prose lost the support of the moderate godly who had pitied the presbyterians up to this point. Two presbyterians were sentenced to death, and although the penalty for one was changed to exile, he died in prison anyway before he could be ejected from the country.

For England's puritans, Whitgift's reign was a time of subversion, protest, and failure. The queen and the archbishop not only opposed godly

---

27. Letter of December 20, 1576, cited in Seaver, *Puritan Lectureships*, 18.
28. P. Collinson, "Grindal, Edmund (1516x20–1583)," *Oxford Dictionary of National Biography* (Oxford: Oxford University Press, 2004).
29. Collinson, *Archbishop Grindal*, ch. 13.

preaching but, like medieval popes, undermined the likelihood of systemic improvement by granting permissions for pluralism, enabling ministers to hold multiple livings sufficiently distant from each other that the pastor could not possibly officiate each cure. Some of the problems with pluralism were better managed under later archbishops through revisions of canon law, but it was often the case that one or more of the parishes of a pluralist had no parson, and no preacher, since the curates appointed in their place were less likely to be equipped to, or permitted to, preach. True, some puritan preachers chose a curacy to avoid the attention from the authorities that a better-paid position might attract.[30] And yet for many curates their task was to administer the sacraments and read homilies approved by the church authorities.[31]

Puritans would always recall this as a painful season for the church in England. After all, as one petition explained, "the word of God preached" brought life, and since the people needed the Word of God applied to them, the minister's "absence from his flock [is] a dangerous and perilous thing."[32] No one missed the point. This tendency to tether salvation to preaching and then preaching to the residency of the pastor was not well received by the queen or by Whitgift. John Penry told the Court of High Commission that nonresident ministers were "odious in the sight of God and man," as they keep the people from "the ordinary means of salvation, which was the word preached."[33] Whitgift was neither slow nor ambiguous in his response: "I tell thee it is an heresy, and thou shalt recant it as an heresy."[34]

The heresy was as much economic as theological. England's system of patronage permitted clergy but also landed gentlemen, well-connected persons, lay corporations, or ecclesiastical officers to be rectors (that is, the one who "owns" and receives by right all the income that each benefice, such as a parish church, was owed from the people of that parish) or vicars (someone who "owns" and receives part of the income from a benefice).[35] From the perspective of a parish, the money that made up these benefices or "livings" was generated by a kind of ecclesiastical tax enforceable by law. From the perspective of a rector or a vicar, who might or might not be a

---

30. Cliffe, *Puritan Gentry*, 169.
31. For the comparison to Rome, see Collinson, *Elizabethan Puritan Movement*, 163.
32. Collinson, *Archbishop Grindal*, 18.
33. Collinson, *Archbishop Grindal*, 19.
34. Collinson, *Archbishop Grindal*, 19.
35. The right of patronage could be held as personal property, could be shared between two or more patrons, or could be held by virtue of an office. Among other resources, The Clergy of the Church of England Database has proved invaluable for understanding this process and for offering definitions of terms. Special thanks to Ken Fincham for answering queries about institution, induction, and other related matters.

clergyman, these livings offered a steady source of income. If the holder of the benefice was a licensed preacher, he was required to preach at or near his parish once each Sunday. If the holder of the benefice was not himself a preacher, he had the legal obligation to provide a preached sermon at least once a month in his parish or parishes (for example, through a curate who was paid a stipend), and on the other Sundays of the month the benefice holder or a curate needed to read one of the homilies of the Church of England. The same rules held for a beneficed preacher who for some legal reason was unable to regularly preach at his own church (for example, a person who had more than one benefice).[36]

As it happened, an educated or godly patron might appoint a highly qualified minister, especially in the church near his home, affording him quality sermons on a Sunday. The process of appointments is discussed more fully below.[37] Here it is enough to know that some patrons had the rights of appointment only, others were also benefice holders, but neither category of patron was required to be conscientious in the appointment of ministers. Some patrons fasted and prayed for an extended time before filling the vacancy—but not for too long since by law they would lose the right of appointment if the position was vacant for more than six months.[38] Others—and occasionally the same persons!—filled the place with the lowest bidder, reserving the remainder of the income coming from the tithes for themselves. Where this was done, the patronage and benefice system encouraged the hiring of low caliber candidates and the practice of pluralism. True, by the seventeenth century a minister who held more than one benefice needed to ensure they were no more than thirty miles apart, and he himself needed to hold at least a master of arts degree—so not every minister could be a pluralist.[39] Nonetheless, the system incentivized ministers to serve more than one parish in order to make ends meet, or to collect more than one living in order to live at (or above) the social standing that was expected of a clergyman and his family, even if those livings were so far apart that one could not possibly pastor both flocks.[40] Pluralism was a problem during Parker's reign. Grindal only began to address it, and the situation only slowly improved as the sixteenth century gave way to the seventeenth.

Whitgift's death brought the comparative relief of Archbishop Richard Bancroft (1604–1610)—at least after the confrontational Hampton

---

36. *Constitutions and Canons Ecclesiastical* (London, 1604), canons 46 and 47. The process by which one became a parish minister is discussed in chapter 4.
37. See chapter 4.
38. Cliffe, *Puritan Gentry*, 175–76.
39. *Constitutions and Canons Ecclesiastical*, canon 41.
40. The Reformation left the system of patronage intact in most places in Europe.

Court conference between the king's bishops and puritan leaders. Then came an even more encouraging season under Archbishop George Abbot (1610–1633), at least with respect to the promotion of preaching. But under both bishops, any renewed interest in preaching had more to do with the court than with Canterbury. During his time in Scotland, King James VI and I appears to have acquired an appreciation for sermons. Upon assuming the English throne, he even took steps to bring Scottish preachers into English cathedrals to foster a better preaching ministry in England. In this environment strong statements about preaching could come from almost any quarter without fear of reprisal. Thus, William Bradshaw confidently argued that the greatest work done by Christ and His apostles, and the greatest work done in the church, was preaching.[41]

Those who objected to the prominence that preaching enjoyed under James found it prudent to wait for a different monarch before publicly venting their frustration. Thus in 1626, and with a new king, Charles I, on the throne, the anti-puritan Henry Valentine finally found the courage to protest what he saw as an ongoing tendency on the part of the godly to "shrink up all religion into preaching."[42] Valentine waited for the political winds to change before making his complaint, but his concerns were probably not new and may have been inflamed by the opinions of preachers such as Ralph Kirk, the Manchester curate who as early as 1604 is alleged to have said that "no man was ever saved but by preaching,"[43] or by Nicholas Byfield, who in two separate works argued that people could not enter heaven without the aid of preaching.[44] He might also have heard of puritan-induced nightmares, like the wedding of Lady Russell's son, where yet another sermon was substituted for the customary dance.[45] It was more likely that Valentine would have been exposed to the works of three generations of puritans such as William Perkins (1558–1602), William Ames (1576–1633), and James Ussher (1581–1656), godly leaders in England, the Netherlands, and Ireland who wrote about the importance of gospel proclamation during the reigns of Whitgift, Bancroft, and, later, William Laud.[46]

---

41. Davies, *Worship of the English Puritans*, 183.
42. Seaver, *Puritan Lectureships*, 20.
43. R. C. Richardson, *Puritanism in North-West England: A Regional Study of the Diocese of Chester to 1642* (Manchester: Manchester University Press, 1972), 41.
44. Richardson, *Puritanism in North-West England*, 41.
45. Seaver, *Puritan Lectureships*, 39.
46. W. Ames, *The Marrow of Theology*, trans. J. D. Eusden (Grand Rapids: Baker, 1997), 182–89 (XXXIII–XXXIV). For Ussher's views of preaching, see J. Ussher, *The Whole Works of the Most Rev. James Ussher*, ed. C. R. Elrington (Dublin: Hodges, Smith and Co., 1864), 1:284–87; for an elevated view of preaching as the "Word of God," see 13:558, 562–66; see also important comments in 11:215, 216.

Among the moderate puritans, William Perkins represented the most significant defining influence for later formulations of godly pulpit theology. While simultaneously occupied as a Cambridge preacher and Cambridge fellow, Perkins authored a series of theological and pastoral treatises, including his manual for preachers, *The Art of Prophesying*, in 1592.[47] According to Perkins, "The dignity of the gift of preaching is like that of a lady helped into and carried along in a chariot, while other gifts of speech and learning stand by like maidservants, conscious of her superiority." "If anyone asks which spiritual gift is the 'most excellent,' undoubtedly the prize must be given to prophesying"—by which Perkins simply meant preaching, not the prophesying events of which the queen disapproved. There are two reasons for his elevation of preaching: (1) It "is instrumental in gathering the church and bringing together all of the elect"; (2) It "drives away the wolves from the folds of the Lord."[48] Behind this is the reality that it is "not so much the preacher who is speaking but the Spirit of God in him and by him."[49]

Perkins's writing was important to members of the Westminster Assembly. Many of the statements found in his brief chapters on prophesying would later be echoed in the Westminster Assembly's Directory for Public Worship and its chapter on Scripture in the Westminster Confession of Faith.[50] As well, the assembly was to make use of Perkins's threefold sermon structure (or fourfold if Scripture reading is included). According to Perkins, preaching involves

1. Reading the text clearly from the canonical Scriptures.

2. Explaining the meaning of it, once it has been read, in the light of the Scriptures themselves.

3. Gathering a few profitable points of doctrine from the natural sense of the passage.

---

47. W. Perkins, *The Workes of That Famous and Worthy Minister of Christ in the University of Cambridge, Mr. William Perkins* (Cambridge, 1617), 2:646–73 (citations are taken from W. Perkins, *The Art of Prophesying* [Edinburgh: Banner of Truth, 1996], 3–79). For the best brief summary of Perkins's life, see the biographical essay in Michael Jinkins, "Perkins, William (1558–1602)," *ODNB*. For a study of Perkins's theology of preaching, see J. A. Pipa, "William Perkins and the Development of Puritan Preaching" (PhD diss., Westminster Theological Seminary, 1985). For prophesying, see Collinson, *Elizabethan Puritan Movement*, 168–76.
48. Perkins, *Art of Prophesying*, 3.
49. Perkins, *Art of Prophesying*, 71–72.
50. See chapter 7.

4. If the preacher is suitably gifted, applying the doctrines thus explained to the life and practice of the congregation in straightforward, plain speech.[51]

Implied in this summary is not only the idea that preaching is vital but that it is vital because it provides something that the bare reading of the Word does not. Perkins assumed that the learned minister would be able to explain the text in a way that could benefit hearers, that he will be able to understand and expound the doctrine or doctrines of the text more clearly than the layperson, and that, if he is skillful, he will be able to apply it in a way that the person in the pew would not be able to do for himself or herself. Most of all, the preacher can show how all of Scripture points to Christ. As Perkins says in the beginning of his work, "Preaching the Word is prophesying in the name and on behalf of Christ."[52] As he says at the end of his book, "The heart of the matter is this: Preach one Christ, by Christ, to the praise of Christ."[53] For Perkins, then, preaching is of prime importance because it does things for the church that the reading of the Scriptures alone would not do.

Archbishop William Laud

With the enthronement of Archbishop William Laud in Canterbury, the debate shifted from the efficacy of the Word read and preached to the efficacy of Word and sacrament. In the previous century John Jewel had emphasized a balance between preaching and the sacraments. Later puritans tipped the scales by throwing a few more pounds on the side of preaching, but Laud placed his full weight on the sacraments, completely removing any vestiges of moderation from the debate.[54] Where Ussher was accused of devaluing the Eucharist over against the sermon, Laud elevated the sacraments at the expense of preaching.[55] As Paul Seaver explains, "Archbishop Laud…never one to equivocate,…reversed the puritan position. Reverence is properly accorded to the altar." In Laud's now famous words, the altar is "the greatest place of God's residence upon earth. I say the greatest, yea greater than the pulpit, for there it is 'Hoc est Corpus Meum,' This is my body; but in the pulpit, it is at most but 'Hoc est Verbum meum,' This is my word. And a greater reverence, no doubt, is due to the Body than to

---

51. Perkins, *Art of Prophesying*, 79.
52. Perkins, *Art of Prophesying*, 7.
53. Perkins, *Art of Prophesying*, 79.
54. Seaver, *Puritan Lectureships,* 20; see esp. A. Hunt, "The Lord's Supper in Early Modern England," *Past and Present*, 161 (1998): 39–83.
55. For comment on Ussher's view of the Eucharist, see *Whole Works*, 1:289, note i.

the Word of our Lord."[56] Horton Davies wryly observes that "Laud insisted that all altars should be railed: he never thought of railing off the pulpit."[57]

As under Whitgift, so under Laud, the concern of the most serious Reformers was structural: the government of the church itself needed to be changed. As well, daily offense was found in the Laudian elevation of all things ceremonial. As Marshall would later say, "They did so mix their humane Inventions with Gods Institutions, that we could not have the worship of God according to the pattern, but must wound our consciences if pertake of the Ordinances."[58] The godly would routinely stress that they held the same doctrine as the rest of the Church of England, and they were pleased to cite comments by Archbishop Sandys, King James, and Lancelot Andrewes to that effect.[59] In lobbying for change, they were as loyal to the crown as their neighbors.[60] They were simply not in tune with innovation.[61] Or with the devaluation of preaching.

Arguably, amid all the turmoil over worship and the means of grace in the first half of the seventeenth century, preaching was in fact holding its own. Nonetheless, under Charles and Laud the institution was undervalued, and the godly were especially sensitive because convictions about the necessity of preaching had slowly begun to erode in the early 1600s with the increased publication of godly literature and the correlative rise in literacy. Arguably, this is why objections in the 1630s against the efficacy of preaching were so painful. Previously, when bishops unsympathetic to preaching came home to roost in the church hierarchy, it ruffled the feathers of preaching advocates in their respective dioceses. But as the years went on, those truly committed to the uniqueness of preaching were deeply concerned that if preaching did not improve, and if preachers were not added to the church, thousands of souls would perish. It was surely a knee-jerk reaction to Laudianism that led the (soon to be) Westminster divine Richard Heyrick (1600–1667) to modestly inform his parishioners that "heaven itself cannot show forth a more excellent creature than a faithful preacher."[62] And it was also in response to Archbishop Laud and his

---

56. Seaver, *Puritan Lectureships*, 20 (citing Laud).

57. H. Davies, *Worship and Theology in England: From Andrewes to Baxter and Fox, 1603–1690* (Princeton: Princeton University Press, 1975), 138.

58. Marshall, *Power of the Civil Magistrate*, 24.

59. E.g., T. Thorowgood, *Digitus Dei: New Discoveryes; With Sure Arguments to Prove That the Jews (a Nation) or People Lost in the World for the Space of Near 200 Years, Inhabite Now in America* (London, 1652), 79.

60. E.g., Thorowgood, *Digitus Dei*, 81; W. Twisse, *Of the Morality of the Fourth Commandement* (London, 1641), 37, 34 [sic].

61. Twisse, *Of the Morality of the Fourth Commandement*, 37.

62. Richardson, *Puritanism in North-West England*, 71.

policies that on November 17, 1640, Cornelius Burges (d. 1665) and Marshall preached to the House of Commons, each of them bemoaning the lack of preaching in the land.⁶³

The Long Parliament, when it was summoned in the final weeks of 1640, quickly made itself a major patron of preaching, privileging reform-minded preachers and "ordering" them to print their sermons for the public eye. In 1641 the House of Commons, presumably with much encouragement from preachers and a few dissenting votes among its members, went so far as to declare that preaching "is even the way to bring People into a state of Salvation; it is the way to save their souls." The agreed-upon text for the declaration was Romans 10:13–14; the agreed-upon metaphor was the minister sent "as an ambassador, to publish and spread abroad the mind and message of God touching Man's duty, and salvation, and to instruct the Church of God."⁶⁴ That these laymen took such an interest in preaching appears curious, but as Paul Seaver points out, "If salvation depended on preaching, all laymen had a legitimate interest in the minister's ability to preach" and, we could add, the church's ability to find preachers.⁶⁵

The Commons' declaration leaves us on the eve of the assembly and with a functional sketch of the assembly's ecclesial environment. This sketch reveals an established godly tradition that valued preaching for the sake of the church as the ordinary means for salvation. The assembly's debates and the statements of individual divines need to be heard in this context—a context where the importance of preaching and preachers might have been taken for granted by the disputants at the assembly but not, as they would well know, by the church at large.

---

63. C. Hill, *The English Bible and the Seventeenth-Century Revolution* (London: Penguin, 1995), 84–86.

64. Seaver, *Puritan Lectureships*, 20.

65. Seaver, *Puritan Lectureships*, 46.

CHAPTER 3

"Democratick Annarchie"

It is this day ordered by the Lords and Commons in Parliament assembled, that the meeting of the assembly of divines, together with some members of both Houses of Parliament, shall be on Saturday the first of July 1643. at nine of the clock in the morning, in the chappell commonly called, King Henry the seventh his chappell in the city of Westminster: and hereof all parties herein concerned are to take notice, and make their appearance accordingly.

—John Brown, clerk of Parliament

For the English men and women wending their way toward the abbey at half past eight on Saturday morning, July 1, 1643, hoping to hear the opening sermon of the Westminster Assembly, there was reason for thanksgiving that an assembly had been called.[1] But it was hardly an idyllic moment. In the summer of 1643 the economy was suffering severely in many parts of England and Wales, and it had been for many months. Furthermore, in spite of the good weather, it looked as though many of the reapers and laborers would not be home at harvest time. Most people still had food, but the future looked grim. Far worse than the lack of money and food were the stories that were being brought to London. The divines, coming from all over England, could tell of parishioners who had left home and never returned, of houses that were looted, and of property plundered and even burned. Crops were regularly trampled on and pilfered.[2] Some divines and parishioners suffered from soldiers billeted in their homes at the monetary expense and sometimes ruin of homeowners. Occasionally the soldiers left other forms of devastation. Admittedly, a few ministers and merchants ended up with life improvements during the 1640s. But most

---

1. *It Is This Day Ordered by the Lords and Commons in Parliament Assembled, That the Meeting of the Assembly of Divines, together with Some Members of Both Houses of Parliament, Shall be on Saturday the First of July 1643* (London, 1643).

2. J. Guy and J. S. Morrill, *The Tudors and Stuarts* (Oxford: Oxford University Press, 1992), 110.

clergy and citizens suffered in some form or other. Outside of the abbey there was a war going on, and those inside needed to hear prolocutor William Twisse's (1577/8–1646) sermon about a sovereign God and a wise and holy Comforter.

Civil War

It had begun the year before. In 1642 the world, or at least Britain and Ireland, was turned upside down. Long-term economic and ecclesiastical frictions and an interconnected web of political missteps in the three nations of England, Scotland, and Ireland had finally brought every part of the Atlantic archipelago into an agonizing civil war. Noblemen, knights, gentlemen, citizens, burgesses, and commoners of all sorts took up arms against their king, Charles I. Some of their complaints were fiscal and political, but many of their grievances were specifically religious. Some were Parliamentarians wanting to rein in their king; some of their number were budding libertarians; many were Reformed Christians and puritans, wanting a change in worship, discipline, and theology that Protestant King Charles and his Roman Catholic wife strenuously opposed.

In England, a large party followed the king and his supporters to Oxford to defend the rights and liberties of the true religion and the English people (where, in January of 1644, he erected his own Parliament).[3] Meanwhile, the revolutionary citizens flocked to London and Westminster Palace, where the "real" Parliament sat to defend the rights and liberties of the true religion and the English people; the remainder stayed home and tried to defend their liberties and religion by keeping both king and Parliament off their land. It was not always easy to decide which party to follow; they often used the same language and made the same claims.[4] Not a few Englishmen sampled all three options, sometimes all at once—John Morrill cites the case of William Davenport of Bramhall, who sent servants to fight for the king and money to support Parliament while he himself stayed home, presumably to protect his property from marauding troops of either party.[5]

Students of puritanism need to remember that the assembly met during a peculiar time in English social and religious history. The nation was fractured in half by a civil war, with one government in Oxford and a rival government in Westminster. Among the disruptions created by this divide was a lack of control over the printing press and the circulation of

---

3. See R. Cust, *Charles I: A Political Life* (Harlow: Pearson, 2005), 381–85.
4. For the near-identical claims of each party, see J. S. Morrill, *Revolt in the Provinces: The People of England and the Tragedies of War, 1630–1648* (London: Longman, 1999), 52–53.
5. See Morrill, *Revolt in the Provinces*, 54–68, esp. 61.

ideas, for the existence of two authorities did not make printers twice as careful about what they published or pastors more careful about what they preached. Some of the ideas that circulated in print and on the street in the early 1640s were seen as revolutionary political ideas. Others, sometimes promoted by the same people, were judged heterodox theological ideas. Some were new, many were old, but for whatever reason, by 1643, London's muddy streets had proved to be an ideal seedbed for sectarian ideas. Perhaps on that Saturday morning in July the gathered politicians at Westminster Palace worried that defective religion would lead to bad politics, and the theologians meeting at Westminster Abbey fretted that bad politics could somehow lead to spiritual deviation. Either way, the war served as a stimulus both to social and religious radicalism and raised new challenges for reform-minded people.[6] The old image of the problem preacher as a greedy pluralist or a dissolute crypto-Catholic did not need to be abandoned by the godly; the legacy of the Whitgifts and Lauds of England's episcopal leadership would not be forgotten. But soon after the outbreak of war it became clear that Reformed orthodoxy could no longer advance its full forces against foes to the right, for on their left flank were other preachers who, because of ignorance or scandal, offered a message that was subversive of time-honored truths. In other words, by the outbreak of war it was more obvious than ever that the national church was troubled and deeply divided.

On the one hand, the church under Elizabeth and James had been drifting away from Edward's reforms, and then under King Charles had been hurtling toward Arminian theology and, as far as the godly were concerned, Roman Catholic worship. This drift or trajectory of the church found favor with a significant sector of the population and continued to do so throughout the 1640s, a fact that was profoundly disturbing to the godly.[7] The men who would be meeting day by day in the abbey, on this account, faced an opportunity and a challenge. Assembly members were being offered the first chance to make the Church of England more Reformed since the time of Edward VI. And yet, given the reality of a strong antireform party and its successes in recent decades, the assembly's task was not simply to steer English Christians in a more Reformed direction. Rather, it was to first stop the movement of the churches and cathedrals of England—already moving at a brisk trot toward Laudian liturgical conformity—and then reverse the direction completely.

---

6. For social radicalism, see K. Lindley, *Popular Politics and Religion in Civil War London* (Aldershot: Scolar Press, 1997); for religious radicalism, see A. Hughes, *Gangraena and the Struggle for the English Revolution* (Oxford: Oxford University Press, 2004).

7. J. S. Morrill, *The Nature of the English Revolution* (London: Longman, 1993), 148–75.

On the other hand, there was the phenomenon that a Scottish commissioner to the Westminster Assembly, Robert Baillie, termed "democratick annarchie." Baillie, fond of vivid language and apt to exaggerate, tended to sensationalize his reports of events in London. Nonetheless, it was true that for some people, the assembly could never do enough to distance the church from its medieval and Roman Catholic past—they wanted a Reformation more radical than anything England had yet seen.[8] This alarmed those who merely wanted England to complete its Reformation in a way analogous to the Reformations on the continent. They were worried when the local butcher's apprentice began to sound like a radical sectarian— perhaps a "Seeker." The butcher himself was no Seeker, but he appeared to be an Anabaptist with antinomian leanings, and he had convinced a dozen people to start another church in his house—thankfully not in his shop. The rumor was that the odd-jobs man who was usually in front of Saint Paul's was selling anti-Trinitarian pamphlets. If so, he could still be arrested, but in the minds of the godly, London was slowly, or not so slowly, being overrun by schismatic and often heretical teachers.

There has been controversy about the accuracy of extreme pictures such as the one I have painted here. On the one hand, John Morrill suggests that the number of radicals in England was very low: "It is easy to lose sight of the fact that even at the end of the 1640s, the vast majority of the population went into their own parish church or (if they had the kind of choice that town-dwellers had) into a neighbouring church."[9] David Como, on the other hand, has argued that "these are only those cases that have left a discernible mark on the documentary record, and therefore represent what is very likely the tip of the historical iceberg." More to the point, if "by 1633, most of London's antinomians had been silenced, and mainstream puritan divinity reigned supreme," it was also true that "the chaos of the 1640s brought these conflicts once again to the surface."[10]

Certainly, radicals were not to be found behind every large tree or church pillar. They were probably not found in large numbers in the nave of Westminster Abbey on the assembly's opening day. And they were not an entirely new phenomenon: godly ministers, including Henry Roborough (d. 1649), Cornelius Burges, and Edward Reynolds (1599–1676), had actively opposed marginal or fringe elements around the puritan movement already

---

8. E.g., see P. C. H. Lim, *Mystery Unveiled: The Crisis of the Trinity in Early Modern England* (Oxford: Oxford University Press, 2012), 16–68.

9. J. S. Morrill, "The Puritan Revolution," in *The Cambridge Companion to Puritanism*, ed. J. Coffey and P. C. H. Lim (Cambridge: Cambridge University Press, 2008), 76–77.

10. D. R. Como, *Blown by the Spirit: Puritanism and the Emergence of an Antinomian Underground in Pre-Civil-War England* (Stanford: Stanford University Press, 2004), 393.

in the 1620s and 1630s. But the presence of these promoters of unorthodoxy was felt. If in the 1620s and 1630s educated Englishmen were increasingly unclear as to why the Bible had to be expounded when it was so clear to begin with, in the 1640s uneducated Englishmen questioned why, if preaching were needed at all, the preacher had to be trained and ordained. July of 1643 was not the epicenter of the chaos that Como discusses, and the theologically grim scenes and stories in works such as the presbyterian Thomas Edwards's *Gangraena* no doubt contained exaggerations, but radical writers and preachers could hardly be forgotten by the people present in the abbey.[11]

Students of preaching and puritanism need to recognize the realities of Britain's civil strife not only to understand the abnormal political and theological contours of the decades when the puritan movement reached a kind of ascendancy, but also to join historians in pondering questions of cause and effect, since for centuries polemicists and academics have asked if puritans or their opposites are to be blamed for inciting civil war. The other, more obvious reason why this study needs to keep the civil war in view is that it led to the calling of the Westminster Assembly. Parliament summoned the assembly with the hope that it would address England's ecclesiastical problems, offering not cosmetic corrections but renewed hope and vigor to a church plagued with deep structural problems. The men and women gathered in the abbey that Saturday morning, leaning against the pillars in the nave and waiting for the sermon to begin, would have known that too.

Reform by Parliament

As mentioned earlier, the desire to address church structures, and not just ceremonies, had long been a feature of the most ardent reforming spirits since the days of Elizabeth: the governmental organization of the church needed to be renovated; its disciplinary methods had to be repurposed to serve pastoral and remedial ends, and not merely administrative and punitive ones; and a filter had to be created through which prospective ministers and ministers in transition would need to pass. This tripartite approach to change offered real possibilities for suppressing residual popery in all of its forms. But this three-pronged weapon also gave the godly a chance to fight back against deviant theology. Admittedly, most battles with the enemies of orthodoxy were fought first, and chiefly, on the hard turf of ideas. For example, David Como argues that in combating antinomianism,

---

11. For another assessment of radicalism in London, see Hughes, *Gangraena*, esp. p. 170 where Hughes concludes that Thomas Edwards's dire picture of London is likely derived from "actual" or "real" "encounters and communications experienced directly by Edwards or passed on to him by others."

godly divines skirmished on three levels: "At its most basic level" there was "a struggle over the meaning of specific scriptural passages." Second, they could "assimilate antinomianism to some prior manifestation of the heretical spirit." Third, and "in the last resort, puritan polemicists appealed to fear of moral and social breakdown."[12]

This was a war of words, and it offered mixed results. What mainstream puritan preachers really wanted to do—and prior to the Westminster Assembly could not do—was to deal decisively with the teachers themselves. They needed to govern, discipline, and, if necessary, replace these preachers. Prior to the Long Parliament, puritan preachers sometimes took the risky step of turning over an antinomian, Anabaptist, or otherwise erring opponent to the ecclesiastical authorities.[13] But these efforts could easily backfire, bringing trouble on the accuser himself. And besides, restless spirits needed more than an archbishop's court; they needed an opportunity to sit under godly preachers and be influenced by biblical doctrinal formulations.

For the godly, it could not be more obvious that structural changes were needed; the church was in a perpetual state of emergency until something radical could be done. Direct appeals to James and Charles had proved useless. Appeals to Parliament found more willing spirits, but the House of Commons was unable to make headway with either father or son. Thus, the most the godly could do was to try to put out fires in the 1620s and 1630s, knowing full well that neither monarch would seriously entertain any form of government that was not episcopal, or any purge of preachers for anything but gross immorality (or, of course, overt sympathy toward puritanism). Their only hope lay with Parliament, should some change in circumstances provide an opportunity for it to press once again for reform. Even that door closed when Charles managed to rule without Parliament from 1629 to 1640.

At the Assembly

Of the many debates held in the abbey, the contests over proposed structures of church governance are the ones best known today and were most publicized among assembly contemporaries. A majority rejection of episcopacy and majority acceptance of presbyterianism was complicated by a majority

---

12. Como, *Blown by the Spirit*, 394, 399, 403. For the assembly's attempts to quell heterodoxy, see W. G. Gamble, "'If Christ Fulfilled the Law, We Are Not Bound': The Westminster Assembly against English Antinomian Soteriology, 1643–1647" (PhD diss., University of Edinburgh, 2014).

13. E.g., P. Lake, *The Boxmaker's Revenge: 'Orthodoxy', 'Heterodoxy' and the Politics of the Parish in Early Stuart London* (Stanford: Stanford University Press, 2001), 221–30.

desire to accommodate congregationalists at the assembly and by the different shades of presbyterian practice and disagreements about presbyterian theory that emerged in the gathering. Here it needs to be noted only that certain topics of church government were linked to preaching, especially the consideration of church officers. One point on which diverging parties would eventually agree was that preachers would all be involved in the government of the church. There would be overseers of congregations who did not preach; they would be called ruling elders. But at least the problem of a bishop, as an overseer of preachers who did not himself regularly preach (a phenomenon more common under Charles than James), would be put to rest. Indeed, the ministry of the Word would not, except perhaps in academic settings, be separated from the government of the church at all.[14]

Assembly members also agreed that the same kind of systemic overhaul had to happen in the sphere of church discipline: pastoral practice needed to be guided by preachers even if ruling elders were to fully participate in the shepherding of the church. No longer were bishops, often through their legal agents, to exercise a cold, impersonal discipline. Rather, it was to be exercised in conjunction with the local preacher and ruling elders.

The godly needed the help of Parliament to effect these changes, but most men called to be members at the Westminster Assembly did not want to see further encroachments of the state on the church. Protestant states had been trending toward Erastianism since the heady days of the Zurich Reformation. For the majority in the assembly it was a matter of divine right, a matter of scriptural obedience and conscience, that the church alone conduct ecclesiastical discipline and thus combat Erastianism. Of course, it mattered most that the sacraments be guarded from pollution. But it mattered almost as much that this guarding be done in a prompt manner through the agency of the church by its preaching pastors and its eldership. It was a fighting matter, and the assembly kept up a losing battle for eighteen months in 1645 and 1646 before finally making peace with the suboptimal arrangement they were able to wrangle out of the House of Commons.[15]

Oddly enough, one argument against heavy pastoral involvement in church discipline, raised by a member of the House of Commons, was that the work of church discipline could hinder the kind of careful study that was needed for good preaching.[16] Certainly there was truth in the

---

14. For debates over church government, see C. B. Van Dixhoorn, "Presbyterian Ecclesiologies at the Westminster Assembly," in *The Keys of the Kingdom of Heaven: Church Polity in the English Speaking World, c.1636–1689*, ed. H. Powell and E. Vernon (Manchester: University of Manchester Press, forthcoming).

15. Van Dixhoorn, "Politics and Religion in the Westminster Assembly and the 'Grand Debate,'" 129–48.

16. BL Harl. 166 fol. 204a.

recognition of this tension. Church discipline, done rightly, would take considerable time and effort. But the solution to the dilemma of discipline was hardly straightforward. The subjects of discipline would be not only members of the church but also ministers of the church. And if government and discipline were not properly settled in the church, there could be no hope that the character of preachers and the content of their preaching could be wisely and pastorally monitored, corrected, and improved.

The enormity of the task that faced this reforming assembly, and the sorrows of the civil war that had occasioned the gathering, were articulated some time after nine o'clock on July 1, 1643. Fittingly, the key feature of the assembly's opening ceremonies was a sermon. Unsurprisingly, the sermon was not rushed: with the addition of some Scripture reading, prayers, and singing, the service stretched out three hours. The preacher, as advertised, was William Twisse, Parliament's appointed prolocutor or speaker for the new assembly. And at this pinnacle point in puritan history Twisse chose as his text John 14:18, "I will not leave you comfortlesse, I will come to you."[17] It was the Holy Spirit who was the primary Comforter; the comfort that preachers like Prolocutor Twisse had to offer could only be derivative and secondary.

The fact that this godly old preacher chose consolation rather than exaltation at this pivotal juncture underscores the anxiety that he sensed in the city and anticipated among his fellow assembly members. The choice of text was pastorally sensitive, but from a public relations standpoint it could hardly have sounded the positive note that Parliament wanted people to hear. Critical remarks about Twisse's effort were passed from one member to another in the House of Commons, and neither house of Parliament ordered the sermon to be printed, a routine standard of measurement for gauging parliamentary approval.[18] It was an ironic start for an iconic gathering, an assembly of preachers that hoped not only to effect a "further reformation" but to model it. Nonetheless it *was* a start, and it would not take long before the reformation of preaching was addressed by the assembly itself. For the watchmen of the assembly would prove themselves willing to do much more than issue apocalyptic warnings about the neglect of preaching or lofty statements about the power and importance of preaching. They would debate every aspect of the Bible's teaching on preaching, and the wisdom of commonly received practices in the church, as well as popular dictums on preaching held within the puritan community.

---

17. CUL Dd XIV.28(4), fo. 1r. For the time of day, see *Journal of the House of Commons*, 3:150, July 1, 1643: "The House adjourned till Twelve Clock, and went to the Sermon preached before the Assembly; and returned at the said Hour."

18. *MPWA*, 1:1.

PART II
A Reforming Assembly

The central part of this book outlines the assembly's own attempts to purge and to purify the pulpits of England and Wales and to set up a godly ministry that would gradually reform the people of the British archipelago through the agency of powerful pulpit preachers. In the initial stages of reform, this involved identifying preachers who needed to be removed from their parish ministries or places in Cambridge and Oxford fellowships as an aid to Parliament in its "speedy proceeding against blind guides and scandalous Ministers." It also entailed endorsing godly replacements for English and Welsh pulpits and equipping the church to carry on its own work of vetting ministers in the future.

Chapter 4 outlines the ministerial shortage that the reforming church faced and the assembly's "temporary" solution of conducting examinations itself until a more sustainable option was in place. Chapter 5 eavesdrops on the assembly's lively deliberations about the pastor's office, paying particular attention to the assembly's definition of the minister's task with respect to preaching. Chapter 6 examines the assembly's Directory for Ordination, comparing and contrasting the program for future presbyteries with the assembly's own examination practice. The final chapter in this section offers a close reading of relevant portions of the assembly's Directory for Public Worship, an illuminating text that has as much to say to preachers as it does about preaching.

CHAPTER 4

Purifying Pulpits: Assembly Examinations

11. What authors he hath been versed in.
12. Where he hath officiated, and why he leaves.
13. What skill he hath in the tongues and logic.
14. Trial of his knowledge in the chief grounds in religion.
15. That he be put to preach if he have leisure.
16. Trial to be taken how he can work upon consciences.
17. To be asked what he thinks of catechising, and of the right way of visiting of the sick.

—"Rules for the Examination of Ministers"

For one young boy, the arrival of the assembly at Westminster Abbey was exciting—so much so that he asked for permission to miss breakfast in order to hear assembly members preach. Each day, divines preached and prayed from six to eight in the morning at Saint Margaret's Church on the abbey grounds.[1] It was to attend these services that Philip Henry, father of the famous biblical commentator, received a note to regularly excuse him from the dining hall of Westminster School. Matthew Henry records that his father attributed his conversion to those morning sermons, especially the ministry of Stephen Marshall, one of London's favorite preachers throughout the 1640s.[2]

The abbey service was followed most mornings by the preaching of a probationer before a committee of the assembly or the full body. (At times a nervous probationer could run a little long, finally leading the assembly to decide that sermons may not extend beyond nine o'clock, for at that hour the assembly's plenary session formally began.)[3] The fact that the

---

1. M. Henry, "The Life of Mr. Philip Henry," in M. Henry, *The Complete Works of the Rev. Matthew Henry* (Edinburgh: Fullerton & Co., 1848), 2:607.
2. Henry, "The Life of Mr. Philip Henry," 606–8.
3. *MPWA*, 5:54–55.

assembly would find itself examining ministers was not at all obvious on the gathering's first day. The task of examination was not mentioned in the printed summoning ordinance that gave the assembly its mandate, it was not requested in any known petition prior to the assembly, and it was not discussed in either house of Parliament prior to the call of assembly members to Westminster. Furthermore, assessing ministers was bound to slow the assembly's progress in its appointed tasks. The examination of ministers and, later, of ministerial candidates can be understood only in the context of the clerical vacuum that Parliament itself had created and as an answer to the assembly's own first petition to Parliament on July 19, 1643, asking for the removal of "blind guides and scandalous Ministers, by whose wickednesse people either lack or loath the Ordinances of the Lord, and thousands of soules perish."[4]

Supply and Demand

In late 1642, a committee of the House of Commons had been established to relocate ministers sympathetic to Parliament who had fled approaching royalist armies or who were forcibly displaced and were plundered by royalist troops. Extending its remit, the same committee was also charged with removing scandalous or malignant ministers from their posts—those deficient in their "conversation" (conduct) or simply unwilling to ally themselves with the parliamentary cause. Nonetheless, while for many months Parliament ejected what it considered to be scandalous ministers, it shrank from the difficulty of developing a plan for filling the pulpits that were now empty. The summoning of the assembly provided a new opportunity, however, and on July 28, 1643, the House of Commons asked the assembly to examine all preachers who had been plundered by the king's forces and who wished to take the place of those "sequestered," or removed from their parish ministries, by Parliament.[5] As a result, twenty-six assemblymen were nominated as examiners, any five of which could constitute the committee.[6]

The assembly's role in the examination of ministers went through several phases. Although the examination of ministers was to consume a vast

---

4. *MPWA*, 5:11 (Doc. 1).

5. CUL Dd XIV.28(4), fos. 8v-9r; for subsequent legislation, see Shaw, *History of the English Church*, 2:279–81.

6. *Journal of the House of Commons*, 3:183 (July 27, 1643). The ordinance states that the Committee for Plundered Ministers was to nominate only persons approved by the assembly, and the assembly was to establish a committee for this purpose. However, the Committee for Plundered Ministers could eject ministers without consultation. A similar note is recorded in the minutes of the Committee for Plundered Ministers (see BL Add. MS 15669, fo. 2r).

amount of time, the initial task was limited in its scope to ejected ministers only. Parliament would refer a minister to the assembly for examination. If this exam was sustained, the assembly would then refer the person back to Parliament, and a ceremony conducted by an official of a bishop now willing to work with Parliament would institute and induct the man in his new living or benefice.

This initial effort was deemed to be such a success that the assembly's remit for the examination of plundered ministers was soon expanded to include an examination of all ministers changing their living within the church. This was an obvious expansion of the assembly's responsibilities. Faced with a qualitatively deficient ministry nationwide, Parliament (perhaps with prompting) was able to see an opportunity not only to eject the most obviously scandalous ministers but also to insist that all ministers attempting to move from one living to another (and not only those ministers displaced by the war) be examined and certified by the Westminster Assembly to see if they were worthy of their calling.

In time, the structure of certification was standardized. The assembly's vote was essential for a minister's approval. If the assembly voted against a minister he could not serve unless the assembly reversed its decision. Nonetheless, if the assembly approved a minister—that is, certified him as fit for ministry—he did not automatically end up in the church of his choice. Over time, the assembly determined that the congregation had to approve of his appointment, and so too did Parliament.[7]

What the Commons and the assembly achieved was astonishing. They had created a system to sift through the existing ministers of England and assess their characters and skills. This was not in place at the time of the Reformation, and even during the Great Ejection there would not be a national process so comprehensive in its scope. This moment, more than any before it, realized a crucial aspect of the puritan dream—a process, at least, to forcibly encourage godly, assiduous preachers and preaching.

Nonetheless, the ministry of England was not only qualitatively wanting; it was also quantitatively wanting, and although a few ministers could be sourced from Reformed churches overseas, the only real solution to the demand for more preachers in England (and for the army and navy) would have to come from a fresh supply at home. The problem was that neither Parliament nor the assembly had a way available to them to allow for the introduction of new ministers into the church. Institution and induction into a living—together the legal and financial sides of serving in a state church—were civil actions sanctioned previously by bishops and

---

7. See Van Dixhoorn, "Presbyterian Ecclesiologies at the Westminster Assembly."

archdeacons and their assistants; this was something Parliament was willing to direct itself. However, ordination was more clearly an action of the church, and the bishops who had once ordained new ministers were now removed from, or had fled from, their posts.

The process by which one became a clergyman, and in particular a benefice-holding clergyman, appears complex to those unfamiliar with the early modern manifestation of the Church of England. Prior to the outbreak of war and the flight of the bishops from the House of Lords and their episcopal posts, a candidate for ordination in the Church of England needed to present himself to a bishop and meet some basic requirements. He needed to be twenty-three years of age to be ordained a deacon, twenty-four years of age to be ordained a priest.[8] By 1604, to be eligible for ordination he needed to show proof that he was appointed, or about to be appointed, to some ministerial or academic calling, or that he had held a master of arts degree for five years and resided at one of the universities, or that the bishop himself was willing to "keep and maintain him with all things necessary" until he had an "ecclesiastical living" in which to put the man.[9] The ordinand also had to establish that he had satisfactory morals, demonstrated by letters of testimonial, and an adequate education, demonstrated by the completion of a university degree or the ability to give "an account of his faith in Latin, according to the Articles of Religion."[10] (A few of the papers submitted by candidates in preparation for ordination and in testimony of their characters survived from the 1630s and thereafter.)[11]

Also prior to ordination, a candidate was required to subscribe to three articles. The first upheld the monarch as "Supream Governour" of the realm and its dominions, "as well in all spiritual or ecclesiastical things or causes, as temporal." The second announced that the Book of Common Prayer and the government of the church contained "nothing contrary to the Word of God" and may "lawfully be so used." The third stated that the 1562 "Book of Articles of Religion" is "agreeable to the Word of God." The subscription formula itself was unambiguous: "I, N. N., do willingly, and ex animo, subscribe to these three articles above mentioned, and to all things that are contained in them."[12] Rarely could subscription be avoided, and only

---

8. One could not be ordained to the diaconate and then to the priesthood in one day. See *Constitutions and Canons Ecclesiastical*, canon 32.

9. *Constitutions and Canons Ecclesiastical*, canon 33.

10. *Constitutions and Canons Ecclesiastical*, canon 34.

11. D. M. Owen, *The Records of the Established Church in England Excluding Parochial Records* (London: British Records Association, 1970), 17; for examples, see 18–21.

12. *Constitutions and Canons Ecclesiastical*, canons 36 and 37.

Figure 1: Process of Episcopal Ordination in the Church of England, 1603–1640s

Maturity	• Must be twenty-three years of age for ordination as deacon
Sustenance	• Proof of appointment or pending appointment to a ministerial office • *or* proof of an MA degree and residence in a Cambridge or Oxford college • *or* proof that the bishop is willing to provide an income until an appointment becomes available
Morals	• Letters of testimonial regarding morals
Education	• Completion of university degree • *or* ability to give an account of one's faith in Latin
Subscription	• Article 1: Acknowledge the monarch as supreme governor of the church • Article 2: Agree that the BCP and government of the church are lawful, and not contrary to the Word of God • Article 3: Accept the Thirty-nine Articles as agreeable to the Word of God

Ordination as deacon	• At the cathedral or church of the bishop, in the presence of:
	  - the archdeacon, dean, and two cathedral officers
	  - *or* in the presence of four preaching priests with a minimum of an MA
	• Take an oath of the king's sovereignty and answer ordination questions
	• Bishops and other priests lay hands on ordinand and ordain him a deacon
	• *Note*: The right and responsibility to preach is not assumed in this ordination

Maturity	• Must be twenty-four years of age for ordination as priest

Ordination as priest	• At the cathedral or church of the bishop, in the presence of:
	  - the archdeacon, dean, and two cathedral officers
	  - *or* in the presence of four preaching priests with a minimum of an MA
	• Take an oath of the king's sovereignty and answer ordination questions
	• Bishops and other priests lay hands on deacon and ordain him a priest
	• *Note*: The right and responsibility to preach is not assumed in this ordination

then through the interposition of a powerful patron and the complicity of a bishop or his officials.[13]

Ordination to the diaconate or priesthood was to be carried out in the church or cathedral of the bishop in the presence of the archdeacon, the dean, and two prebendaries (the latter two categories being cathedral officers) or in the presence of four preaching priests with a minimum of a master of arts degree. During the service the deacon or priest would take an oath of the king's sovereignty and answer a series of questions, and both bishops and other priests would lay hands on those being ordained.[14]

The next step, for rectors and vicars but not for curates, was presentation—the appointment of the clergyman to a particular benefice (or "living"). The ordained minister was appointed to a benefice by a bishop of a diocese or some other "ordinary."[15] The appointment was a formal act where the patron presented the name of the clergyman whom he wished to see appointed to the benefice.[16] (This request could be denied by the ordinary, but such refusals were uncommon, not least because it could be challenged in civil court and because a "caveat" could be issued by either the patron or clergyman, keeping the ordinary from appointing anyone else to the benefice until the difference was settled in court.)[17]

Following ordination and presentation came institution. Here a bishop or some other ordinary committed a benefice to the care of the minister. The bishop would need proof of presentation from the patron, the clergyman's three subscription oaths, and letters of testimonial.

After institution came induction. It was at this point that a beneficed clergyman took possession of the financial rights associated with the living. Aspects of this final ceremony included the archdeacon or someone with similar authority placing the hands of the appointed clergyman on the doors of the church and tolling the church bell.

This method was enforced by a system of visitations by a bishop who was supposed to call on every place under his authority at least once in

---

13. Cliffe, *Puritan Gentry*, 176.

14. *The Forme and Manner of Making and Consecrating Bishops, Priestes, and Deacons* (London, 1627), sig. A5-A6, B-B3.

15. The "ordinary" is the person who exercises ordinary ecclesiastical jurisdiction over a particular place. In the case of a "peculiar"—that is, a place exempt from the jurisdiction of the bishop of a diocese—jurisdiction was exercised by a bishop from another diocese, some other ecclesiastical dignitary (such as an archdeacon or a cathedral officer), or even, in a few cases, a layman.

16. If the patron was also the ordinary, the "presentation" of a clergyman was not possible. In this case the process of appointment was called a "collation," which was nonetheless still followed by "induction" (what Presbyterians would call "installation." "Installation" in the Church of England referred only to bishops or officers of cathedrals).

17. That patrons were rarely challenged is also asserted in Cliffe, *Puritan Gentry*, 169.

three years, during which visit he would confirm young people, listen to the complaints of church wardens about ministers or church members, and require all ministers to display their papers for any activities or positions licensed by the church.[18] An expected fee was payable upon each bishop's first visit, after which the fee was reduced by half for all subsequent visits. If a new bishop was consecrated for the diocese, the fee schedule reset, with full payment once again due for his first visit and a half payment for all subsequent visits.[19]

Even though the fees payable to a bishop were modest, the system was not without its challenges. In the first place, the process of institution, that of assuming a benefice, could be prohibitively expensive. Ministers often had to pay the legal costs that their patrons incurred in drawing up a deed of presentation. Then there was a fee of institution to be paid to the bishop and his servants and a fee of induction to be paid to the archdeacon and his official. First fruits had to be paid to the Crown, a sum equal to a year of the minister's income. And an official inspection needed to be made of church property—including the minister's residence, barns, and the church building. Repairs had to be made by the incumbent or his estate or else the incoming minister would be fined for keeping the property in ill repair and forced to bear the costs of that repair. And the timing of one's institution mattered: if one came to a new living after harvest, when the tithes of the year had already been paid, he would incur all of these costs without receiving his annual income for another year.[20]

In the second place, the money that exchanged hands fell short of simony, but it did support a self-sustaining ecclesiastical bureaucracy that was in itself objectionable and open to abuse.[21] Ministers were not exactly buying their offices from the bishops or paying for the privilege of being ordained. Furthermore, the fee structure applied to any vocation controlled by the church (such as teaching in schools or midwifery), not simply to ordained persons. Nonetheless, an expansion of the number of people who

---

18. *Constitutions and Canons Ecclesiastical*, canons 86, 111, and 116.

19. *Constitutions and Canons Ecclesiastical*, canon 137.

20. R. A. Marchant, *The Church under the Law: Justice, Administration and Discipline in the Diocese of York, 1560–1640* (London: Cambridge University Press, 1969), 27–28. The systems of churchwardens, church repairs, and tithing were maintained during the interregnum. See Shaw, *History of the English Church*, 2:252–60.

21. The bishop of Norwich, for example, was to be charged by the House of Commons with "extorting of undue fees." See *Journal of the House of Commons, 1547–1629* (London: His Majesty's Stationery Office, 1802), 1:705.

Figure 2: Process of Obtaining a Benefice before 1643

Presentation and Appointment	• Patron presents priest to a bishop (or similar official) for a benefice (also known as a living) • Priest pays legal fees incurred by patron
Institution	• Priest pays institution fee to the bishop • Priest shows proof of presentation, three subscription oaths, and letters of testimonial
Induction	• Priest pays induction fee to archdeacon (or similar official) • Priest pays first fruits (equivalent of first year's income) to Crown • Archdeacon (or similar official) places hands of priest on the doors of church and tolls church bell • Priest takes possession of financial resources and responsibilities of benefice • *Note*: The right and responsibility to preach is not assumed in this process

had to pay would not salve sensitive consciences nor make an episcopal visit any more welcome.[22]

It should be noted that in this entire process, the clergyman's abilities and right to preach were not assumed. Obtaining a license to preach was a separate process, not included in or assumed by ordination, although by the seventeenth century an increasing number of ministers were licensed to preach.[23] If a clergyman were to be licensed to preach, his license came directly from the archbishop, or his local bishop, or from one of the two universities. But many ministers —even most ministers—were not permitted to preach. That this was troubling to parishioners was assumed in canon 57 of the canons of 1603. There parishioners were warned that they must

---

22. These were not the only costs of an episcopal visit. Dinner had to be supplied for the bishop and his administrators, and unless the churchwardens were themselves wealthy, this cost was passed on to the local church. Marchant, *Church under the Law*, 134–35.

23. Particularly challenging for those trying to understand the process described here is a certain ambiguity or fluidity in terminology. Letters of institution were in effect both a license to serve in the church and a legal confirmation of institution, but not a license to preach. At the same time, episcopal record books recording licenses for clergy note licenses to serve as a curate, or to preach, but not licenses to serve as the incumbent. See Owen, *Records of the Established Church*, 21. I am grateful to Ken Fincham for his help in interpreting canons 36 and 137 in particular.

not refuse to have their children baptized or to avoid taking Communion from a minister simply because he did not preach.[24]

Of course, ordination by bishops would have required a return to ecclesial aspects of these old ecclesiastical structures, including the laying on of the hands of a bishop and his associates, subscription to the canons of the church, and the disconnection of preaching from ordination. This was a proposal that the majority in the Westminster Assembly and in Parliament would not entertain.[25] And yet ordination by any other method demanded the creation and coordination of something new, which would strain the limited relational capital that members of Parliament could afford in the midst of a civil war. Once again, the matter was referred to the Westminster Assembly for its consideration, and by the autumn of 1643, the assembly was forced to grasp the thorny question of a theory, or at least a method, for ordination.

The assembly's answer was a temporary expedient: ordination solemnized by a committee of ministers nominated by the assembly and appointed by Parliament. (Only later would the assembly recommend that ordination be an action of presbyteries, thus creating a permanent mechanism for introducing new ministers into the church.) The remainder of the process, from appointment to induction, was not discussed by the assembly; it became a matter for Parliament itself to reform should it wish to do so, although the assembly would urge Parliament to keep better track of those they did institute and induct.[26]

Parliament accepted the expedient but undermined the importance of the assembly's text for ordination by insisting that the assembly continue examining candidates and ministers even after presbytcries were established. This was no mere pebble in a presbyterian shoe. The whole

---

24. For the efforts of the House of Commons to increase the number of preachers by appointing licensed preachers in parishes (supported by voluntary contributions), see *History of the English Church*, 2:182–85. Even more puzzling for the authorities was the phenomenon of people with a preaching minister visiting a neighboring church with an even better preacher; the wide variance in the quality of preachers was yet another issue that most bishops ignored. See Cliffe, *The Puritan Gentry*, 178–79.

25. All canons not enforced by civil statute were suspended by the House of Commons in May 1641. See *Journal of the House of Commons, 1640–1643* (London: His Majesty's Stationery Office, 1802), 2:152 (May 21, 1641). Furthermore, episcopal "administration of admission, institution, collation, or induction" was forbidden of the archbishop by Parliament at least from May 1643, and by other bishops even earlier. See *Acts and Ordinances of the Interregnum, 1642–1660*, ed. C. H. Firth and R. S. Rait (London: His Majesty's Stationery Office, 1911), 157–58; and, e.g., *Journal of the House of Commons*, 2:907 (Dec. 30, 1642).

26. See *MPWA*, 4:428–29 (Feb. 15, 1647; Sess. 792). For Parliament's ad hoc administration of patronage, institution, and induction, see Shaw, *History of the English Church*, 2:175–286.

assembly was given no relief from the duty of examination, not even after presbyteries were conducting full, multiday examinations of candidates themselves. This redundancy was emblematic of the tensions between Parliament and the assembly. The politicians wished to retain this newfound level of control over the ministry of the church through the agency of the assembly; the pastors wished to establish the self-government of the church without the interference of the civil magistrate. The unhappy solution, at least in the experience of many of those being examined, was to endure two sets of examinations.[27]

Godly Connections

When Parliament first assigned the assembly the task of examining preachers, a committee was created for the examination of ministers (and later, ordinands also) and began to function almost immediately, with John Ley (1584–1662), formerly a prebendary and subdean of Chester Cathedral, evolving into the role of chief examiner. At Dr. Thomas Temple's (1602–1661) request, the membership of the committee was reconstituted on June 4, 1644. Additional examiners were proposed, and liberty was granted to any member of the assembly to join and vote in the committee at any time.[28] Ley remained the de facto chair of the committee—indeed it came to be called "Mr. Ley's committee," and it remained under his guidance until late 1647.[29]

The records of the assembly's examination committee, like the records of almost all other assembly committees, appear to be lost. Nonetheless, through occasional reports of problems with ministers and through the gradual process of regularizing examinations with additional rules and structures, a picture of the assembly's examination procedures emerges. The first significant ruling about examinations came at the end of September 1643, when the assembly decided that its committee for ministerial examinations was to obtain the approval of the full assembly prior to recommending anyone for ministry, thus requiring the committee to make

---

27. It appears that in those areas of the country where presbyteries were not formed, the assembly's examination would be followed by ordination by a pro tempore committee of ministers and not a presbytery, which would have given some satisfaction to congregationalists resistant to the permanent establishment of presbyteries. Joel Halcomb's brief but illuminating essay "The Examination of Ministers" outlines the way in which the examination and approval process was managed between the Committee for Plundered Ministers and the Westminster Assembly (*MPWA*, 1:217–26).

28. *MPWA*, 3:129 (June 4, 1644; Sess. 231).

29. Beginning January 14, 1648, and without explanation, the assembly began to appoint a new chair for the committee each week. See *MPWA*, 4:723 (Sess. 993 and subsequent Friday sessions).

some kind of report to the full assembly about a person's "sufficiency" before a certificate of approval could be issued in the name of the assembly.[30] Already in the summer of 1643 the examination process relied heavily on letters of reference or testimonials (which sometimes, confusingly, were also called "certificates"). This practice was in continuity with what had been required of ordinands and ministers in the past. If these testimonials or references were deemed satisfactory and if the minister or his referees were known to the assemblymen, the minister would preach a sermon before the assembly or a committee of the assembly prior to the commencement of a plenary session.[31] In most cases letters of testimonial were considered sufficient to begin the process of examination, but if a testimonial was not deemed satisfactory, the minister was not admitted to examination and was instead asked to produce better letters of recommendation.[32]

Further study of the letters of reference sent to the assembly is needed before we can understand the importance of personal histories and connections between assembly members and referees. Nonetheless, it is apparent that the divines were so confident of their knowledge of the puritan network that they would refuse letters of reference if the author was not known to them, as in the case of a Mr. Atkinson who was to "bring a testimoniall of his piety from knowne men."[33] Occasionally the assembly wanted a letter from ministers closer to the current address of the minister.[34] In fact, in its early months the assembly came close to insisting that testimonials regarding the person's life must come "from those places of his abode." But with the displacements that accompanied the war, members saw too many difficulties with such a restriction rigorously applied, and the assembly's scribe deleted the clause.[35]

The assumptions that a godly man could always find a godly divine to recommend him and that the assembly's web of godly connections was sufficiently broad to reliably identify such a divine were telling. If a man was unacquainted with a godly minister known to the assembly who could

---

30. *MPWA*, 2:152–53 (Sept. 28, 1643; Sess. 64).

31. The minutes do not mention these sermons, and the first sermon mentioned by Lightfoot was preached on August 3, 1643: "This morning we had a Sermon[,] for the Committee for examination of ministers had appointed one to preach upon this text[,] 2 Chron. 16:9." See CUL Dd XIV.28(4), fo. 12r.

32. The majority of the surviving testimonials are in the Parliamentary Archives at Westminster Palace.

33. *MPWA*, 4:839 (June 20, 1650); Atkinson is himself sufficiently obscure that he was left unidentified in the recent edition of the assembly's minutes. For other examples of men referred for testimonials from known persons, see, for example, *MPWA*, 4:444–45, 470 (Mar. 1, 22, 1647; Sess. 800, 812).

34. E.g., *MPWA*, 4:602–3 (June 18, 1647; Sess. 865).

35. *MPWA*, 1:178 (Oct. 9, 1643; Sess. 70).

testify to his good character, he was not running with the right crowd. If the best that he could do was to bring a reference from known men with dubious credentials in godly circles, the assembly was immediately concerned about what this might say about the examinee's character, and the gathering would send the hopeful minister away with a requirement that he obtain letters of reference from "approved" or "godly" persons.[36] It is possible that this process of getting a letter from a "known" or "godly" man was intended to be a formative moment creating a positive influence: there was hope of the minister coming under the sway of godly men, perhaps growing in holiness. It would either be good for his character development or could lead to some needed repentance. Such repentance was sometimes needed. A Mr. Woodward was asked to write a paper about "his fall & his repentance." In this case the paper was deemed unsatisfactory, and the assembly decided not to proceed with an examination nor, it appears, with any further testimonials.[37]

There were other obvious reasons to request letters from known and godly men. Connection to certain names could suggest that a candidate had spent time with ministers involved in approved forms of puritan postgraduate education. Preparation for godly preachers was often furthered in informal "seminaries," such as the ones described by Tom Webster, or in the form of continuing education at prophesyings or godly conferences described by Webster and Patrick Collinson—all venues where people were encouraged and equipped to become better preachers.[38] Such known connections and assumed experiences must have played a substantial part in the assembly's examination process since ministers were occasionally approved without coming to the abbey.[39]

It was also possible that the assemblymen thought that unknown ministers might be willing to lie about a candidate's age, a minister's level of education, or some other necessary qualification. Worse, ministers who were unknown might not exist. For any number of reasons, then, the assembly would at times make further inquiries not about the examinee, but about his referees.[40] But these were exceptions to the rule. The hope was that useful information could be gleaned from persons mentioned in, or the authors of, godly testimonials.

---

36. E.g., *MPWA*, 4:718 (Dec. 24, 1647; Sess. 980), p. 839 (June 20, 1650).

37. *MPWA*, 4:840–41 (June 20, 27; July 11, 1650).

38. Webster, *Godly Clergy in Early Stuart England*, 15–59; Collinson, *Elizabethan Puritan Movement*, 168–76, 208–39.

39. There are over one hundred occasions mentioned in volume 3 of the minutes where preachers are given certificates from the assembly without appearing at the abbey.

40. See the case of Thomas Long in *MPWA*, 4:734 (Feb. 16, 1648; Sess. 1014).

A Method of Examination

By mid-autumn of 1643 the assembly recognized that it needed to further codify its procedures for the examination of ministers, and a committee appointed for the purpose returned to the assembly with a list of twenty-one rules, recorded by John Lightfoot (1602–1675) in his journal. The first six were uncontroversial for assembly members: "1. That the chairman of that committee begin with prayer. 2. That the party examined shall be dealt withal in all mildness and gravity. 3. That the examination be made by the chairman: and if any other of the Assembly present desire to propose a question, he shall propose to the chairman, and the chairman to the…" at which point in the sentence the journal trails off. It resumes: "4. That attention be given by those that are present. 5. That the party be questioned whether he be in orders, and by whom ordained. 6. Whether he have brought sufficient testimony for his good conversation?"[41]

Each of the rules had an obvious purpose. The time of prayer recognized that the persons examining and the person being examined relied on God's help in order to do their task well. The call for kindness and respect in the second rule acknowledged the position of power (and potential for pride) that the examiners had assumed by virtue of their mandate to examine fellow ministers. The third and fourth rules required an environment that was ordered and not chaotic, permitting full involvement of the committee but in a manner that would not distract the one being examined. The fifth rule required fact checking; it could also reveal information about the man's piety. Something could be learned about a man based on the bishop who had been willing to ordain him. Different stories were implied if hands were laid on a man by the worldly John Bridgeman, the popish Godfrey Goodman, the Calvinist John Williams, or the godly John Prideaux. The sixth rule appears to have provided a preliminary check that he had adequate testimonial of his character.

The seventh rule was actually a question, "Whether he will officiate in his own person, viz. by preaching and administration of the sacraments?"[42] The main thrust of the inquiry was to determine if the minister was merely collecting a living for his own income or if he was hoping to serve as a preacher and pastor of a local congregation. It appeared to be a straightforward attempt to preclude pluralism, but Marshall proposed that with an added phrase it be specified that the minister would administer the sacraments only after "he hath instructed them & made them fit."[43] Marshall did not want the minister to make a sweeping commitment to administer

---

41. Lightfoot, *Journal*, 47–48 (Nov. 10, 1643).
42. Lightfoot, *Journal*, 48 (Nov. 10, 1643).
43. *MPWA*, 2:300 (Nov. 10, 1643; Sess. 93).

the sacrament of the Lord's Supper without knowing "whether he shall find some that are not fit to receive" it.[44] Thomas Coleman (1597/8–1646) objected to the proposed rule and the proposed amendment, as they presumed that the assembly would advocate both "residency" and a "mixt communion," where pastors would distinguish between parishioners with a credible profession of faith and those without.[45]

Three dozen speeches followed, with twenty-seven members offering their thoughts, including members who rarely ever spoke in the assembly. The debate was complicated by poor moderating. It was not clear what question was on the floor, and speakers did not always indicate if they were speaking about the committee's seventh recommendation about residency or Marshall's proposed revision, which had to do with the administration of the sacraments to worthy participants only. At the conclusion of the discussion, the first part of the seventh rule was supported by the majority over the objections of those who thought it redundant (given the fact that they were supposed to be examining a man for a specific pastoral charge), or that the assembly did not have authority to fight against pluralism, or that the gathering was preempting a proper debate on the subject of resident ministry. Debate over the second part of the seventh rule, requiring the administration of the sacraments, was focused on the administration of the Lord's Supper, but Philip Nye (bap. 1595, d. 1672) also reminded the gathering that baptism would need to be withheld from some people. He was incensed, however, when he discovered that the seventh question was designed by the committee not simply to eliminate pluralists but also to flush out any separatists and Anabaptists.[46]

Marshall's proposed revision received far more attention than the original rule. It was supported by some of the congregationalists, with the notable exception of Nye, who wanted an opportunity to argue that it was the congregation, and not the pastor alone, who would determine if a person was to be kept from the table. It was opposed for varying reasons by a bevy of presbyterians. Nonetheless, a revised form of Marshall's proposal, that the one examined be asked if he would "administer the sacrament to those that are fit," was "voted affirmatively." Lightfoot complained that all of this "cost some large debate, and that exceeding long indeed, for it took up all the day."[47]

Even then, it was the eighth proposition, that the minister "hold the church of England for a true church, and the ministry of the church of

---

44. Lightfoot, *Journal*, 48 (Nov. 10, 1643).
45. *MPWA*, 2:300 (Nov. 10, 1643; Sess. 93).
46. *MPWA*, 2:300–304 (Nov. 10, 1643; Sess. 93).
47. Lightfoot, *Journal*, 48; *MPWA*, 2:300–304 (Nov. 10, 1643; Sess. 93).

England a true ministry," that divided the assembly's presbyterians and congregationalists along a ragged line. Supporters of congregational polity thought that a visible church was a local congregation, properly ordered. They would admit that there were true ministries in churches and true churches in England. But to require the admission that the Church of England was itself a true church threatened their basic ecclesiological commitments and felt like an episcopal subscription formula. Supporters of presbyterian polity responded that the Scriptures did refer to the visible church as a regional aggregate of congregations and that a true church could have dirty spots in it. The congregationalists were given the floor to make their case, but older members of the assembly would not brook any ambiguous formula, such as the ones that Nye proposed, which would also leave room for separatism. Proposition eight was duly voted.[48] The remaining rules were "passed without any debate":

9. If he give an affirmative; then his testimonial to be taken into consideration, whether valid or no.

10. If any thing be doubtful about the testimonial, then the committee to report upon it to the assembly.

11. What authors he hath been versed in.

12. Where he hath officiated, and why he leaves.

13. What skill he hath in the tongues and logic.

14. Trial of his knowledge in the chief grounds in religion.

15. That he be put to preach if he have leisure.

16. Trial to be taken how he can work upon consciences.

17. To be asked what he thinks of catechising, and of the right way of visiting of the sick.

18. Inquiry after the nature of the place.

19. Upon his withdrawing, those that are present, to give their censure of his answers.

20. His certificate to be first published in the assembly, and to be despatched without paying anything.

21. That no chairman be made for this, but by the assembly.[49]

---

48. Lightfoot, *Journal*, 48–49; *MPWA*, 2:305–11 (Nov. 13, 1643; Sess. 94).
49. Lightfoot, *Journal*, 49–50 (Nov. 13, 1643).

The ninth, tenth, and twelfth aspects of the examination process are designed to further the assembly's understanding of the minister's reputation and ministry history as well as his hopes or ambitions in wishing to move from one pastoral charge to another. Ministers do sometimes wish to leave difficult situations where it would be better for them to remain, or to seek a new charge for inadequate or even problematic reasons. Rules eleven, thirteen, and fourteen require the examiners to determine if a man is sufficiently learned to engage in the varied work of ministry. Thus the committee was to find out what he read, how he reasoned, what he knew about key doctrines, and whether he could work with the original languages of Scripture (Hebrew and Greek) and the usual language of scholarship (Latin).

The next three rules treat facets of practical theology. The assembly tested his preaching skills before the congregation (if there was time), his ability to serve as a physician of souls ("work upon consciences"), and his ability to catechize and visit the sick. The closest that the Westminster Assembly ever came to outlining its priorities for pastoral care was in rules sixteen and seventeen. Together these two rules touched on three problems in living that were typically addressed in post-Reformation pastoral care: that of sin, ignorance, and suffering. Some demonstration of proficiency in all three of these categories was required to meet a minimum standard of care.

Only after gleaning all of this information did the assembly think it would be in a position to ask "after the nature of the place" where the man wanted to serve. The last three of this final cluster of rules pertain to the operation of the examination committee and its relationship to the assembly.

Of the fourteen direct questions of the minister or about his testimonials, most are slanted toward basic fact finding, questioning theological positions more than theological depth. These questions could be asked and answered briefly and, if there were no material concerns about the minister being questioned, could be completed in an hour or two. Trial of his knowledge on the fundamentals of religion and on his ability to handle cases of conscience, like any other parts of the examination, would take much more time.

For much of the assembly's history, the gathering concluded the process with a simple vote to accept or reject the minister. Only in the latter years did a third option, that of placing the candidate on probation, become increasingly popular. Candidates began to be "approved of" for periods of six, nine, or twelve months.[50] A more detailed study of the ordinands themselves is needed to determine if the rump assembly—that part of the assembly remaining after the execution of the king, a remnant dominated

---

50. E.g., *MPWA*, 4:884–85 (Mar. 18, 25, 1652).

by congregationalists instead of presbyterians—used probationary approval as a means of admitting less qualified candidates into the ministry or as a means of enforcing more stringent requirements.[51]

Problematic Cases

Most of the work of examination rested on the assembly's committee, although more than two dozen times the assembly appointed special committees to deal with difficult cases, including assembly members.[52] Some candidates or ministers under examination proved especially problematic. Others had powerful patrons or political connections that made rejection

---

51. For Baxter's comments on the type of person approved by the assembly, see R. Baxter, *Reliquiae Baxterianae, or, Mr. Richard Baxters Narrative of the Most Memorable Passages of His Life and Times* (London, 1696), part 1, p. 74.

52. Committee to investigate Mr. Anderson, *MPWA*, 2:290–92 (Nov. 8–9, 1643; Sess. 201–202), see also 282n1; committee concerning Mr. Moulines, Lightfoot, *Journal*, 147 (Feb. 13, 1644); committee to find a fit man for Hempstead to replace the Anabaptist George Kendall, *MPWA*, 2:575 (Mar. 4, 1644; Sess. 167); committee to communicate with Committee for Plundered Ministers about Charles Anthony and Mr. Needham, formerly denied certificates, *MPWA*, 2:577 (Mar. 5, 1644; Sess. 168); committee to deal with Richard Vines and his refusal to be master of Pembroke College, Cambridge, *MPWA*, 3:21 (Apr. 16, 1644; Sess. 201); committee to consider Thomas Bedford, *MPWA*, 4:138–39 (May 21, 1646; Sess. 644), supplemented, *MPWA*, 4:172–73 (June 18, 1646; Sess. 661); committee to consider Thomas Reynolds, *MPWA*, 4:150–51 (June 2, 1646; Sess. 650); committee to consider Thomas Watts, *MPWA*, 4:152–53 (June 3, 1646; Sess. 651); committee for John Gobert mentioned, *MPWA*, 4:192–93 (July 6, 1646; Sess. 671); committee for Henry Greenwood mentioned, *MPWA*, 4:290–91 (Sept. 22, 1646; Sess. 714); committee for William Launce, *MPWA*, 4:376–77 (Dec. 24, 1646; Sess. 761), supplemented, *MPWA*, 4:386–87, 743 (Dec. 31, 1646, Mar. 13, 1648; Sess. 764, 1030); committee for Sidrach Simpson, *MPWA*, 4:398–99 (Jan. 13, 1647; Sess. 773); committee to consider the ministers who have gone to Wales, *MPWA*, 4:440–41 (Feb. 26, 1647; Sess. 799); committee to consider John Dicks, *MPWA*, 4:450–51 (Mar. 4, 1647; Sess. 803); committee to consider Thomas Pike, *MPWA*, 4:472–73 (Mar. 23, 1647; Sess. 813); committee to consider Samuel Hall, *MPWA*, 4:500–501 (Apr. 13, 1647; Sess. 826), supplemented, *MPWA*, 4:502–3 (Apr. 14, 1647; Sess. 827); new committee for Hall, *MPWA*, 4:578–79 (June 3, 1647; Sess. 855), supplemented, *MPWA*, 4:594–95 (June 15, 1647; Sess. 862); committee for Robert Bacon, *MPWA*, 4:525 (Apr. 30, 1647); committee for Stephen Jerome mentioned, *MPWA*, 4:642–43 (July 15, 1647; Sess. 882); committee to consider Andrew Harward, *MPWA*, 4:709 (Nov. 25, 1647; Sess. 959); committee to consider John Wallis, *MPWA*, 4:716 (Dec. 17, 1647; Sess. 975); committee to consider Robert Henson, *MPWA*, 4:728 (Feb. 2, 1648; Sess. 1004); committee to consider Mr. Pierce, *MPWA*, 4:730 (Feb. 7, 1648; Sess. 1007); committee to consider Thomas Wilmot, *MPWA*, 4:735 (Feb. 21, 1648; Sess. 1017). The names recorded in this list are provided as they are in *MPWA* or Lightfoot's journal. I catalog only the establishment of a committee and those occasions where the committee is supplemented or reestablished. In some instances, the initial constituting of a committee is not mentioned; later references by Lightfoot or elsewhere in the minutes are the only indication of its existence; in each of these cases I state that the committee is "mentioned." For the purposes of enumerating the committees by subject, I count each new committee, even if it is a new committee to replace a former committee, as a separate or distinct committee.

of the candidate or minister a delicate matter. However, the task of examination was also difficult because the charge to examine ministers was interpreted broadly, both by Parliament and by the assembly. One committee was formed to try scholars applying for Cambridge fellowships.[53] Four were created to resolve conflicts in churches (yet another task well outside the assembly's original remit).[54] Additional committees were established to find ministers for Ireland, Wales, the north of England, and for Inns of Court (training and social centers for lawyers) such as the Inner Temple in London.[55] From time to time the assembly was also required to find preachers for the army and for the navy, matters so urgent that they were discussed in plenary sessions. Eight additional committees were appointed for other examination-related tasks, including a committee to investigate ministers who were obtaining livings (whether as vicars or rectors) without the assembly's permission, a committee to establish a registry to track the institution and induction of ministers (the register is now lost), and a committee to examine how the examination committee could be more efficient.[56]

---

53. *MPWA*, 3:39 (Apr. 29, 1644; Sess. 207). Oxford was under control of the king's forces at the time that this committee was formed.

54. Committee to consider schism in French church mentioned, Lightfoot, *Journal*, 93 (Dec. 29, 1643); committee to present a letter from Guernsey to the Commons, *MPWA*, 3:125 (May 28, 1644; Sess. 228); committee to consider petition and letter from St. Peter's Port, Guernsey, *MPWA*, 3:713 (Nov. 24, 1645; Sess. 541); committee to hear the differences between Aldeburgh and Wattisfield, *MPWA*, 3:645 (Aug. 8, 1645; Sess. 483).

55. Committee to provide a minister for the Temple, *MPWA*, 3:126 (May 31, 1644; Sess. 229); committee to consider ministers for York, *MPWA*, 3:249 (Aug. 26, 1644; Sess. 273), supplemented, *MPWA*, 3:260 (Sept. 3, 1644; Sess. 277); committee of York and Durham, *MPWA*, 3:369 (Oct. 4, 1644; Sess. 297), disputed, *MPWA*, 3:402 (Oct. 16, 1644; Sess. 305), called "the Committee for the North" and supplemented, *MPWA*, 3:449 (Nov. 15, 1644; Sess. 323), supplemented, *MPWA*, 3:629 (July 8, 1645; Sess. 464), supplemented, *MPWA*, 3:640 (July 31, 1645; Sess. 477), supplemented, *MPWA*, 4:326–27 (Nov. 3, 1646; Sess. 734); committee to consider ministers for Ireland, *MPWA*, 3:582 (Apr. 18, 1645; Sess. 420); committee to consider ministers for Wales, *MPWA*, 4:687 (Sept. 17, 1647; Sess. 918).

56. Committee to consider the Lords' order and the petition from Wapping, *MPWA*, 3:172 (July 1, 1644; Sess. 248), supplemented, *MPWA*, 3:686 (Oct. 13, 1645; Sess. 517); committee of western members to consider the letter from the commanders of the Lord General, *MPWA*, 3:176 (July 2, 1644; Sess. 249); committee to attend upon the Committee for Plundered Ministers mentioned and supplemented, *MPWA*, 3:421 (Oct. 24, 1644; Sess. 310); committee to investigate ministers who have obtained livings without the assembly's permission, *MPWA*, 4:184–85 (July 1, 1646; Sess. 668); committee to petition for a registry of ministers to inhibit the institution and induction of scandalous ministers, *MPWA*, 4:428–29 (Feb. 15, 1647; Sess. 792); committee to consider ministers that come to the assembly for approbation from royalist quarters, *MPWA*, 4:448–49 (Mar. 3, 1647; Sess. 802); committee to consider the expedition of the examination of ministers, *MPWA*, 4:468–69 (Mar. 19, 1647; Sess. 811), called the "Committee for the Consideration of the Examination of Ministers" and supplemented, *MPWA*, 4:470–71 (Mar. 22, 1647; Sess. 812), called the "Committee for Review" of the examination of ministers, mentioned, *MPWA*, 4:490–91, 644–45, 722 (Apr. 6, July 16, 1647; Jan. 12, 1648;

Occasionally a committee was called to adjudicate disputes involving Westminster divines. It appears that in these cases assemblymen could get the better deal or the benefit of the doubt. In one such circumstance the people of Maidstone, in Kent, asked their godly minister, Samuel Smith, to find another church so that they could have their old pastor, Thomas Wilson (c. 1601–1653), back in the pulpit.[57] (Wilson had been suspended from his ministry for various acts of nonconformity to the Laudian regime.)[58] Even with this awkward vote of nonconfidence, Smith was not eager to move on, but Wilson persuaded the incumbent to submit to a panel of "six judicious Ministers of the assembly," three of which could be chosen by Smith. The panel decided that Wilson, a member of the assembly, should get his old church and that Smith should move on and serve as pastor of a nearby parish.[59]

At times the biggest roadblock to reform proved to be Parliament itself. The assembly often faced challenges with regard to ministers favored by one of the houses but rejected by the assembly, and assembly members felt keenly the political or legal liabilities of rejecting ministers. After a breach of confidentiality with an apparent leak of information over the weekend, the assembly began the week of January 19, 1646, by ordering that "when any information is given in this assembly by any members of it against any minister to be examined, the name of the member of the assembly shall not be made knowne to the party complained of or any other by any member of the assembly."[60] Draft rejection letters in the minutes also suggest a desire for cautious wording, as the number of interlineations and erasures in the rough notes of the assembly's minutes indicate.[61]

Local disputes could often have broader implications. Keith Lindley refers to an instance of a "disagreement over the choice of lecturer for St Martin in the Fields in 1645 [which] turned the parish into a battleground between rival supporters of lay and clerical authority," with part of the congregation siding with some prominent members of the congregation (who happened to be members of the House of Peers) and the other part

---

Sess. 821, 883, 991); committee to consider inconveniences mentioned by the Committee for Plundered Ministers, *MPWA*, 4:722 (Jan. 11, 1648; Sess. 990).

57. For Smith's institution as curate of the parish, see *Journal of the House of Commons*, 3:63 (Apr. 28, 1643).

58. J. Eales, "Wilson, Thomas (c. 1601–1653)," *Oxford Dictionary of National Biography* (Oxford: Oxford University Press, 2004).

59. G. S[winnock], *The Life and Death of Mr. Tho. Wilson, Minister of Maidstone* ([London], 1672), 23–24.

60. This polished order follows an incomplete order containing one of the few instances of underlining in the minutes: "That <u>when anything</u> spoken in this Assembly by way of testimony against any minister to be examined…" *MPWA*, 3:741 (Jan. 19, 1646; Sess. 575).

61. E.g., the case of Jonadab Birch, *MPWA*, 4:467 (Mar. 18, 1647; Sess. 810).

with its minister, Daniel Cawdrey ([1587/8–1664] who happened to be an assembly member). Lindley mentions a similar case involving another Westminster divine, Andrew Perne (c. 1595–1654).[62] These were parochial squabbles engaging members of the established political class, indirect conflicts with parliamentary authority. Sometimes, however, Parliament and the assembly clashed directly over the approval of certain ministers. The House of Lords requested, and persisted in requesting, that the assembly accept William Launce to fill a sequestration, a place vacated by a minister deemed ignorant or scandalous by Parliament. Launce had come into conflict with the assembly (and Parliament) in October 1643 when he refused to encourage his parishioners to sign the Solemn League and Covenant and then snubbed George Gibbs (c. 1590–1654), another member of the assembly, who was sent to Launce's church on October 17 to promote the Covenant.[63] What is more, Launce was supposed to have sat as a member of the assembly, but he had refused to take his seat, at least after the autumn of 1643. Launce's name was still written on the roll of the assembly as late as November 2, 1643, but it was struck off sometime later.[64] Having ensconced himself in the assembly's bad graces, when he finally sought a prominent London church in November 1646, the assembly held up his approval for the parish for twenty months. Even then, when the majority were worn down and finally capitulated, agreeing to approve Launce for a living, multiple divines registered their dissenting votes.[65]

The assembly, after a similar struggle with Parliament and similar reluctance among its members, steadily refused to approve of Samuel Hall. The results were disastrous. On February 10, 1647, Hall provided his examiners at the assembly with what they considered inadequate testimonials of his faith and life.[66] The following day the assembly sent a memo to the inhabitants of Thaxted, in Essex, who must have been apprised of Hall's efforts to gain the town pulpit, and gave them a fortnight to produce any arguments for or against Hall.[67] On March 12, 1647, the assembly stalled Hall for another week; the decision to delay his examination was then overturned and he was examined, suggesting that Hall's testimonials from known ministers were ambiguous enough for the majority of the assembly to be willing at least to allow him to proceed to examination.[68] Nonetheless, he was not approved, and his case dragged on for months with both houses

---

62. Lindley, *Popular Politics*, 273–74.
63. *MPWA*, 2:207 (Oct. 18, 1643; Sess. 77).
64. *MPWA*, 2:262.
65. *MPWA*, 4:765–66 (June 9, 1648; Sess. 1078).
66. *MPWA*, 4:424–25 (Feb. 10, 1647; Sess. 789).
67. *MPWA*, 4:426–27 (Feb. 11, 1647; Sess. 790).
68. *MPWA*, 4:458–59 (Mar. 12, 1647; Sess. 806).

of parliament and their respective committees calling on the assembly to explain its decisions and to accept Hall.

The assembly countered by appointing ever-larger committees to respond to Parliament and explain why the majority could not approve of his continuing ministry. Hall eventually was installed in the Thaxted church by authority of the besieged Parliament of July 1647 (a Parliament that met without its speakers), but when the speakers returned to Parliament in August, all orders and ordinances of July were made null and void, including the order to place Hall in Thaxted. But by now, enough people in Thaxted were willing to have Hall as a minister that when sequestration officers from Parliament came to the church to remove Hall, they were shouted down by the men of the church and attacked by a group of women who clambered over the front pews in order to reach the pulpit and defend their pastor. Other members of the congregation, presumably those who had opposed Hall all along and were in support of his removal, expressed their shock at the behavior of their fellow parishioners and placed a well-timed complaint with the House of Lords, carefully emphasizing the impropriety and disorder of the women's behavior in the attack as much as the attack itself.[69] As Keith Lindley has argued in other contexts, violence in parishes was not uncommon before and during the civil war, especially where the traditional structures and practices of church and society were threatened by change.[70] The assembly's role in examining ministers and Parliament's role in installing them were examples of such obvious changes. Yet the assembly concluded that the possibility of a godly ministry in England was worth even the potential for further civil disobedience, and thus promoted the process needed for the installation of godly ministers in pulpits across the country.

---

69. PA, HL/PO/JO/10/1/238, Main Papers, August 27, 1647.
70. Lindley, *Popular Politics*, 33–73.

CHAPTER 5

The Pastor's Office: Assembly Debates

Res.: That it is the office of a Pastor to feed the Flock by preaching of the Word according to which he is to teach, convince, reprove, exhort, & comfort. 1 Tim. 3:2; 2 Tim. 3:16, 17; Tit. 1:9.

Res.: That Catechising, which is a plain laying down of the first principles of the Oracles of God, Heb. 5:12, or of the Doctrine of Christ is a part of preaching pertaining to the Pastors office.
—minutes for November 6, 1643, Session 89

Someone in the Jerusalem Chamber had asked if it was a pastor's duty to read the Scriptures publicly in the weekly worship services of the church. It was November 1643, and the Westminster Assembly was trying to build a biblical system of church government from the ground up. In the summer months of 1643 the gathering had been revising an existing text of the Church of England, the Thirty-nine Articles. But in late September the Solemn League and Covenant had been signed between the English and Scottish Parliaments, drawing the two rebel parties into a military and ecclesiastical alliance and setting them on a shared course of church reform. From early October the assembly, at the behest of Parliament, had turned its attention to the subject of church government and the creation of new texts for the two churches as well as Protestant Ireland. Church government requires church officers, and a discussion of church officers entails a discussion of what they are to do—such as a possible role in leading worship—which is how the gathering got around to discussing the public reading of the Scriptures.

Preaching and Reading

Among the assembly's members Thomas Temple and Thomas Gataker led the way in insisting that it was the preacher's duty, and his alone, to read the Bible in public worship. This could have been a relatively inconsequential comment if the two Thomases had not added that the preacher is to read because the reading of the Scriptures is the preaching of the Scriptures.[1] In recent memory, the people who argued that Bible reading was a form of Bible preaching blurred lines as a way of defending those ministers who read the sermons of others and did not write and preach their own. The equation of reading with preaching was a traditionally anti-puritan argument promoted by Laudians, who were among those who "would have the word only read, and that there should be no preaching or expounding of it."[2] Members of the assembly were disappointed to hear this argument articulated by their peers, and they produced a variety of arguments in response. Charles Herle (1598–1659) pointed out that in Nehemiah 8, reading and preaching are distinguished. Joshua Hoyle (bap. 1588, d. 1654), who would often express alarm with Gataker's ideas, declared that his former teacher's equation of reading and preaching was "dangerous."[3] Herle and Thomas Wilson also argued that faith is ordinarily worked by preaching of the Scriptures, not reading.[4] Romans 10 and the series of questions found in verse 14 were sufficient, for them, to establish the necessity of preaching: "How then shall they call on him in whom they have not believed? and how shall they believe in him of whom they have not heard? and how shall they hear without a preacher?"

Wilson's view, not unheard of in godly circles, was that no more of the Bible should normally be read in a worship service than the minister was able to preach in his sermon since the Scriptures needed to be explained and pressed home to the hearts of the hearers.[5] William Bridge (1600/1–1671) agreed, and his revealing comment that he was unwilling to call it sin to read more than one preached testifies to the strength of his conviction.[6] That kind of assertion, in turn, disturbed William Price (d. 1666), who insisted that he was not "an advocate for an Illiterate Clergy" but that he could not "with patience heare the reading of the word of God soe much undervalued as I have this morning." There was skill in reading it and profit in hearing it.[7] Wilson, the object of these remarks, answered that his

---

1. *MPWA*, 2:265–66, 274, 278.
2. W. Greenhill, *An Exposition Continued upon the Sixt, Seventh, Eighth, Ninth, Tenth, Eleventh, Twelfth, and Thirteenth Chapters of the Prophet Ezekiel* (London, 1649), Epistle Dedicatory.
3. *MPWA*, 2:265–66, 275 (Nov. 2, 3, 1643; Sess. 87, 88).
4. *MPWA*, 2:266–67 (Nov. 2, 1643; Sess. 87).
5. *MPWA*, 2:272, 283 (Nov. 3, 7, 1643; Sess. 88, 90).
6. *MPWA*, 2:275 (Nov. 3, 1643; Sess. 88).
7. *MPWA*, 2:275 (Nov. 3, 1643; Sess. 88).

"vehemency" in making his point was not "passion"—and he toned down his argument considerably.[8]

In an effort to explain his earlier comments, and in strong opposition to Wilson's inculcation of a dependency on preaching, Gataker noted that puritans only played into the hands of papists when they promoted such a low view of the "bare reading" of the Scriptures. He was no admirer of recent trends in the church, but were not Protestants the supposed champions of the Bible's perspicuity and sufficiency? What is more, Gataker showed (at least to his own satisfaction) that the New Testament revealed the people of God reading sections too long to preach, and he noted that the apostle Paul insisted that his letters be read in the churches.[9] No one at the assembly doubted that these letters were indeed Scripture—or believed that patristic preachers always expounded entire epistles.

The force of these arguments was indirect but nonetheless significant. One way of demonstrating that the Scriptures could be read profitably by themselves, without explanation, was to permit a larger portion of the Bible to be read publicly than is preached publicly. The practice of reading a portion of Scripture that was not preached could be edifying, advocates argued; it was also an apologetic against Roman Catholic views on the alleged insufficiency of the Scriptures, and most assembly members were willing to argue that more of the Scriptures might be read than preached in a typical worship service. There were also other practical concerns to take into account: Philip Nye was concerned that to restrict the passage read to the passage preached would not sufficiently expose people to the breadth of the Scriptures.[10] Others agreed, and Herbert Palmer (1601–1647) expressed his pleasant surprise that so many in the assembly were in favor of "public reading"—that is, reading beyond the passage preached, for "In committy it is denied."[11]

The extent of the passage read could exceed the portion preached. But the original question remained: Who is to read the Scriptures in a service of worship? Obviously some people thought that only the preacher should do it. Some assembly members thought anyone may do it.[12] Thomas Goodwin (1600–1680) thought that the pastor could do it if no one else was

---

8. *MPWA*, 2:276 (Nov. 3, 1643; Sess. 88).

9. *MPWA*, 2:273 (Nov. 3, 1643; Sess. 88). For a similar observation about puritan and Roman Catholic comments on the need for biblical interpretation, see Hunt, *Art of Hearing*, 40, 52.

10. *MPWA*, 2:275 (Nov. 3, 1643; Sess. 88).

11. Sess. 87, *MPWA*, 2:268 (Nov. 2, 1643; Sess. 87); see also further speeches by Cornelius Burges, Theodore Bathurst, John Ley, and Thomas Gataker in *MPWA*, 2:265, 272, 278, 283 (Nov. 2, 3, 7, 1643; Sess. 87, 88, 90).

12. Joshua Hoyle and Stephen Marshall (*MPWA*, 2:265, 268, 271) and perhaps Temple, Nye, and Wilson (*MPWA*, 2:266, 271–72; Nov. 2–3, 1643; Sess. 87–88).

available.[13] Conversely, Cornelius Burges thought the pastor should do it unless he was not available, but, even then, the pastor must ensure that it be done well by whoever was charged with the responsibility.[14] A number of members argued that a special class of person read the Scriptures in the days of the Old Testament and that this suggested that ministers of the gospel should do it in the days of the New. Wilson countered that arguments based on the reading and preaching practices of the Levites (such as those in the days of Ezra and Nehemiah) could not be straightforwardly applied to New Testament ministers. This was a hermeneutical concern that others shared, even if they did not arrive at the same outcomes as Wilson.[15] The majority of the assembly was convinced that some kind of "public person" must read the Scriptures, whether it was the pastor or someone to whom the pastor would delegate to the task, such as a deacon or sexton or candidate for the ministry.[16] But the majority also concluded that the reading of the Scriptures was not an absolutely essential part of a minister's office. It could not definitively be proved from Scripture. And the existence of physically, rather than spiritually, blind preaching pastors (mentioned by both Richard Heyrick and Hoyle) proved that one could be an effective minister without engaging in the public reading of Scripture.[17]

It was Burges who saw a way to make peace with almost everyone through a simple declaration that the reading of the Scriptures itself is a "public ordinance" of God. This formulation honored the idea that the reading of the Scriptures was a stand-alone component of a worship service. And it implied, without actually saying so, that a public officer in the church ought to read the Scriptures. Burges was also trying to correct the idea (current only among the godly) that "reading is denied to be the ordinance of Christ, without exposition." A clutch of divines spoke in favor of the phrase, and the day after he proposed it, Burges could say that it

---

13. *MPWA*, 2:278 (Nov. 6, 1643; Sess. 89).

14. *MPWA*, 2:271 (Nov. 3, 1643; Sess. 88).

15. See William or Thomas Carter's speech in *MPWA*, 2:282 (Nov. 7, 1643; Sess. 90).

16. See the speeches of Lazarus Seaman, William Gouge, Henry Wilkenson Sr., Cornelius Burges, Herbert Palmer, Edmund Calamy (who thought it was not necessary but was at least "convenient"), Peter Smith, and Jean de la Marche. It is probable that William Twisse, Francis Woodcock, and John Lightfoot held a similar position. Richard Heyrick, Thomas Young, Joshua Hoyle, and perhaps Charles Herle did not insist that a pastor read the Scriptures, but it is not clear if they insisted that a public officer read them. See *MPWA*, 2:266–69, 271, 274, 276, 277–79, 281 (Nov. 2–7, 1643; Sess. 87–90). In the debate about the subdirectory for preaching in the Directory for Worship, others added themselves to this number: Samuel Rutherford, one of the Carters, George Gillespie, and Alexander Henderson (*MPWA*, 3:139–41 [June 13, 1644; Sess. 238]). The Scottish commissioners were all in favor of candidates for the ministry reading Scripture publicly.

17. *MPWA*, 2:266, 278 (Nov. 2, 6, 1643; Sess. 87, 89).

"apeared to be the sence of the Assembly."[18] Wilson was not happy, and Bridge found reason to hesitate: even if the reading of the Scriptures was an ordinance of God, was reading beyond the scope of preaching it an usual feature, or was it a "standing ordinance," one which would form a normal part of weekly worship?[19] But almost everyone else concurred with Burges.

In defining the office of a pastor, the assembly was, one vote at a time, constructing a rudimentary draft of a directory for church government, and it is there that the assembly's conclusions can be found. The portion treating the office of a pastor (reproduced in appendix 1) includes sections on blessing the people, administering the sacraments, praying (which was seen to be an especially close partner in ministry to preaching), and ruling in the church. However, the description of the pastor's office begins with statements about the reading and the preaching of the Scriptures.

The assembly voted that "the publick reading of the word in the congregation is an holy ordinance in Gods church" (using Burges's phrase) even "though there follow no immediat[e] explication of that which is read" (addressing Temple's and Gataker's concern).[20] Could this reading be delegated to any public person? In the end, the assembly thought not, for it declared "that the public reading of the Scriptures belongs to the pastors office."[21] This was another victory, and a surprising one, for Temple and Gataker. Behind the scenes Temple had patiently guided the assembly to this position—probably only one of many occasions where his skill in either drafting a document or presenting its scriptural support worked in his favor.[22]

Nonetheless, the discussion was not quite over. It was the assembly's practice, following any debate about the substance of a matter (such as the minister's duty to read the Scriptures or to preach), for the gathering to enter a second phase of discussion, in which the assembly officially adopted the best scriptural support for the position for which they had successfully voted. The assembly's votes on the reading responsibilities of the pastor follow this pattern, with the resolution voted first in session 89 and the

---

18. See speeches by Cornelius Burges and perhaps Herbert Palmer, Edmund Calamy, William Gouge, Thomas Gataker, Philip Nye, William Price, and Samuel de la Marche (*MPWA*, 2:265, 267, 269, 271, 274–76 [Nov. 2–3, 1643; Sess. 87–88]); and votes in *MPWA*, 2:6 (Nov. 3, 1643; Sess. 88).

19. *MPWA*, 2:272, 275–76 (Nov. 3, 1643; Sess. 88).

20. Votes in *MPWA*, 2:6 (Nov. 3, 1643; Sess. 88).

21. Votes in *MPWA*, 2:7 (Nov. 6, 1643; Sess. 89).

22. Thomas Temple is the only significant member of the Westminster Assembly to have escaped the attention of historians and biographers alike, and he is the only important assembly member who is not included in the *Oxford Dictionary of National Biography*.

biblical support adopted in a later session: "Res[olved]: That the publick reading of the Scripture belongs to the pastors office."²³ And,

> Sess. 90. Nov. 7: Ord[ered].: 1. That the Priests and Levites in the Jewish Church were trusted with the publick reading of the word, as is proved. Deut. 31:9, 10, 11; Nehem. 8:1, 2, & 13.
>
> Ord.: 2. That the ministers of the Gospell have as ample a charge & commission to dispense the word as well as other ordinances, as the Priests & Levites under the Law. Proved Isai. 66:21; Matt. 23:34 where our Saviour intituleth [entitles] the officers of the New Testament whom he would send forth by the same names of the Teachers of the old.
>
> Ord.: These propositions shall be brought to prove, That therefor (the Duty being of a morall nature) it followeth by just consequence, that the public reading of the Scriptures belongs to the pastors office.²⁴

Wilson, who disagreed with the majority position that the pastor was particularly charged to read the Scriptures, sat at the back of the room, warning his colleagues that it would "be hard" to prove from Scripture what they had now voted.²⁵ The presence of naysayers like Wilson, always present at the second stage of the assembly's debates, no matter what the topic, served a useful function in forcing careful rather than overly crude or creative scriptural justifications for the ideas held by the majority party. In this case Wilson argued that the pastor is not uniquely called to publicly read the Scriptures, for priests and Levites were "not tipes of ministers, but of Christians."²⁶

Although in essential agreement with Wilson's assertion that Christians are the priests and temple servants of the new covenant, most members of the assembly still wanted to see some special relevance in the office of Old Testament teacher for the office of New Testament preacher. They emphasized continuities between the two testaments implicitly by describing the priests and Levites of "the Jewish Church." They argued their case explicitly, first from the lesser to the greater, asserting that "the ministers of the Gospell have as ample a charge & commission to dispense the word as well as other ordinances, as the Priests & Levites under the Law," and then by noting New Testament appropriation of Old Testament terminology. Of particular relevance in drawing this conclusion was the promise in Isaiah 66:21 that the Lord would one day take some of the Gentiles "for priests and for Levites," which the assembly saw fulfilled in Jesus's warning to the

---

23. *MPWA*, 2:7 (Nov. 6, 1643; Sess. 89).

24. *MPWA*, 2:7 (Nov. 7, 1643; Sess. 90).

25. *MPWA*, 2:281 (Nov. 7, 1643; Sess. 90). For Wilson's likely seating location, see *MPWA*, 1:44, 208–10.

26. *MPWA*, 2:283 (Nov. 7, 1643; Sess. 90).

scribes and Pharisees, that He would "send you prophets and wise men and scribes" (Matt. 23:34), noting that Jesus "intituleth the officers of the New Testament whom he would send forth by the same names of the Teachers of the old." Jesus did, indeed, use Old Testament names for New Testament apostles and preachers.

Significantly, in concluding that the public reading of the Scriptures is a ministerial task, the assembly did not appeal to direct examples but argued instead that it reached its conclusion "by just consequence." Curiously, and parenthetically, it added that the duty to read publicly was "of a morall nature."[27] Lazarus Seaman (d. 1675), who was the strongest advocate for the delegation of reading to any public officer and not simply to the pastor, found something slippery in the assembly's argument and protested that a "moral equity" was hardly enough to make reading the Scriptures a pastoral duty.[28] Many months later Temple, speaking for a committee during the drafting of the Directory of Public Worship, softened the statement of the assembly, both meeting Seaman's objection and answering Bridge's earlier question: he explained that only when people conceive of the regular reading of the Word as an office is it the minister's office.[29] This was a conditional statement that offered an expansive concession to Bridge and those who shared his point of view. In 1647 the assembly Larger Catechism would go even further, merely stating that "all are not to be permitted to read the Word publicly to the congregation"—which was much less specific than the catechism's corresponding statement that "the Word of God is to be preached only by such as are sufficiently gifted, and also duly approved and called to that office."[30]

In spite of these later clarifications, the 1643 debate over the office of the pastor is significant for those who wish to understand the importance of preaching for the Westminster divines, not because it is unusual but because it was typical. Throughout the debate, members of the assembly were approaching questions of polity and practice from different vantage points. Some were eager to stress the supremacy of preaching as a means of grace, in defiance of the Laudian legacy of the past decade. Others disagreed over approaches and implications of the connection between the two Testaments of Scripture. Still others, some of them ancient veterans of a war with older enemies, were alert to the key issues that divided Protestants and Catholics during the Reformation and could return to trouble the church once more. Popery was not an abstraction for old divines such

---

27. Votes in *MPWA*, 2:7 (Nov. 6, 1643; Sess. 89).
28. *MPWA*, 2:284 (Nov. 7, 1643; Sess. 90).
29. *MPWA*, 3:139 (June 13, 1643; Sess. 238).
30. Compare WLC 156 and 158.

as Thomas Gataker, whose own father watched (and came to admire) Protestants being tortured in the homes of his Roman Catholic relatives.[31]

Preaching Deacons and Preaching Catechisms

Considering old enemies, obviously not all remnants of Roman Catholicism were equally problematic. For example, the idea of a preaching deacon as a probationary office leading toward a full priestly ministry was debated in the assembly later in 1643, with full recognition of its Roman Catholic heritage but without any sense of alarm, probably because this practice (unlike a low view of Scripture) had patristic roots.

Some members denied that the office of deacon was established for the care of the poor (including the Erastians John Lightfoot, Thomas Coleman, and John Selden [1584–1654], and perhaps the non-Erastian, Edmund Calamy); others agreed that the office was established for the care of the poor, but only temporarily or locally (including Herbert Palmer and Peter Smith); most or all of these members were in favor of maintaining the episcopal tradition of preaching deacons. Nonetheless, a majority of members denied that preaching was the purpose of the diaconate, and some of them were willing to press their case on the assembly floor (including Richard Vines [1599/1600–1656], Thomas Wilson, Thomas Hill [d. 1653], and perhaps Thomas Young [c. 1587–1655]) and argued that the object of a perpetual office of deacon was to care for the poor (including Joshua Hoyle, William Rayner, William Gouge, Richard Vines, Thomas Young, Hill, Wilson, Charles Herle, and probably Richard Heyrick).[32] The assembly concluded that "it doth not pertain to the office of a Deacon to preach the word, or administer the Sacraments."[33]

Debates over the idea of a preaching deacon were of a lower order of importance to the assembly than understandings of preaching that minimized the value of Bible reading. Only the latter left members alarmed by assertions that seemed to minimize the clarity and sufficiency of Scripture, dishonor the Word of God, and, although no one would say it, make every preacher a kind of pope. As it happened, efforts in the assembly to broaden the definition of preaching were not restricted to the (unsuccessful) equation of reading and preaching. At this point in the assembly's deliberations, the majority in the assembly was actually willing to say that catechizing, by which it meant "a plain laying down the first principles of the Oracles of God…or

---

31. S. Ashe, *Grey hayres crowned with grace* (London, 1655), 41.
32. See *MPWA*, 2:462–70 (Dec. 15, 1643; Sess. 116).
33. *MPWA*, 5:58 (Doc. 19); see also *MPWA*, 5:131 (Doc. 45).

of the Doctrine of Christ," was a form of preaching.[34] This was a surprising assertion given Laud's recent legacy of limiting churches to a morning sermon and insisting that if there were to be a Sunday afternoon sermon that it be an exposition of the church's catechism rather than an exposition of a scriptural passage. It was also surprising given the general opposition of the godly to Laud's decision, for while seizing the opportunity to catechize, they perceived Laud's ruling as an attack on preaching.[35] (It offers little surprise, then, that the assembly would return to this topic at a later point.)

The case for catechizing as preaching was inconsequential compared to the much broader definitions of preaching occasionally mentioned by a minority in the assembly—assertions that make sense only in the context of the assembly's debates about church government. Notoriously, the assembly engaged in a protracted debate in the early winter of 1644 on the probable size of the church in Jerusalem during the period following the first Christian Pentecost. The presbyterians at the assembly offered arguments for a large number of converts in Jerusalem and a correspondingly high number of preachers. As the presbyterians saw it, high numbers of converts implied multiple Christian congregations in Jerusalem. The multiplicity of congregations was in turn significant because the New Testament refers to these many congregations as one church and shows church leaders making joint decisions—what appeared to be a presbyterian kind of visible unity of multiple congregations, united by cooperative church government.

Congregationalists in the assembly saw the danger to their own position in this historical construction and thus tried to limit the total number of converts in Acts. They argued for the plausibility of one large meeting place (the temple) and a minimum number of preaching pastors (since there was only one congregation). The significance of that debate to this study is that the minimization of the number of pastors in Jerusalem led some congregationalists to suggest that passages mentioning preaching activity needed to be taken generally, perhaps referring to a kind of preaching that laypeople could do.[36] This need to permit room for lay preaching made the congregationalists more flexible with respect to some of the qualifications for preachers, even leading them to welcome lay preaching in some

---

34. *MPWA*, 5:205 (Doc. 77); see also *MPWA*, 5:55, 130 (Docs. 19 and 45).

35. For concerns about forced catechetical preaching, see J. Davies, *The Caroline Captivity of the Church: Charles I and the Remoulding of Anglicanism 1625–1641* (Oxford: Clarendon, 1992), 139 (see also pp. 136–46). Davies corrects others who ascribe this injunction to Charles. See Seaver, *Puritan Lectureships*, 263; and Webster, *Godly Clergy in Early Stuart England*, 144. For the relationship between catechesis and preaching, see votes in *MPWA*, 2:7 (Nov. 6, 1643; Sess. 89); and *MPWA*, 2:279–80 (Nov. 6, 1643; Sess. 89).

36. See William Bridge's comments on Acts 8:4 and on the teaching of Priscilla and Aquila (*MPWA*, 2:570 [March 1, 1644; Sess. 166]).

contexts.[37] It may also help to explain Goodwin's unexpected comment, in an earlier debate, that when "those nobles & commons that sit here…speake their mind in divinity…I count it a prophesying & preaching."[38]

---

37. E.g., J. A. Halcomb, "A Social History of Congregational Religious Practice during the Puritan Revolution," (unpublished PhD thesis, University of Cambridge, 2009), 56: "While the origins of many gatherings can be located with a particular minister and his preaching, there is overwhelming evidence for lay activism in gatherings without ministerial oversight."

38. *MPWA*, 2:216 (Oct. 19, 1643; Sess. 78).

CHAPTER 6

Ordaining Preachers:
The Directory for Ordination

He shall be examined touching his skill in the Originall tongues, and his tryall to be made by reading the Hebrew and Greek Testaments, and rendring some portion of some into Latine; And if he be defective in them, enquiry shall be made the more strictly after his other learning, And whether he hath skill in Logick and in Phylosophie. What Authors in Divinity he hath read and is best acquainted with; And tryall shall be made in his knowledge of the grounds of Religion, and of his ability to defend the Orthodox Doctrine contained in them, against all unsound and erronious opinions, especially these of the present age: of his skill in the sense and meaning of such places of Scripture, as shall be proposed unto him, in cases of Conscience; and in the Chronologie of the Scripture, and the Ecclesiasticall History.

—"Rules for Examination," Directory for Ordination

By mid-October 1643 the requests for additional parish ministers had become so urgent that John Ley mentioned the possibility of recommending men for ministry who were not yet in priestly orders. Ley's suggestion assumed that regular preaching could be done without ordination. William Gouge, the first to speak to the motion, offered the strongest opposition to the idea: "Not only for the sacraments, but for the preaching of the word there must be an outward call," which for Gouge entailed ordination.[1]

The Ordination of Ministers

Over two days of discussion the Westminster Assembly was divided as to both its estimate of the most pressing needs of the war-torn church and the best remedy to meet those needs. A group of men citing English, European, and patristic precedent suggested that candidates for the ministry or

---

1. *MPWA*, 2:196 (Oct. 13, 1643; Sess. 74).

preaching deacons could be sent to preach.[2] But other members countered that the request that had come to the assembly was for men to officiate a cure—people wanted pastors for the parishes and not simply preachers for their pulpits. Thomas Wilson retorted that in cases of dire necessity, a parochial ministry of Word could continue without a ministry of the sacraments: people do not "perish for want of sacraments, but they 'perish for want of knowledge'" (Hos. 4:6).[3]

But how to promote that knowledge? William Rayner (c. 1595–1666) thought the assembly's action in examining and sending a man might constitute a sufficiently official outward call.[4] Lazarus Seaman suggested that Parliament could temporarily serve as a kind of commissioning body.[5] Wilson, a presbyterian, and Thomas Goodwin, a congregationalist, thought that even without such formalities gifted laypeople could be sent to preach in needy parishes.[6] As many as nine members spoke in favor of men preaching, under certain conditions, without an outward ministerial call.[7]

Yet theory did not easily translate into practice. Proposals included the possibility of a special commission of ministers to ordain candidates for the ministry (shot down by nervous congregationalists), or ordination at the hands of expatriate French Reformed ministers in London (dismissed by Jean de la March), or shipping men north for ordination by the Scottish kirk (criticized by the English presbyterian Seaman). Eventually men began to change their minds. Seaman, Herle, and Ley, all three of whom had been hypothetically in favor of sending unordained men to preach, now spoke in favor of waiting: the assembly should first develop its own policy for ordination.[8] No one suggested ordination by bishops.

In counseling the assembly to wait, these three additional men formed a majority with the pro-ordination party, which insisted that a preacher have an outward call before being sent to serve in a parish and that he be ordained by preaching presbyters prior to serving as a pastor. This group also concluded that an opportunity for promptly increasing the pool of ordained men in England was not within immediate reach. They included

---

2. Thomas Young, Lazarus Seaman, and perhaps Peter Smith and Cornelius Burges. *MPWA*, 2:211–14 (Oct. 19, 1643; Sess. 78).

3. *MPWA*, 2:215 (Oct. 19, 1643; Sess. 78).

4. *MPWA*, 2:196 (Oct. 13, 1643; Sess. 74).

5. *MPWA*, 2:212 (Oct. 19, 1643; Sess. 78).

6. *MPWA*, 2:215–16 (Oct. 19, 1643; Sess. 78).

7. In addition to those already mentioned, Charles Herle and John Ley can be added. *MPWA*, 2:212 (Oct. 19, 1643; Sess. 78).

8. For a temporary body for ordination and objections, see *MPWA*, 2:211, 214–15; for ordination by French ministers or the Scottish kirk, and objections, pp. 214–15; for Seaman, Herle, and Ley favoring delay, p. 212, although Ley gets back on the fence in p. 214 (Oct. 19, 1643; Sess. 78).

in their number Thomas Gataker who, influenced by stories of debates on the subject at the Synod of Dort, was unsure if deacons should ever have been permitted to preach in the English church in the first place and was unconvinced that bishops really had a right to give a preaching license to someone unordained. William Price felt constrained to add that the assembly would "doe preaching a great deale of dishonour if we hould that preaching may be without imposition of hands."[9]

It also made sense in the autumn of 1643 to delay a decision about ordination because the two days of debate over the possibility of ordination pro tempore had been interrupted by orders requiring the assembly to cease debating the Thirty-nine Articles and to discuss the text of the Solemn League and Covenant (thus including Scotland in this second Reformation), and then to begin settling the discipline and government of the church. Nonetheless, the insistence in this debate that the assembly come up with orderly, sustainable, and perhaps also respectable solutions to pressing practical problems would continue to characterize the counsel of most of the assembly's older members.

Nevertheless, the difficulty extended even beyond this. Although in hindsight we know that they managed it for a decade, in 1643 the continued examination of every potential preacher in England appeared to be an unsustainable task for the assembly. What is more, most assembly members, while grateful for the opportunity to be agents of an immediate reformation, wanted the work of examination itself to be shifted to the church, where it properly belonged and could be continued on a more settled basis.

By late January 1644 the assembly resolved that "in extraordinary cases something extraordinary may be done" to satisfy the need for the ordination of ministers, "yet keeping as near as may possibly be to the Rule." Two days later they concluded, "there is at this time an extraordinary occasion." By mid-April they had in hand a theological rationale for ordination as well as a draft of a directory for ordination, and submitted both to the houses of Parliament.[10] The assembly had labored for months on the doctrinal basis for ordination, and key questions had cut jaggedly across the membership of the assembly. None of this is visible in the two texts submitted to Parliament.

The propositions regarding church government (constituting the "Doctrinal Part of Ordination of Ministers") were tightly structured and defended

---

9. *MPWA*, 2:213. For further insistence that an outward call is necessary for all preaching, see comments made by William Gouge, Herbert Palmer, Thomas Temple, and John Lightfoot in pp. 213, 215 (Oct. 19, 1643; Sess. 78).

10. Votes in *MPWA*, 2:15 (Jan. 23, 25, 1644; Sess. 139, 141).

from Scripture.[11] The assembly had expended a huge amount of time writing and refining them because they expressed basic ecclesiological commitments. These commitments included key principles as well as some specific practices, but only practices (such as the laying on of hands) that were identified in Scripture and related to the subject of ordination in particular.

The assembly's entire proposal for examining potential ministers, trying their gifts, and asking set questions (constituting the Directory for the Ordination of Ministers) was intended to be an outworking of biblical principles and applied wisdom; it was a statement of ecclesiastical polity.[12] This latter, longer part of the assembly's submission to Parliament had only been delegated to a committee on April 3, 1644. Work did not begin in earnest until, a little more than a week later, members began to worry that the practical aspects of the directory might delay the submission of the whole.

These worries were ill-founded. By April 18, after a few afternoons' work, Thomas Temple could report that the "Particulars" were "not compleated in it, but" there were "such things as will be suddenly dispatched." It really was a matter of "knitting" some propositions together and "fully digesting" a few questions. The directory was in a developed enough state to be read, and Dr. Cornelius Burges offered that once the questions to be asked of the ordinand were completed, there were only a few tweaks that would be necessary. This was a little optimistic, but after a second day of debate, which John Lightfoot records in some detail, and after some laughter at a poorly phrased addition from Herbert Palmer, the text was declared ready for Parliament.[13] No doubt the assembly was able to produce its practical "directory" quickly because it was able to draw on the experience that it had gained in examining ministers.

Unfortunately, and to the assembly's lasting disappointment, its two texts, the "Doctrinal Part" and the directory, did not receive equally friendly treatment from the House of Commons. The Commons cut the directory loose from its doctrinal moorings, rejecting a consideration of the "Doctrinal Part of Ordination" entirely. After further exchanges with the assembly, Parliament produced in October 1644 a stopgap measure for ordination consisting of the (now revised) Directory for the Ordination of Ministers only. This ordinance was revised in turn thirteen months later when the examination and ordination of candidates was assigned to newly established presbyteries, but, as the assembly was to recognize, the doctrinal, ecclesiological part of the assembly's work would never be reunited to

---

11. *MPWA*, 5:63 (Doc. 20).
12. *MPWA*, 5:64 (Doc. 20).
13. *MPWA*, 2:664 (Apr. 3, 1644; Sess. 192), 2:682 (Apr. 11, 1644; Sess. 198), 3:27 (Apr. 18, 1644; Sess. 203); Lightfoot, *Journal*, 249–54 (Apr. 17–19, 1644).

the practical, polity part of the directory or even seen by the public.[14] As a result, the change of government presented to the church would appear to the public to have behind it only the weight of parliamentary authority, and not the authority of the Scriptures.

The Directory for Ordination

An examination of the assembly's Directory for Ordination (found in appendix 2) shows that the assembly obviously required the presbyteries to vary somewhat from the assembly's own practice of examination. For example, the directory altered standard questions posed to examinees to reflect the fact that the candidate for ordination would obviously not already be in orders and would not have officiated in any church prior to his examination.

The directory might also assume that candidates for the ministry would require a more in-depth examination, as men coming before a presbytery could be unknown quantities and would have limited preaching and no pastoral experience. The directory also needed to account for the fact that the temporary ordination committee, and later the presbyteries, would not enjoy as broad a network of contacts as did the assembly itself. After all, the assembly could hardly have anticipated that it would continue its own examinations while local presbyteries carried on the same task. What is clear is that the gathering's Directory for Ordination of Ministers contains a synopsis of the assembly's ideals and probably sheds further light on some of the assembly's own practices as well as its vision for later presbyteries, for in drafting proposed rules for incoming or transferring ministers the assembly was undoubtedly drawing on its own experience and reflecting its own examination standards.

The directory begins with a preface and is followed by nine rules. The preface stresses that it is obvious from the Scriptures "that no man ought to take upon him the Office of a Minister of the Gospel, untill he be lawfully called and ordained thereunto." If that is what the Word of God requires, the assembly argues, then "the work of Ordination is to be performed with all due care, wisdome, gravity, and solemnity." Those ordaining the preacher are doing God's work, and it is clear that the divines are intent on stressing the magnitude of this task. After such a strong statement about the teaching of the Scriptures and its significance with respect to ordination, it is remarkable how gently the divines treaded when they actually came to introduce their directives, both the general ones in the preface and

---

14. Part 1 (the doctrinal part) is in *MPWA*, 5:63–64; the directory is on pp. 64–69 (Doc. 20).

Figure 3:
Process of Presbyterian Ordination in the Church of England, 1644–1660

Maturity	• Must be twenty-four years of age for ordination as a minister
Education	• Must be a university graduate
Call/ appointment	• Must have an appointment to minister at a particular place (or as a chaplain or college fellow)
Morals (1644–1653)	• Letter(s) of testimonial regarding morals presented to the assembly
Examination (1644–1653)	• Assembly examines candidate • Assembly hears him preach • Assembly issues a certificate
Morals	• Letter(s) of testimonial regarding morals presented to a body of ministers to ordain, 1644–1646; or to a presbytery or the former body where no presbytery is operational, 1646–1660 (hereafter, simply, "presbytery")
Examination	• Presbytery examines the candidate • Presbytery hears him preach • Evidence assessed as to whether he has taken the Solemn League and Covenantt • Candidate preaches before ministers and the congregation that is calling him • Ministers assess candidate's gifts in relation to congregation calling him
Congregational interaction	• Preach three days before the congregation • Converse with the people, who will try "his gifts for their edification" • Allow people to "better…know his life and conversation" • Notice posted by presbytery permitting people to bring objections against candidate

Figure 3: (*continued*)
Process of Presbyterian Ordination in the Church of England, 1644–1660

| Ordination as minister | • A solemn fast to be held by the congregation
• At the church in which he is to serve a sermon is preached (or in any church if he is being ordained as a chaplain or college fellow)
• The candidate answers questions regarding his faith and duty
• A minimum of seven ministers lay hands on the ordinand, setting him apart to the ministry with a short prayer or blessing
• A brief exhortation is given to the candidate by the minister who preached
• A brief exhortation or charge is given to the people to receive, maintain, and encourage their pastor, followed by a prayer, psalm, and blessing
• "No money or gift of what kind soever" is to be paid by ordinand or by anyone on his behalf, except to a registrar who files his papers, and that fee is not to exceed ten shillings |

the specific rules in the body of the document. They merely state that they "humbly tender these Directions as requisite to bee observed."[15]

In broad outline, the divines first state that the person to be ordained must be nominated by the people of the congregation or commended to the presbytery for a particular place. In either case, he must appear before the presbytery with the appropriate documentation—namely, a testimonial (or more than one) that would provide evidence of

1. "Taking" or signing the Solemn League and Covenant
2. Diligence and proficiency in study
3. University degrees
4. The amount of time spent in university
5. Age (the person must be at least twenty-four)
6. The person's "life and conversation"[16]

It is noteworthy that the assembly was so concerned about a preacher's ability to study. That sermon making, preaching, and pastoring are intellectual exercises is evidenced in half of the points that the testimonials

---

15. *MPWA*, 5:64 (Doc. 20).
16. *MPWA*, 5:64–65 (Doc. 20).

were to provide. As well, the continued requirement that preachers must be at least twenty-four years old indicated that they could not easily enter a pulpit immediately upon graduation from university. These were features that the assembly no doubt looked for in their own perusal of testimonials.

Perhaps the first and sixth points are the most jarring for modern readers. The requirement that a candidate commit himself to the religious and political platform of Parliament (in the form of the Solemn League and Covenant) serves as a kind of date stamp for this civil war text. Yet in the 1640s there was no thought that the Solemn League and Covenant was to die in a decade. It was seen by many signers as a perpetual agreement between the English and Welsh and their northern and western counterparts in Scotland and Ireland, a guarantee that the three nations would never go to war again over the form and substance of religion, for the simple fact that they would share the same religion. What is more, if the church was to be purged of crypto-Catholics and sectarians, something like this covenant was useful. Nonetheless, this stipulation also kept godly Royalists and episcopalians out of pulpits and was almost undoubtedly intended by some presbyterians to put pressure on congregationalists also.

The final feature of the required testimonial is striking in what it does not say. Although the variation amounts to only a couple of letters in a word, inquiries about "life and conversation" were significantly different than inquiries about "life and conversion." The assembly wanted sincere Christian preachers, genuine believers in the pulpit, as is seen in their rules. Many puritans did experience dramatic conversions. Yet not once in ten years did the assembly do anything but record matters relating to life and conversation, and they did not want presbyteries doing anything different. Perhaps a study of the surviving testimonials sent in support of the ministers and ordinands who came before the assembly would alter this picture: it is possible that these testimonials indicated explicitly or implicitly (by the character of the one writing the recommendation) that the examinee had a conversion experience. Men in or entering the ministry were to be converted, but the assembly certainly does not appear to have ever inquired about conversion narratives or experiences in a way analogous to American congregationalists or to the revival preachers of the First Great Awakening in America and the Evangelical Revival in Britain, such as George Whitefield, Gilbert Tennent, or John and Charles Wesley. This is one indication that there were differences among puritans and that the later puritan piety of the early eighteenth century should not be read back into much, perhaps most, of mid-seventeenth-century puritanism.

Having satisfied the presbytery with testimonials, the candidate was then to be examined by the presbytery itself. The examiners for the

Figure 4: Process of Obtaining a Benefice from 1643 to 1660

Election	• Congregation chooses a minister, followed by the appointment of the House of Commons (without presentation, institution, and induction)
or	
Presentation and Appointment	• Patron nominates minister to Parliament • Opportunity for a just exception against candidate is offered to the congregation • Minister probably pays legal fees incurred by patron
Institution	• Minister probably pays institution fee to official appointed by Parliament • Minister shows proof of presentation from patron and proof of taking Solemn League and Covenant
Induction	• Minister probably pays induction fee to same official • Minister pays first fruits (equivalent of first year's income) to Parliament • Official probably places hands of the minister on the doors of church and tolls church bell • Minister takes possession of financial resources and responsibilities of the benefice

presbytery were to put a series of five questions to him in a logical order. First there would be enquiries "touching the Grace of God in him." (Curiously, William Rathbone [d. 1644], objected to the phrase, but the rest of the assembly was firm: some examination was needed to see if the man was a Christian.)[17] Second, he was tested to see if "he be of such holinesse of life as is requisite in a Minister of the Gospel." After all, there are people who are Christians but have not sufficient growth in grace to serve as examples to other Christians and as shepherds to other sheep. Third, harkening back to the matter of the testimonials, the candidate was to be examined "touching his learning and sufficiency." Fourth, if he was deemed capable of ministry, he was asked about "the evidences of his calling to the holy Ministery." The divines believed that no one could be called who was not gifted, but there were gifted people who might not be called—the call and the gift could not be equated. Fifth, "and in particular," the examiners were to inquire about "his fair and direct calling to that place," a proviso perhaps

---

17. For Rathbone's objection, see Lightfoot, *Journal*, 251 (Apr. 18, 1644).

intended to determine if there was anything untoward in the way in which the candidate came to be preferred over any competitors to the post.[18]

Having outlined the information to be provided in testimonials and the questions to be asked of candidates, the precise content of the examination was laid out in the directory's nine rules. Significantly, most of these rules have been followed in some fashion by presbyterian churches over the centuries and—except for the fifth rule, now fallen into disuse—are continued in some form by churches today. They are as follows:

1. That the Party examined bee dealt with in a Brotherly way, with mildness of spirit, and with special respect to the gravity, modesty, and quality of every one.

2. Hee shalbee examined touching his skill in the Original tongues, and the trial to bee made by reading the Hebrew & Greek Testaments & rendring some portion of them in to Latine. And if hee bee defective in them, enquiry shalbee made the most strictly after his other Learning, and whether hee hath Skill in Logick and Philosophy.

3. What Authors in Divinity he hath read, & is best acquainted with; and trial shalbee made of his Knowledg in the chiefe grounds of Religion, & of his ability to defend the Orthodox Doctrine contained in them against all unsound & erroneous opinions, especially those of the present Age; of his skill in the sense & meaning of such places of Scripture as shalbee proposed unto him in Cases of Conscience, in the Chronology of Scripture, & the Ecclesiastical History.

4. If hee hath not before preached in publique, with approbacion of such as are able to judg, he shall at a competent time assigned him, expound before the Presbytery such a place of Scripture as shalbee given him.

5. Hee shal, with in a competent time also, frame a Discourse in Latine upon such a Common Place, or Controversy in Divinity, as shalbee assigned him; and exhibit to the Presbytery such Theses as expresse the summe thereof, & maintaine a Dispute upon them.

6. Hee shal preach before the People, the Presbytery, or some and the Ministers of the Word, appointed by them, beeing present.

7. The Proportion of his guifts in relation to the place unto which hee is called, shalbee considered.

---

18. *MPWA*, 5:65 (Doc. 20).

8. Besides the trial of his guifts in Preaching, hee shall undergo an Examination in the premisses, two several dayes; and more, if the Presbytery shall judg it necessary.

9. And as for him that hath bin formerly Ordained a Minister, & is to bee removed to another charg, Hee shall bring a Testimonial of his Ordination, & of his Abilities, & Conversation, whereupon his fittnes for that place shalbee tryed by his preaching there, and (if it shalbee judged necessary) by a further examination of him.[19]

The first rule is directed more to the presbytery than to the candidate and shows considerable understanding of the plight of a nervous ordinand. Indeed, it echoes the language of the assembly's own rule, drafted at an earlier point, that people be "dealt withal in all mildness and gravity."[20] But here familial language is used to remind ministers that this potential peer and colleague is not to be treated as a student before his teachers but as a brother before his brethren. The assembly had a near-constant stream of men queuing in the hallways of Westminster Abbey, either waiting to be called in for examination or awaiting the results of their exams. It appears that the divines understood the human side of this process even if some requirements, especially rules two and three, focus chiefly on the life of the mind.

The fourth and fifth requirements were to illustrate the person's ability to communicate his learning in both popular and scholarly contexts. It is not at all clear that the Latin lecture and disputation needed to be performed with real excellence for the person to pass this stage in the exam. Indeed, some of the conversations in the assembly suggest otherwise.[21] Rather, here (and in rule two) his ability in Latin would assure the assembly that he could access books of Protestant theology. As well, the quality of his work would help the presbytery discern the man's "parts" or abilities so that they could help him determine where he should minister and how. If he was called to be a preacher in, say, a university town, he should excel not only in preaching but in scholarship. This idea is part of what is envisioned in rule seven. Perhaps there was another potential benefit to the disputation that is less obvious. Presbyteries in the 1640s were to function like presbyteries now—with a multitude of committees—and the disputation could have the (perhaps unwanted) side effect of identifying fresh candidates for committee work.

Both presbyterians and congregationalists agreed that if the candidate was to be approved by a congregation, then he needed to preach before

---

19. *MPWA*, 5:65–66 (Doc. 20).
20. Lightfoot, *Journal*, 47 (Nov. 10, 1643).
21. E.g., *MPWA*, 2:229–31 (Oct. 27, 1643; Sess. 83).

them. And lest the people be swept off their feet by eloquent nonsense, rule six stipulates that ministers of the Word were to be on the spot to hear this sermon too. After the completion of the final sermon (or sermons), the presbytery could establish whether the person was sufficiently gifted for the place—and then finish his trials with a minimum of two days of theological examination. This was captured in the eighth rule, which called for an examination "in the premises," or basic doctrines. If the examination in the premises is inclusive of all the other parts of the examination, it is to be suspected that more days would often be necessary. Modern presbytery exams, in many denominations, can hardly be sustained in all their parts over a two-day period, and the Westminster divines insisted on a Latin discourse and disputation as well. But this two-day examination appears to be additional to, and not a part of, the other aspects of the examination. Needless to say, the directory envisaged a considerable amount of work on the part of the presbyteries.

What is immediately apparent in the assembly's instructions for presbyteries is that where they overlap with the assembly's own procedures, the rules for presbyteries are far more detailed and more rigorous than the rules employed in the assembly for its own examinations. In examining ministers, the assembly made preaching optional. In scrutinizing candidates for ministry, the presbyteries were to make it mandatory. The assembly questioned a minister about his knowledge "in tongues," but the presbytery was required to offer rigorous tests of those abilities. And there were also curious procedural differences. The assembly asked about an ordained minister's commitment to catechizing and his method of visiting the sick, whereas the ministerial candidate, although surely expected to perform the same tasks, was not asked these questions. On the other hand, the assembly's rules do not mention the need to test existing ministers in their knowledge of the Bible or church history, whereas the directory requires examinations in both for candidates for the ministry. The most significant difference, however, between the assembly's rules and the directory's procedures had to do with existing ministers. The assembly's rules for itself required substantial examination for everyone who came before the body. The directory's procedure for examining a candidate was a two-day examination in the basic facts of theology, but in the case of an established minister who wished to accept a call to a different congregation, the examination could be waived if a presbytery saw fit. There were other parts to the Directory for Ordination not discussed here (including a stipulation that no fees or gifts be collected related to the ordination of ministers).[22] There were also aspects

---

22. *MPWA*, 5:68 (Doc. 20).

of ministerial and church life avoided by the directory. Most significantly, while the process of ordination changed, the rights of patrons were upheld (although qualified by a congregation's right of refusal). And institution and induction—likely with the payment of fees—was continued, in most cases, under the oversight of Parliament, whose officials appointed for the task gradually replaced the role of bishops and cathedral officers.[23]

If presbyterian ordination was a change for ordinands, it was entirely new for local congregations. In the first place, they had an opportunity to get to know the candidate and decide whether they wanted him as their pastor. After the presbytery had approved a man for a call to a local church, he was to stay with the congregation for three days, preaching, meeting with people, and "making tryall of his gifts for their edification." Through this they would "better...know his life and conversation." Following this assessment the congregation was given notice (read publicly and nailed to the church door) of a time by which they could state any exceptions against the candidate.[24]

Assuming that there were no "just exceptions against" the candidate, the congregation was then called to further participate in the process by fasting and praying. After a sermon by one of the ministers appointed to ordain, the congregation was called de facto to serve as witnesses to the candidate's answers to a series of questions or "demands." Although the precise wording of these answers was not stipulated—in contrast to earlier oaths of canonical obedience and later presbyterian ordination vows—something analogous was offered as he expressed his faith and duty in eight areas "by the help of God." The ordinand was to indicate (1) his faith in Christ; (2) his persuasion of the truth of the Reformed religion; (3) his sincere intentions and purposes in entering this calling; (4) his resolution to be faithful in prayer, reading, meditation, preaching and ministering the sacraments, and all ministerial duties; (5) his zeal and truth for the gospel; (6) his zeal and truth for the unity of the church against error and schism; (7) his care that

---

23. Parliament considered giving the presbyterian classes the right of institution. See *Journal of the House of Commons, 1646–1648*, 5:649 (July 28, 1648). Normally officials appointed by parliament assumed the rights and privileges of institution and induction; occasionally even these steps in the process were simply suspended by order of parliament. See *Journal of the House of Commons, 1644–1646*, 4:634 (Aug. 5, 1646) and *Journal of the House of Lords, 1644*, 7:564 (Sept. 2, 1645). Prior to 1646 the House of Lords also continued to employ bishops for institution and induction on an *ad hoc* basis. See *Journal of the House of Lords, 1644*, 7:273 (Mar. 15, 1645) and 7:599 (Sept. 25, 1645). Months later the Lords would overturn the institution and induction of a bishop. See *Journal of the House of Lords, 1645–1647*, 8:30 (Dec. 6, 1646). It appears that only in July 1649 did Parliament begin to consider the fee structure involved in institution and induction. See *Journal of the House of Commons, 1648–1651*, 6:263 (July 18, 1649).

24. *MPWA*, 5:66 (Doc. 20).

he and his family would be examples to the flock; and (8) his resolution to continue in his duty even during trouble and persecution.[25]

Following his answers, ministers would lay hands on the ordinand, setting him apart to the ministry with a short prayer or blessing. The minister who preached would then offer a brief exhortation to the candidate, followed by a brief exhortation or charge given to the people to receive, maintain, and encourage their new pastor. The service concluded with a prayer, a psalm, and a blessing. For the first time they would have seen a man being set apart for gospel ministry in their own local church, rather than hearing about an action that took place at a distant cathedral. And for the first time, a ministry of preaching was entailed in every ordination.[26]

If for the congregation the novelty of the event was seeing it at all, for the historian, the most striking feature of the assembly's proposed procedures may be the absence of a set doctrinal standard to which these ministers were to conform or subscribe. It was not only left to the presbytery's discretion to waive an examination in the case of an ordained minister who needed to be installed in a new congregation, but it was also given complete discretionary powers to decide whether a minister was orthodox or not. It could be argued that the assembly envisioned this as a temporary situation—after all, the first directory was authored in 1644. That year fell in the awkward period when the Thirty-nine Articles had fallen out of use (it was not officially outlawed) and the production of a full confession of faith was still in progress. Of course, the assembly was in favor of confessional standards for the church (it was writing one: the Confession of Faith). Nonetheless, it is not clear what the divines thought about the various subscription options that they and Parliament would eventually have had to consider if the course of history had not so dramatically changed later in the decade. As it happens, Parliament did not approve of the assembly's doctrinal texts, and thus the gathering's members were not asked to subscribe to the documents that they themselves produced.

Nonetheless, it may be informative that the assembly thought that the church was capable, at least for a time, of discerning godly and orthodox men without the aid of a confessional standard. Perhaps this has relevance for debates that continue in some Presbyterian churches about whether presbyteries should have the power to discern whether preachers can differ from, or hold any exceptions to, the Westminster Confession of Faith or whether the granting of such power signals the beginning of a slide toward

---

25. *MPWA*, 5:66 (Doc. 20).
26. *MPWA*, 5:67 (Doc. 20).

unorthodoxy.[27] Perhaps one can conclude (or concede) only the petite point that if a committee for examining candidates and ministers in a church with a long confessional heritage has an orthodox chair and good members and has examined thousands of men for ministry, that the committee is likely to be able to do its job well even without a current confessional standard as a reference point for candidates and examiners.

At the same time, the assembly, in establishing these rules, was drawing a line in the sand, and the more radical reformers on the fringes of this puritan revolution would have seen it, as would those who were willing to make space for them in the church. For all the emphasis on godliness, the changes that were made to the ordination process, the expansion of input on the part of congregations, and the increased participation on the part of a potential minister's peers, one thing was clear: the entire process of credentialing ministers and assessing candidates excluded lay preachers from exercising any kind of public ministry within the church.

---

27. E.g., I. Hamilton, *The Erosion of Calvinist Orthodoxy: Seceders and Subscription in Scottish Presbyterianism* (Edinburgh: Rutherford House, 1990).

CHAPTER 7

Directions for Preaching:
The Directory for Public Worship

Preaching of the Word, being the power of God to salvation & one of the greatest & most excellent workes belonging to the Mi[ni]stry of the gospell, should be soe performed, that the workeman neede not be ashamed, but may save himselfe & them that heare him.
—"Of The Preaching of the Word," Directory for Public Worship

Illuminating as the Westminster Assembly's discussions about the office of pastor can be at points, the real debate over preaching itself only resumed in the summer of 1644 as the gathering drafted a Directory for Worship for England and Scotland and, as a result, Ireland—although Irish concerns and practices are never mentioned by the assembly.

The Directory for Public Worship has many features worthy of notice, at least three of which warrant mention in relation to preaching. In the first place, the directory is not always very clear, as Horton Davies and others have noted, about whether it is giving directives as suggestions, or directives as commands.¹ Sometimes the directory says a minister *may* do something, in other places it says he *shall*. Practices are variously termed "necessary" or "requisite" but also "expedient," "convenient," or "sufficient."² A deliberate attempt was made to express differing degrees of confidence for different practices featured in the directory, and this is evident from the first day of debate on the Directory for Preaching (and elsewhere).³ In the second place, the directory is really a compilation of directories. After the directory's completion, it was more often referred to as a whole; while it was being crafted, the minutes of the assembly refer to the individual directories that make up that whole—for example, a directory for prayer, a directory for

---

1. Davies, *Worship of the English Puritans*, 130.
2. See the assembly's own explanation in A Directory for the Publique Worship of God, 7.
3. *MPWA*, 3:128 (June 3, 1644; Sess. 230).

visiting the sick, and a directory for administering the sacraments.[4] In the third place, the directory took the unusual step of including its directives for preaching in a text intended to guide people in corporate worship.[5]

Debates about Preaching

A directory for preaching in a directory for worship was uncommon, and Alexander Mitchell flagged this fact in his history of the assembly.[6] But Mitchell was not the first to do so, for Jeremiah Whitaker (1599–1654) noted the same thing on the floor of the Westminster Assembly, calling on the gathering "to consider whether it be fit to have a directory for preaching" at all.[7] John Lightfoot's journal records that in defense of his motion, "Mr Whittacre opposed…a Directory for preaching, as needless and not expected: and he queried of what use of this Directory should be."[8]

Usually the chair or a member of a committee presenting a report would defend its own work. However, in this case Samuel Rutherford

---

4. The final form of the Directory for Public Worship begins with one section on the assembling and behavior of worshipers and then devotes a section to the public reading of the Word of God. The following three sections are all connected to preaching: one each on prayer before and after the sermon, and one section on the sermon itself.

5. For studies of the Directory for Public Worship that have some discussion of its section on preaching, see B. D. Spinks, "Brief and Perspicuous Text; Plain and Pertinent Doctrine: Behind 'Of the Preaching of the Word' in the Westminster Directory," in *Like a Two-Edged Sword: The Word of God in Liturgy and History*, ed. M. Dudley (Norwich: Canterbury Press, 1995), 91–111; R. S. Paul, *The Assembly of the Lord: Politics and Religion in the Westminster Assembly and the 'Grand Debate'* (Edinburgh: T&T Clark, 1985), 359–74, esp. 364–65; A. F. Mitchell, *The Westminster Assembly: Its History and Standards* (London: James Nisbet, 1883), 212–45, esp. 238–41; and H. Davies, *Worship and Theology in England*, 412–13. C. P. Venema has contributed an article in which he notes the particular emphasis that the Westminster Catechism and Larger Catechism place on preaching: "The Doctrine of Preaching in the Reformed Confessions," *Mid-America Journal of Theology* 10 (1999): 135–83. A similar point is made by A. D. Strange in "Comments on the Centrality of Preaching in the Westminster Standards," *Mid-America Journal of Theology* 10 (1999): 185–238. Strange includes an excursus on eighteenth-century preaching (pp. 205–12) and appends the text of the Directory for Public Worship (pp. 233–38). For a discussion of the preaching of the assembly itself, see Norris, "The Preaching of the Assembly," 63–81. Norris sums up the fuller argument of J. F. Wilson's *Pulpit in Parliament: Puritanism during the English Civil Wars: 1640–1648* (Princeton: Princeton University Press, 1969), 137–65. For further discussion of preaching before Parliament, most of which was done by Westminster divines, see E. W. Kirby, "Sermons Before the Commons, 1640–42," *American Historical Review* 44, no. 3 (1939): 528–48; and Hill, *The English Bible and the Seventeenth-Century Revolution*, 79–108. H. R. Trevor-Roper presents a fascinating study of the fast sermons in *Religion and Reformation and Social Change* (London: Macmillan, 1967), 294–344.

6. Mitchell, *History*, 238.

7. *MPWA*, 3:130 (June 4, 1644; Sess. 231).

8. Lightfoot, *Journal*, 277 (June 4, 1644).

(c. 1600–1661) immediately took the floor and played the Scottish trump card: the Solemn League and Covenant. Rutherford stated that a directory for preaching was needed for "uniformity" and held that without it "a speciall article of the covenant [was] called in question."[9] From there Rutherford characteristically launched into a three-point sermonette on the nature of Christian liberty and its application to the proposed Directory for Public Worship. Cornelius Burges's response is lost, but John Arrowsmith's (1602–1659) rejoinder is not. Arrowsmith appreciated Whitaker's point and the possibility that a directory for preaching might unduly restrict the liberty of preachers. After all, "ther is difference betwixt uniformity in praying & in preaching. The one is possible, the other is not." But this did not mean that there should be no directory, for, Arrowsmith adds, "this [matter] of preaching directs only for the pastors work."[10] Herbert Palmer, without adding any clarity to the discussion, did add that "the generality of the godly ministers in this kingdome have been uniform in their preaching."[11] Eventually the inclusion of a subdirectory on preaching within the larger directory for worship was passed; presumably there were enough ungodly preachers needing the assembly's advice.

Conversations such as this reveal an eagerness to improve the quality of preaching. There is no evidence that Parliament required such a directory for preaching, and the divines were not (in spite of Rutherford's puzzling claim) under any obligation to prepare such a work under the Solemn League and Covenant. The Covenant mentions a "confession of faith, form of church-government, directory for worship" and a directory for "catechising"; it says and assumes nothing about a directory for preaching.[12] No previous communication between the Church of Scotland and the Westminster Assembly mentions preaching either.[13] Yet the assembly,

---

9. *MPWA*, 3:130 (June 4, 1644; Sess. 231).

10. Arrowsmith seems to hold out a softer understanding of the directory, one that provided suggestions, not demands.

11. *MPWA*, 3:130 (June 4, 1644; Sess. 231).

12. *A Solemn League and Covenant, for Reformation, and Defence of Religion* (London, 1643).

13. The various acts of the Scottish General Assembly, which considered making its own directory for worship, and later correspondence with the English, frequently mention the need for a common confession, form of church government, catechism, and directory for worship, but from 1641 to 1644 no specific mention is ever made of a directory for preaching or of preaching as one element within a directory for worship. See *The Acts of the Assemblies of the Church of Scotland, from the Year 1638, to the Year 1649, Inclusive* ([Edinburgh?], 1682), 107, 131, 142, 147, 172–73, 177, 196. Significant for understanding Rutherford's response to Whitaker, however, the June letter of the Scottish Commissioners to the Scots Assembly does mention that, among other things, "the method of Preaching" has been discussed but is not far enough along for the assembly's perusal (*Acts of the Assemblies*, 226–27). The General Assembly in its response does not register any surprise about the preaching directory, and

in a display of initiative, determined that good preaching was so essential and bad preaching so common that some directives were necessary. This came at a price. In spite of initial hopes for the speedy passage of the Directory for Preaching, it was passed only after, in Robert Baillie's words, "a world of debate"; the directory occupied the assembly as a whole for the space of six days.[14]

The deliberations occupying the assembly and its committee for the Directory for Preaching (under Stephen Marshall's leadership) revolved around the basis, structure, and content of the sermon and the use of foreign languages or scholarly quotations in the sermon,[15] not the relative importance of preaching itself. For example, in a burst of compassion, the committee attempted to shorten sermons by stating that "the preacher shall handle so much for each time, as may be kept in memory by the hearers." This brief suggestion "cost large debate, about long sermons" since many, and in the end most, of the divines did not want "the people's memory" to "be the stint of sermons."[16] The committee also suggested that the truth preached in a sermon be "principally intended in the place [i.e., a particular biblical text]." Lightfoot and others found this to be objectionable and cited the New Testament's use of the Old as proof that one can move beyond the "principal intent" of the author. The committee also spoke of "the several parts of the text" from which the sermon would be preached. Again Lightfoot protested: he held that a sermon text could consist of one word, such as "amen." The assembly complied and changed the wording to the singular.[17]

Within the Directory for Public Worship, the subdirectory for preaching was not alone in its promotion of the preacher's work. The subdirectory for reading of the Scriptures, harkening back to an earlier debate, insisted that not so much of the Scriptures be read that preaching be "streightned" or constrained.[18] The subdirectory for the sanctification of the Lord's Day includes counsel not only to be at the worship service but also to hold "repetitions of the sermons" at home, telling heads of families to call "their

---

comments instead on the need for a directory for the ordination of ministers (*Acts of the Assemblies*, 237–39). This may indicate an assumption on the part of the Scots that a directory for worship would as a matter of course say something about preaching, except that, as Mitchell has pointed out, this had never been done before (Mitchell, *History*, 238).

14. Baillie, *Letters*, 2:191. In a May 31 letter Robert Baillie writes, "We trust, in one or two sessions, to through also our draught of preaching: if we continue this race, we will amend our former infamous slowness" (Baillie, *Letters*, 187). For the six sessions, see *MPWA*, 3:121–23 (May 24, 1644; Sess. 226), 128–37 (June 3–7, 1644; Sess. 231–234), 142–48 (June 17, 1644; Sess. 240).

15. See chapter 8.

16. Lightfoot, *Journal*, 277 (June 4, 1644).

17. Lightfoot, *Journal*, 278 (June 4, 1644).

18. *MPWA*, 5:96 (Doc. 36).

families to an account of what they have heard."[19] This was a practice that some of William Gouge's parishioners had found even more useful than his sermons—a telling comment given that Gouge was one of London's most famous preachers.[20]

The discussions in crafting the subdirectory for preaching hardly exhaust the gathering's comments on preaching, a subject mentioned more than four hundred times in the assembly's surviving minutes. Nonetheless, it is in these debates that the evident concern of the divines to reform preaching is most clearly expressed. There is a steady urgency to get the assembly's directions right because men needed to preach the Scriptures faithfully and authoritatively or, as Arrowsmith put it, "as the oracles of God," and because assembly members hoped pastors would use their directory.[21] The same concern is apparent in the subdirectory itself, which highlights the importance of preaching. "Preaching of the word," the opening line declares, is "the power of God unto salvation, and one of the greatest and most excellent Works belonging to the Ministry of the gospell."[22]

The Directory for Preaching and the Character of the Preacher

Of course, the best location for understanding the assembly's ideals for preaching, often expressed as ideals for preachers, is in the subdirectory itself, titled "Of the Preaching of the Word," where the assembly clearly expected the one who preaches to be a scholar, a worshipper, an orator, an apologist, a pastor, and a servant.[23]

Even before he enters a pulpit, the preacher is called to be a scholar. Referring readers back to the Directory for Ordination, the assembly explained that "according to the Rules of Ordination" a minister must "in some good measure" be "guifted for soe weighty a service." He is to have "skill in the originall languages & in such arts & Sciences as are hand maides to Divinity." He is to have "knowledg in the whole body of Theology, but most of all in the holy Scriptures." He is to be able to understand and to summarize Scripture, to analyze and divide texts, to ensure that the truths he expounds are "contained in or grounded on that text" he preaches, and to "cheefly insist upon those doctrines which are principally intended" in the passage he addresses.[24] Nonetheless, he is to be the kind

---

19. *MPWA*, 5:122 (Doc 43).
20. Hunt, *Art of Hearing*, 76.
21. *MPWA*, 3:135 (June 7, 1644; Sess. 234).
22. *MPWA*, 5:100 (Doc. 36).
23. The following citations quote from the edition of the directory found in the Oxford edition of the papers of the Westminster Assembly.
24. *MPWA*, 5:100 (Doc. 36).

of scholar whose teaching is "expressed in plaine termes" because he is a scholar whose work is for the benefit of others and not just for himself or his peers.²⁵

In the paragraphs most clearly emphasizing a preacher's scholarly abilities, the assembly also underscored that he is a worshipper. In fact, immediately after stressing that a preacher is to be a student of truth and an expert in the Bible, the directory states that the preacher must have "his senses & hart exercised in them above the common sort of beleevers." He is to trust in "the illumination of gods Spirit & other guiftes of edification." In "reading & studying of the Word" and in seeking God "by prayer, & an humble hart," the preacher is always to be "resolving to admitt & receive any truth not yet attained, when ever God shall make it knowne unto him." Assembly members considered preparation for preaching as an act of piety, a sanctifying experience of personal worship. And thus "he is to make use of" and "improve" on "his private preparations, before he deliver in publique" what he has studied.²⁶ That is to say, he is to be "persuaded in his owne heart that all that he teacheth is the truth of Christ" and "earnestly both in private & in Publique recomending his labours to the blessing of God, & wachfully looking to himselfe & the flocke wherof the Lord hath made him overseer."²⁷

Preachers are not mere professionals, paid to study topics and prepare sermons. Nonetheless, they are to be orators, men able to construct and deliver addresses that are organized and persuasive. The assembly expected sermons to have introductions, well-ordered arguments, and illustrations that engender "spiritual delight."²⁸ The directory directs the preacher to exhort and dehort (or dissuade), to explicate and to insist.²⁹ The liability of the label "orator" is that it could suggest that preaching is but a type of rhetoric. This the assembly would reject. The subdirectory insists that the preacher communicate in a manner "that the meanest may understand, delivering the truth not in the entiseing words of mans wisdome, but in demonstration of the spirit & of power, lesse the crosse of Christ should be made of none effect."³⁰ The preacher's "gesture[s], voice & expressions" were to be appropriate to his ministry.³¹ The preacher must abstain "alsoe from an unprofitable use of unknowne tongues, strange phryases & cadences of sounds & words, sparingly citing sentences of Ecclesiasticall or other

---

25. *MPWA*, 5:101 (Doc. 36).
26. *MPWA*, 5:100 (Doc. 36).
27. *MPWA*, 5:103 (Doc. 36).
28. *MPWA*, 5:100–101 (Doc. 36).
29. *MPWA*, 5:101–2 (Doc. 36).
30. *MPWA*, 5:102 (Doc. 36).
31. *MPWA*, 5:103 (Doc. 36).

humane writers, ancient or modearne, be they never so elegant." It was not elegance that the assembly was after. While they knew preaching would be "a worke of great difficulty…requireing much prudence, zeale, & meditation," what the assembly really wanted were men who could preach in such a way that "auditors may feele the word of God to be quicke & powerfull," to discover the "discerner of the thoughts & intents of the heart." And "if any unbeliever or ignorant person be present, he may have the secrets of his hart made manifest, & give glory to God."[32]

The directory also insists that a preacher is to be aware of and respond to error, that there is an apologetic dimension to his work. There is no assumption on the part of the directory that people who come to worship will believe whatever the preacher says. That is why the sermon is to employ "places of scripture, confirming the doctrine" and why these places "are rather to be plaine & pertinent then many." The preacher is to offer "Arguments or Reasons" that are "solid, &, as much as may be, convincing." What is more, "If any doubt, obvious from scripture, reason, or prejudice of the hearers, seeme to arise, it is very requisite to remove it, by reconciling the seeming differences, answering the reasons, & discovering & taking away the causes of prejudice & mistake." Of course, there are preachers who have made it their hobby to refute heresy, and so the assembly also added, sensibly, that "it is not fitt to detaine the hearers with propounding or answering vaine or wicked cavilles, which as they are endlesse, soe the propounding & answering of them doth more hinder than promote edification." Or to put it another way, "In Confutation of false doctrines, he is neither to rayse an old heresy from the grave, nor to mention a blasphemous opinion unnecessarily. But if the people be in dang[e]r of an error he is to confute it soundly, & endeavour to satisfy their Judgments & consciences against all objections."[33]

Unsurprisingly, the assembly speaks to preachers in such a way as to remind them that both in his motivations and in his concerns the preacher is a pastor. The preacher is to address the people in such a way that they sense his "loving affection" and his "godly zeale & hearty desyre, to doe them good." He is to walk "before his flocke as an example to them…wachfully looking to himselfe & the flocke wherof the Lord hath made him overseer."[34] And he is to be mindful of both their weakness and sinfulness. His sermons are not to be too complicated. He is "neither to burden the memorie of the hearers in the begining with too many members of division, nor to trouble their mindes with obscure termes of Art." His concern

---

32. *MPWA*, 5:101 (Doc. 36).
33. *MPWA*, 5:101 (Doc. 36).
34. *MPWA*, 5:103 (Doc. 36).

is for their souls. In his preaching he will "make most for the edification of the hearers."[35] A good preacher not only calls them to their duties but helps them to see how to get there.[36] He is to point out the misery and danger of sin, to offer comfort against temptations, "troubles and terrors." He is to answer the objections that troubled hearts will likely raise against his preaching. Through "his residence & conv[e]rsing with his flocke" he will select the best uses and applications of texts and doctrines "such as may most draw their soules to Christ, the fountaine of light holines & comfort."[37]

Above all, the preacher is a servant, or "minister." And while preaching is "one of the greatest & most excellent works," it remains work. The preacher is a "workeman," one who hopes not to be ashamed in his Master's assessment of his labors. He is a minister of Christ, but he is also a servant of God's people. He is to work hard to make sure that his sermon is not a "burden" for the memory of hearers to bear, or trouble for their minds, and he is to have in view their edification and benefit.[38] He is to offer a "removal service"[39] for doubts, "taking away the causes of prejudice & mistake," or whatever else might hinder the progress of his congregation. As a servant, he must not "rest" with easy applications but give something that will be truly useful, even if "it prove a worke of great difficulty to him selfe."[40]

The preacher as servant is the subdirectory's major motif, and it ends with a stirring call to faithful labor: "The Servant of Christ, what ever his method bee, is to performe his whole ministry.... Painfully, not doeing the worke of the Lord negligently." He is to serve on behalf of the "meanest" of his listeners. Echoing Jesus's parables about laborers, the preacher is told by the assembly to be ever "looking at the honor of Christ" and "the conversion, edification & salvation of the people, not at his owne gaine or glory: keeping noething backe which may promote those holy ends."[41] As a servant he is to be wise, grave, and loving, "that the people may see all coming from his godly zeale & hearty desyre, to doe them good." In the end, he is to recommend "his labours to the blessing of God.... Soe shall the doctrine of truth bee preserved uncorrupt, many soules converted & built up & himselfe receive many fould comforts of his labours even in this life & afterward the Crowne of glory laide up for him in the world to come."[42]

---

35. *MPWA*, 5:100 (Doc. 36).
36. *MPWA*, 5:101 (Doc. 36).
37. *MPWA*, 5:101–2 (Doc. 36).
38. *MPWA*, 5:100 (Doc. 36).
39. *Removal service*: a moving company.
40. *MPWA*, 5:101 (Doc. 36).
41. *MPWA*, 5:102 (Doc. 36).
42. *MPWA*, 5:103 (Doc. 36).

The Directory for Preaching and Sermon Structures

While the conclusion of the preaching portion of the directory echoes the kinds of themes that could be delivered in an ordination or installation sermon, the body of the directory's practical instructions (as J. I. Packer, Davies, and others have noted) takes its cue from William Perkins, holding closely to the three-part sermon structure of exegesis, doctrinal extraction, and application found in *The Art of Prophesying*. Drawing a direct line between Perkins and the Westminster Assembly, Packer writes that the puritan "principles in preaching, first formulated by Perkins in his *Arte of Prophecying*, found their best balanced expression in the Westminster Assembly's Directory for the Public Worship of God."[43] John F. Wilson argues that during the civil war the "plain style" of the preachers appointed by Parliament "may be traced back to their patriarch, William Perkins." Wilson makes an explicit connection between Perkins's preaching instructions and those found in the assembly's directory.[44]

Nonetheless, the recommendation of a Perkinsian tripartite sermon structure in the Directory for Preaching—the plain-style structure so standard among godly preachers and later to be employed in a manual for preachers written by an assembly member[45]—was opposed by three of the assembly's most prominent members. Anthony Tuckney (1599–1670) did not want the assembly to tie a "preacher to the forme of doctrine, reason and use."[46] Lightfoot recalled that both Thomas Gataker and Gouge joined in Tuckney's protest "concerning the prescription of preaching by doctrine, reason, and use, as too strait for the variety of gifts, and occasion doth claim liberty." Their arguments had some effect as the assembly decided on "an addition in the close or preface—that this method is not to be prescribed to every man, nor upon every occasion, but is recommended upon the experience of the benefit that hath accrued by it." He added that "it cost a good deal of time before we could find terms for it."[47]

---

43. J. I. Packer, *A Quest for Godliness: The Puritan Vision of the Chirstian Life* (Wheaton, Ill.: Crossway, 1990), 280.

44. Wilson, *Pulpit in Parliament*, 139, 141–42; cf. Norris, "The Preaching of the Assembly," 67–68; and Davies, *Worship and Theology in England*, 163–64.

45. W. Price, *Ars Concionandi Regulis Perspicuis, & Exemplis Palmariis, & Multifariis, Concinnata & Instructa* (Amsterdam, 1656). Price outlines the processes involved in exegesis of the text (including contextual and genre-related factors), and analysis, exposition, and interpretation of the text. He discusses the transfer of this information to the sermon itself and the identification of themes and doctrines. He then discusses application in its various types, and then concludes by discussing matters of form and style. Throughout he provides extensive examples of his own exegesis and sermon outlines.

46. *MPWA*, 3:131 (June 5, 1644; Sess. 232).

47. Lightfoot, *Journal*, 278.

While many of the preaching debates can easily be understood, at times little can be determined beyond the fact that there were two sides. This is the case on Monday, June 3, 1644, when the divines discussed whether preachers should expound a "text or argument." Some opposed the idea of preaching from an argument (i.e., a doctrinal statement) "because it gives liberty to preach without a text."[48] The result of the discussion is known: the directory explicitly states that the sermon is to come from a biblical text.[49] The actual content of the debate is unknown, and its main outlines can only be suggested by known contextual factors. The decision to advocate text-based sermons may have indicated a growing discomfort with the assembly's earlier decision to subsume catechesis under preaching. Alternatively, the majority of divines may have been unhappy with preachers who routinely expounded one biblical text and then preached a series of sermons on the argument or doctrine(s) of that text rather than on the text itself.[50]

If this was the assembly's point, it must be conceded that these sermon series were not unpopular with everyone. For the preacher, these thematic expositions on a biblical text made easy the increasingly frequent transition of sermon series to book-length studies. The book market was equally pleased: one of Jeremiah Burroughs's sermon series turned book, titled *The Rare Jewel of Christian Contentment*,[51] enjoyed at least a dozen printings in the seventeenth century alone and continued to be printed in the eighteenth, nineteenth, and twentieth centuries. But arguably Burroughs (bap. 1601?, d. 1646) was blurring the old distinction between goose and gander since what was good for the bookstall was not necessarily good for the parish church.

For example, Burroughs preached a sermon series on a half dozen words in Isaiah 66:2. As can be seen from its printed form, the series began with a couple of pages of thoughtful exegesis and explanation of the text. Yet from that point forward in the series there is no return to careful biblical

---

48. *MPWA*, 3:128 (June 3, 1644; Sess. 230).

49. *MPWA*, 5:100 (Doc. 36). This comment in the minutes informs another discussion where Godfrey asserts (contra Philip Schaff) that the Larger Catechism was not intended as a document for preaching in the churches, as was the practice of continental churches with the Heidelberg Catechism (see Godfrey, "The Westminster Larger Catechism," in *To Glorify and Enjoy God*, 131). The minutes here support Godfrey: if the assembly deliberately voted against preaching from doctrinal propositions, then it is most unlikely that they would intend the Larger Catechism for this purpose.

50. Robert Baillie argues that this approach is most commonly adopted by the Independent. See his *A Dissuasive from the Errours of the Time* (London, 1645), 118. Additional research is needed to confirm the accuracy of the impression that the congregationalists were proportionately more likely to produce these sermon sagas on individual biblical texts or phrases than other puritans.

51. J. Burroughs, *The Rare Jewel of Christian Contentment* (London, 1648).

study, and the Bible is used only to illustrate and enforce arguments made by the preacher. Not only is the biblical text no longer that which propels the sermon series, it is also the case that the series functions structurally as a single sermon. For example, the second "sermon" ended on point five, subsection 2, and so the third "sermon" begins with subsection three. The approach of a series of propositional sermons required parishioners to be present for the whole offering in order to appreciate the parts, both in terms of biblical foundations and in terms of the coherence of the series. For those who attended multiple sermons per week, memories were taxed with recalling multiple sermon series in progress. Nonetheless, this process could be aided by careful sermon notes, and it was not inherently more difficult than the task of reading three or four books at a time (a practice with which many readers are probably familiar).[52]

An additional challenge sometimes attended propositional preaching: the fact that each sermon series often focused on one topic only. Although many facets of the one topic were displayed by the best preachers, the sermon series itself could not stand alone as a well-rounded theological presentation. Each series required the supplementation of other series if the church was to have a biblically balanced diet. In *Gospel-Fear*, for example, Burroughs discusses the person of God and provides a detailed exposition of what people are to do but has little to say about Jesus Christ and what He has done for sinners. For weeks, even months, one would have to listen to sermons about sin or the law until the tide would finally change once more and the emphasis would return to Christ and the gospel or to some other biblical topic. To be sure, many people could not only tolerate but also enjoy propositional sermons crafted by a talented preacher like Burroughs. But he had few equals as a preacher, and it is not hard to see why the Directory for Preaching sought to distance itself from preaching built on doctrinal propositions or on the brief exegesis of a single text that would be only a dim memory by the close of a sermon series many months later.

Continuing Education?

The assembly's Directory for Preaching offered an important means for putting godly ideals into practice. It was the capstone of the assembly's reforming work with respect to preachers and preaching, and the only thing approaching an attempt to actually help the incoming and continuing preaching ministry of England. Combined with the Directory for Ordination and its attempt to define the preacher's task relative to the other duties of his office,

---

52. E.g., see the sermon notebook of Robert Legard, which reveals more than one overlapping sermon series while he was a student at Cambridge University (FSL MS V.a.432).

and with examinations intended to increase the supply of godly and learned ministers, there was a chance for real change in the church.

These two directories were to be employed in tandem, but they assumed different audiences. The Directory for Ordination was intended to be used chiefly by ministers, reminding them of the minimum standards that must be met to permit entry into the pulpit. The Directory for Preaching, on the other hand, was addressed to the public and designed to help them see what kind of people their preachers ought to be and the kind of sermons that their preachers ought to deliver. Where taken seriously, it could serve to help a local pastor improve his sermons. It could also lead parishioners to expect more of their preacher. The Directory for Preaching had the capacity to facilitate the kind of destabilization that can occur after a famous preacher visits a congregation and offers them a taste of particularly good preaching. Having been exposed to a gourmet sermon, a return to rice-and-beans preaching can sometimes be hard for a congregation to swallow. The Westminster Assembly must have known this but thought it was either worth the risk or even helpful for congregations who were not being nourished by their preacher and perhaps even needed to find a replacement.

The unresolved puzzle of the assembly's reform of preaching is that the replacement of ministers was given so much prominence in the reform of the church. The assembly considered removal rather than renewal. Beyond the Directory for Preaching, it lacked any practical program to improve the existing ministry of the church. The directory had the potential to be a useful teaching text, but why did the gathering stop there? Seventy years before, when working for reform from within the system of episcopacy, puritans attempted to *train* ministers. They helped to teach the blind guides how to see for themselves and then how to preach to others. This was the purpose of the prophesyings, those entertaining educational venues for preachers that even bishops would bless and that William Grindal defended at the cost of his archiepiscopal post.

Nonetheless, with all of its suggestions for change, the assembly failed to implement or officially encourage any system of remedial education for deficient preachers. The Westminster Assembly never once lobbied to restore continuing education structures, like prophesying, so valued by an earlier generation of the godly. Perhaps wars, and above all civil wars, encourage binary thinking, such as the ejection of inadequate preachers and their replacement with other ministers. Perhaps the war so stretched resources that educational projects were not feasible. And yet an assessment of ministers and ministerial candidates without a sufficient provision for retooling was not ideal—or was too idealistic. The closest the assembly ever came to offering supplementary helps to ministers was in its directory, and as their forefathers recognized, if preaching were to be improved, something more personal and practical than a directory would be needed. Perhaps research will show that, without the assembly's prompting, prophesyings enjoyed a widespread revival during the 1640s, but we can be confident that the assembly will not get the credit for it.

The assembly would continue its examination of preachers through the entirety of its history. Indeed, from 1649 to 1653 it appears that the assembly did nothing else. The assembly's insistence on doing everything that it could to reform the preaching ministry of England says something about the priorities of the gathering itself. In total, the examination of ministers required the formation of forty-seven different committees from 1643 to 1653 and the expenditure of more man-hours than any other task. It also marks an astonishing moment in English church history. Joel Halcomb observes that "estimates derived from the extant records of the committee for plundered ministers"—a parliamentary committee that worked closely with the Westminster Assembly—"suggest that the assembly conducted as many as 5,000 examinations—an astonishing number considering that there were 8,600 parishes in England and perhaps 10,000 ordained clergy in England and Wales, many of them serving chaplaincies, cathedral chapters, and the two universities." This continuous and near systematic attempt to purge the Church of England of preachers who were ungodly, unlearned, and, on a less firm biblical basis, anti-Parliamentarian was a key part of the continuing reformation that the godly had long wanted and that the assembly was able to attempt. "Attempt," because the assertion of this study is not that the assembly successfully accomplished its program of reform but rather that these reforms are a useful, indeed essential, metric for gauging the priorities of the assembly itself. That said, Halcomb is surely correct to conclude that "the greatest upheaval caused by the assembly may not have been effected in the Jerusalem Chamber, but in the Jericho Parlour, where candidates and ministers were vetted for places in the newly Reformed Church of England."[53]

---

53. J. A. Halcomb, "The Examination of Ministers," in *MPWA*, 1:218. The Committee for Plundered Ministers was a committee of the House of Commons first tasked with taking care of clergymen supportive of Parliament whose property or source of income had been adversely affected by the war. The committee then took on the additional task of ejecting scandalous ministers from their pulpits in territory controlled by Parliament. Over time it became one of the committees most frequently employed of the House of Commons to communicate with the Westminster Assembly.

PART III
In Theory

The final part of this study explores the ideas expressed in the Westminster Assembly's reforms. It is composed of topical treatments on the subject of preachers and preaching and draws on the printed works and speeches of assembly members. Various aspects of pulpit theory are considered while acknowledging that these are neither universal nor consistently applied. The remaining chapters are a study of theory, not practice—an examination of statements on preachers and preaching, not a study of ministers and their sermon manuscripts.

Chapter 8 focuses on the prerequisites of a godly preaching ministry. Chapters 9 and 10 explain why assembly members thought so highly of preaching and how they compared it to similar means of grace. Chapters 11 and 12 argue that for most assembly members every sermon needed to bring their hearers to Christ, but that there was more than one way of doing so. The final constructive chapter highlights the importance of the Holy Spirit for effective preaching, while noting that members were not dogmatic about modes of sermon delivery.

CHAPTER 8

On Preachers: Godly, Trained, and Ordained

That this honourable house will goe on in their Care & indeavour for the placing of a Godly & able ministry in every parrish with all convenient speed.
—"Petition to the House of Commons"

[B]e exhorted to pray to God, that he would raise up many Pauls in his church, godly and learned Ministers, that by godliness may subdue sinne, and by learning may conquer heresies; such as these are both burning and shining lights; such as these are Stars indeed, both for the light they give, and the purity of their conversation. Happy is the church of God, when such Stars shine in her. If we have godly Ministers, and not learned, then the subtil Papist and Heretick, will be ready to prevail. If we have learned, but not godly, then all holy order will be neglected, then prophaneness and impiety will lift up its head; but both together make a blessed Church.
—Anthony Burgess

It is axiomatic that the reformation of the pulpit urged by the Westminster Assembly called for pious preachers. From its first petition, the assembly asked that "unable, idle or scandalous" ministers be replaced by "able and faithful ministers."[1] In the assembly's writings faithful preachers are most often called "godly ministers," but they are also described as "godly and reverend divines," "godly divines," men with "godly wisdom," "godly and faithful ministers," "godly brethren in the ministry," "godly brethren," "godly and able" ministers, "godly, grave judicious and learned ministers of the Word," or "godly and conscientious ministers." When complimenting their Scottish friends, the assembly spoke of "Honourable, Reverend, learned, and godly" ministers; when discussing potential candidates for ministry, they spoke of

---

1. *MPWA*, 5:11 (Doc. 1).

"godly and hopeful men"; when considering the next generation training for the ministry, they wrote about "godly and hopefull students."[2]

Godliness

An emphasis on godliness was hardly surprising given the literature that assembly members studied. Each of the apostle Paul's pastoral epistles placed a priority on a pastor's purity over his abilities and learning, and pastoral classics circulated in the godly underground emphasized the same. Oliver Bowles (c. 1577–1644), a patriarch of the assembly, dedicated more than a third of his manual for preachers on the pastor's life and devotion (a manuscript of the text was printed during the assembly's tenure at Westminster).[3] It is significant that this discussion occupies the first part of Bowles's book. Godliness is part of the *praeparatio* of the preacher, and Bowles argues that it includes a commitment to gravity, reverence, setting a good example in the company that he keeps, avoiding bribes, loving the Scriptures, and remaining resident among the people whom he serves.

For the assembly, the ideal man for the pulpit needed to be knowledgeable, but knowledge without zeal was not sufficient. Every parish needed "a godly and zealous preacher," and the assembly insisted on the necessity of personal holiness as a distinguishing characteristic of every person it approved for a preaching ministry.[4] At first glance, it seems surprising that the assembly's commitment to holiness does not appear in its rules for examination. That oddity is explained by the fact that no one could reach examination unless the assembly had first satisfied itself by means of testimonials that the person being examined was, in fact, evidently godly in his "life and conversation."[5]

And yet there is evidence, too, that even after having received testimonials of godliness, the assembly engaged in further questioning on the topic and considered it essential that it do so. The Committee for Plundered Ministers, a committee of the House of Commons that, in spite of its name, was specially dedicated to the sequestration (removal) of problematic

---

2. For "godly ministers," see *MPWA*, 5:36 (Doc. 14), p. 68 (Doc. 20), p. 119 (Doc. 42), and p. 228 (Doc. 81). For the other descriptors, in order of appearance, see p. 28 (Doc. 12), p. 20 (Doc. 3), p. 27 (Doc. 12), p. 39 (Doc. 14), p. 105 (Doc. 36), p. 119 (Doc. 42), p. 176 (Doc. 61), p. 235 (Doc. 83), p. 177 (Doc. 61), p. 196 (Doc. 72), p. 199 (Doc. 73), p. 334 (Doc. 128), p. 11 (Doc. 1), and p. 28 (Doc. 12).

3. O. Bowles, *De Pastore Evangelico Tractatus: in quo Universyn Munus Pastorale; tam quoad Pastoris Vocationem, & Praeparationem; quam Ipsius Muneris Exercitium* (London, 1649).

4. A stock phrase for the godly. See, for example, S. Rutherford, *The Divine Right of Church Government* (London, [1646]), 600.

5. See chapter 6 and appendix 2.

ministers and installation of all ministers, was also the usual liaison between the assembly and the Commons for all matters relating to the operation of the assembly. For three years, the Committee for Plundered Ministers required the assembly to examine preachers, both candidates and ordained ministers, for their learning and godliness. But in the spring of 1646, the committee changed its mind about the merits of examinations for godliness and required the assembly to examine preachers with respect to their learning only.

The test case was with Thomas Watts. The assembly was not satisfied with Watts's letters of testimonial. The Committee for Plundered Ministers, in response, requested that the assembly examine Watts for his "sufficiency in learning notwithstanding any allegations against him in conversation." It was an entirely unrealistic request, exposing a tin ear to the long history of puritan demands for a godly ministry. The assembly appointed a committee to draft an answer. But while the assembly's committee was deliberating, the Committee for Plundered Ministers began to issue other orders for examinations of learning without respect to the candidate's life.[6]

Given the problem with Watts, the assembly was disturbed over the potential implications of ignoring a minister's "conversation" and its impact on the ministry of the church. Members wanted to ensure that they were promoting both a learned *and* godly pulpit ministry (and they did not trust Parliament to make judgments in either category). The assembly resolved on June 5, 1646, that "because of the new forme of the order of the Committee" it would not approve of any additional ministers or candidates until the problem was resolved.[7] That meant that poor Stephen Geree, hoping to become the rector of Abinger, Surrey, was forced to wait, even though the assembly had approved him for ministry.[8]

Naturally, in blocking requests from the House of Commons, the assembly could continue business as usual with the House of Lords. A Mr. Owen was examined for ministry in Wales as the request came from the Earl of Pembroke; the gathering both approved him for ministry and recorded their approval in the normal manner.[9] In the meantime, the assembly drafted a paper in response to the Commons' Committee for Plundered Ministers, arguing for the rights of the church to decide whether a preacher was sufficiently godly to serve as a preacher.[10] On June 9 they sent a message to the Committee for Plundered Ministers stating that it

---

6. *MPWA*, 4:148–49, 152–57 (June 1, 3–5, 1646; Sess. 649, 651–653).
7. *MPWA*, 4:156–57.
8. *MPWA*, 4:157.
9. *MPWA*, 4:158–59.
10. *MPWA*, 4:152–57.

was "noe way proper" for them to be "informers"—perhaps a charge that had been leveled at them from some quarter—but most proper for them to issue certificates touching both godliness and learning, as they had previously done, and "not proper" for them to obey the orders sent by the committee to the assembly. Dr. Peter Smith (1586–1653) was sent alone to the committee to press the assembly's case.[11] The assembly had chosen its man wisely, for it achieved what it wanted. "Henceforth" the assembly had "power…to certify both learning and conversation." Furthermore, the Committee for Plundered Ministers agreed to recall the orders sent to the assembly for examination in learning only and to reissue them as requests for examination in doctrine and life.[12] The assembly, in return, released the names of examined and approved ministers. Watts was not among them.

Training

The assembly's June 1646 exchange with the Committee for Plundered Ministers happened to be about *godliness*, no doubt reflecting a frustration that the assembly was too rigorous in its standards for ministerial holiness. Nonetheless, had the Commons relaxed the requirement for the examination of *learning*, there is every reason to think the assembly would have responded with an equal amount of stubborn resistance. After all, the ministers they idealized and admired were not only godly and wise but "able" and "learned"—those who had "prepared themselves" for ministry.[13] Thus, when Stephen Marshall found himself defending Thomas Goodwin, "an eminent Preacher of the Gospel of Christ," he characterized his friend as a "learned godly" minister, and both adjectives were important.[14]

All members of the assembly were outspoken and unambiguous about the need for an educated clergy. Bowles argued that for the pastor "*requiritur omnigena scientia*," or at least "*desiderantur*,"[15] and he makes the case in the first of three books that all kinds of knowledge are required, including Hebrew, Greek, and Latin, but especially a knowledge of the Scriptures (a subject to which he gives an enormous amount of attention).[16] Fellow assembly member John Lightfoot argued that study was needful for anyone to be a preacher since it was necessary even for the apostles. They engaged

---

11. *MPWA*, 4:160–61.
12. *MPWA*, 4:162–63.
13. In the order listed, *MPWA*, 5:105 (Doc. 36), p. 11 (Doc. 1), p. 177 (Doc. 61), p. 20 (Doc. 3), p. 196 (Doc. 72), p. 334 (Doc. 128), and p. 11 (Doc. 1).
14. S. Marshall, *A Defence of Infant-Baptism* (London, 1646), 143.
15. "All kinds of knowledge are required," or at least "desired."
16. Bowles, *De Pastore Evangelico Tractatus*, 71.

in "hearing, study, conference, and meditation," and they were with Christ Himself for a full year before being sent out to preach.[17]

Negatively, Goodwin opposed "those who decry learning and study."[18] He took note of Paul's instruction to Timothy to study (2 Tim. 2:15) and argued that extempore preaching only, without study, is contrary to Scripture. He also commented (perceptively) that those who argue against study still rely much on what they have heard and discussed.[19] No one comes into the pulpit with a blank slate (although parishioners occasionally hear sermons that cast doubt on this general rule)! Daniel Featley (1582–1645) was concerned that there were too many preachers who thought they had studied when they plundered a concordance and climbed into a pulpit. He implies that there is a connection between a lack of preparation and absurd gesticulations and overlong sermons. These were the kinds of preachers who managed to kill listeners even at funeral sermons with their "prolixitie."[20] In practice, a learned preacher might need to disagree with the marginal notes in English Bibles, and he should have the training that would enable him to do so.[21]

John Arrowsmith discusses the need not only for training but also for ability. The three things necessary for a "lawfull calling" are ability, inclination, and separation (ordination). In Arrowsmith's mind, "He that is Un-gifted, I dare be bold to say, he is Un-sent."[22] This follows from another of Paul's instructions to Timothy that "the things that thou hast heard of me among many witnesses, the same commit thou to faithful men, who shall be able to teach others also" (2 Tim. 2:2). Not everyone is an able teacher.

Training for a preacher did not consist merely of thorough Bible instruction, though it could be nothing less than that. Obadiah Sedgwick (1599/1600–1658) leaves no doubt of his opinions when he says, "I am not of his minde who would have preachers study no booke but the Bible."[23] Robert Harris (1580/1–1658), in a milder tone, apologized to the readers of his *The Way to True Happiness* for not properly citing the authors he quotes: "Once for all, let me tell you, I reverence Antiquity as much as [those] who

---

17. Lightfoot, *Works*, 3:67.
18. T. Goodwin, *Of the Constitution, Right Order, and Government of the Churches of Christ*, in *The Works of Thomas Goodwin* (Eureka, Calif.: Tanski Publications, 1996), 11:379.
19. Goodwin, *Of the Constitution*, 11:378–79.
20. D. Featley, *Sacra Nemesis, the Levites Scourge, or, Mercurius Britan* (Oxford, 1644), 62.
21. E.g., A. Tuckney, disagreeing in a sermon with the note "set down in the Margin of your Bibles" in *Death Disarmed: And the Grave Swallowed Up in Victory* (London, 1654), 5.
22. J. Arrowsmith, *Theanthropos, or, God-Man: Being an Exposition upon the First Eighteen Verses of the First Chapter of the Gospel according to John* (London, 1660), 99.
23. O. Sedgwick, *Christ's Counsell to His Languishing Church of Sardis* (London, 1640), To the Reader.

doth most, and make use of as many Ancients and Moderns as my purse can buy, and strength will bear: If I rather read than name them, it is for your sake, and so I pray you take it."[24]

While the members of the assembly agreed that learning and ability needed to be cultivated through education, not everyone outside the Jerusalem Chamber, where the gathering debated, agreed. In debating whether a minister, as a teacher, could properly use his gifts in schools and universities, George Walker (bap. 1582?, d. 1651) commented that "Divers men amongst us deny the necessity of learning & universityes."[25] Although members in the assembly had denied the legitimacy of some of the biblical proof texts submitted in support of university education, and others had argued against "any severe distinction betweene universityes & churches," none had argued against formal training or preparation for ministry, and Walker no doubt had in mind those "amongst us" in London, or England, and not those among the assembly's members.[26]

The three usual arguments brought against the need for a learned ministry were the existence of an unlearned ministry found in the Bible, for both Testaments mention uneducated prophets and apostles; the powerful outpouring of the Spirit on believers in the New Testament age; and the abuse of learning by enemies of the church. If simple fishermen could serve as apostles and if the Spirit of Pentecost was still working in the church and if bishops caused so much havoc in the church, why should godly people insist on the need for an educated clergy?

Of course, as Anthony Burgess (d. 1664) readily admits, it was true that God sent out prophets and apostles who were not educated men. But those who were sent out by Jesus lived and trained with Jesus Himself for an extended time before they began to teach. What is more, they received the Holy Spirit—and evidenced that reception in a special manner. Also worthy of note, he explained, was that the twelve disciples did not continue in their various trades. Once commissioned they dedicated themselves entirely to the task they had undertaken. Admittedly, the apostle Paul did not. He was a tentmaker. But in Paul God had chosen an unusually learned man. In this variety God showed that He "can make use of all."[27]

Even more significant to assembly members when considering biblical preachers was the fact that prophets and apostles, although under the

---

24. R. Harris, *The Way to True Happiness* (London, 1653), 98.
25. *MPWA*, 2:353 (Nov. 21, 1643; Sess. 100).
26. See speeches by Thomas Wilson and Philip Nye in *MPWA*, 2:353.
27. A. Burgess, *An Expository Comment, Doctrinal Controversal and Practical upon the Whole First Chapter of the Second Epistle of St Paul to the Corinthians* (London, 1661), 7.

direct inspiration of the Holy Spirit, still required normal instruction.[28] There were schools of prophets. There were Jewish schools for teaching in Jesus's day, and Paul seems to have thought it added to his usefulness to have sat under Gamaliel.[29] Burgess, drawing a customary distinction between extraordinary and ordinary ministers, notes that even those "with extraordinary gifts, did make use of study, and labour, and diligent paines." Placing both Paul and Timothy in that category, he notes that "Paul exhorts Timothy, to give himself to reading, that his profiting may appear to all men, 1 Timothy 4:13, 15," and "Paul himself made use of his Parchments." Burgess concludes from this "that those Lamps which were inlightened by God himself, did yet need the continuall oyl of their labour and paines. And if this is true of the extraordinary gifted persons, how much more of the ordinary? The Nurse that feeds not, cannot long give milk; so neither the Minister that studieth not."[30]

As it happened, scriptural evidence indicated that a reliance on the Holy Spirit had not removed the need for proper training even for prophets and apostles, let alone normal preachers. But Burgess promised not to be envious if the Spirit-led people around him "were inabled to speak in all strange tongues, and were inabled to work miracles for the confirmation of their Doctrine." If they could "demonstrate such an extraordinary effusion of Gods Spirit on them," good.[31] Furthermore, he was willing to agree that "the Spirit of God is the alone Sanctifier of all gifts and abilities." But the Spirit didn't seem to be working in any special manner among the adversaries of a learned ministry. They were not speaking in tongues. They did not even understand Hebrew and Greek. And if they could "not look for the Spirit of God in such an immediate way, it must be by a mediate and acquired way. And this ordinary way doth not exclude Gods Spirit, but supposeth it."[32]

When considering the divines' stress on learning, a June 1644 debate about displays of scholarship in the pulpit illustrates their ideals for the church.[33] The debate involved an assumption, a worry, and a proposed resolution. All assumed that the preacher would be familiar with scholarly and biblical languages along with standard Reformation and patristic works. This, along with other forms of learning, was actually required in

---

28. Burgess, *Expository Comment*, 49.
29. See speeches by Nye, Seaman, Walker, and Lightfoot in *MPWA*, 2:353 (Nov. 21, 1643; Sess. 100); and Burgess, *Expository Comment*, 6.
30. A. Burgess, *The Scripture Directory, for Church Officers and People* (London, 1659), 75–76.
31. Burgess, *Expository Comment*, 7.
32. Burgess, *Expository Comment*, 49.
33. *MPWA*, 3:131–37 (June 5, 1644; Sess. 232–234).

the Directory for Ordination, framed the year before. The worry seemed to have been about ostentatious displays of scholarship in preaching. The proposal of the committee that drafted the subdirectory for preaching within the larger Directory for Worship was to prohibit or warn against citing authorities such as Calvin or Augustine in sermons and quoting Latin, Greek, and Hebrew words or phrases from the pulpit.

Edmund Calamy was quick to inveigh against the committee's proposal. According to the record of the debate found in the assembly's minutes, Calamy reasoned that "if I must use my owne deductions & make use of my owne parts why may not I make use of Calvin?" He suggested that he might profitably "use the name of Calvin and Austin [Augustine]," and, in fact, there were "many reasons to prove the lawful use of it." For example, "sometimes it is to good edification as to show it is noe new opinion." Mentioning "the author doth show it is not my opinion alone, & then it doth secretly put a Reverence upon their opinion." Arrowsmith completely agreed. Displays of learning are permissible, and he cited Augustine (in Latin) to show that this is not a new opinion in the church.

Herbert Palmer was on the other side of the fence from Arrowsmith and announced that he was "not convinced but that it is unlawfull" to cite other names in the pulpit. He reminded his brothers "that we may make use of humane learning, farre be it from me to contradict it." But "whether necessary or fitting to quote the names of those whom we may make the use of. I conceive we may not doe it. It is not according to the patterne of the scriptures; Paul did not doe it. Consider in what case he useth these; if we will follow the apostle, it must be in the like case." He did not need to add that the name of Paul did give an argument authority.

Before sitting down, Palmer stated once more that "for that reason doe I thinke it unlawfull," and with some rhetorical flourish asked, "Doe I preach to gaine authority by man or by the authority of the word of God in their hearts? If the authority of Mr. Calvin shall make my people believe my word, I had rather have had my mouth stoped [caulked] for that time."[34] It is perhaps for that reason that he chose not to cite William Perkins in support of his point, although the master of English preaching agreed that scholarship should be employed in the creation of sermons but disguised in their delivery.[35]

According to Lightfoot, Palmer "vehemently" urged his perspective on the assembly; he was insistent because he was almost alone in opposing the citation of "authorities" in sermons (usually a reference to leading church

---

34. *MPWA*, 3:134–36 (June 7, 1644; Sess. 234).
35. Perkins, *Art of Prophesying*, 71.

fathers and Reformers, not to medieval and post-Reformation authors).[36] A similar picture emerges with the use of Hebrew and Greek in the pulpit, and it was Palmer, again, who most forcefully argued for their prohibition. As Palmer saw it, the Directory for Ordination was a sufficient protection for a learned ministry; nothing more needed to be proved in the pulpit. In fact, the use of all displays of learning brings the "word of God into contempt." For that reason he had an "eternall quarrel" with exhibitions of erudition. At most, in consideration of the example of the apostle Paul, he would grant that it might be permissible "by way of condescension to the infirmity & disease of the people" who think they need such proof of learning—but it had to be an act of mercy ministry, with the same motives as the apostle himself, who was willing to be all things to all men.

But Palmer was not entirely alone. His most articulate supporter was Samuel Rutherford, who tried to employ a regulative principle of sorts: if displays of learning are useful, then they ought to be commanded, not permitted, in the Directory for Worship. Rutherford knew well that to pitch the matter so high as to insist on it was to argue against its inclusion at all. Rutherford also noted the age-old distinction between the study and the pulpit, or the kitchen and the dining room: "The pot may be used in the bilyng but not brought in with the porridge." Alexander Henderson (c. 1583–1646), and perhaps Thomas Wilson, agreed with them. But seventeen or eighteen other divines spoke in favor of the use of Hebrew and Greek in a sermon, provided that it was done carefully, that it was translated, and that the preacher tailored his use of languages to the congregation in front of him. Henderson was willing to conform to the assembly's cautious advocacy of foreign tongues, and at the end of the debate it was an early utterance of Joshua Hoyle that prevailed: "It should be done sparingly, but it would go ill under the name of the Assembly if we should wholy put it off."[37]

It is evident from the debate that those arguing against citations of authors and the use of foreign languages were still advocates of learning, were themselves learned, and took care to make both of those facts clear to the others. Lively debate in the assembly about the examination of ministers reveals that these sentiments were backed up in practice. While exceptions were occasionally permitted, hopeful preachers that came before the assembly had to be conversant in Hebrew, Greek, and Latin in addition to being

---

36. Temple, Calamy, Gataker, Marshall, Herle, Burges, and probably William Gouge and perhaps Philip Nye all opposed Palmer, while Samuel Rutherford supported him. See *MPWA*, 3:135–37, 143–44, 147. But Lightfoot reports that on this question Nye agreed with Palmer. See Lightfoot, *Journal*, 282 (June 7, 1644).

37. See *MPWA*, 3:133–37, 142–43, 144–48; and Lightfoot, *Journal*, 281–82, 285 (June 7, 17, 1644; Sess. 234, 240).

able to display a firm grasp of Scripture and theology. Agonizing debates over ministers who came before the assembly's examination committee and wanted to move to a new charge but had "forgot their Greeke" highlight the importance of learning to the divines.[38] Was there to be a different standard of language examination for those already in the ministry than for those wishing to enter? What if the person could read and understand Latin but not speak it? Did it matter where the person was to preach? The context of each of these debates also highlights the fact that these were not ivory-tower discussions. A real person was pacing about the abbey, waiting for the assembly's answer.[39]

Ordained Ambassadors

Examinations in godliness and tests of learning were intended as steps and helps toward an appointment to ministry and the setting apart of the man for a ministerial calling—what presbyterians and others called "ordination." It is well known that the assembly was divided on the necessity and nature of ordination. The most vocal advocates at the assembly of a special appointment to the ministry, at least after the departure of the gathering's episcopalians, were the presbyterians.

In his posthumously published *Treatise of Miscellany Questions*, George Gillespie (1613–1648) underscores the need for an ordained ministry by taking up the challenge of a "fierce furious Erastian" who was teaching that "neither is there any such thing now to be acknowledged, as a speciall distinct sacred calling, or solemn setting apart of men to the ministrie of the Word and Sacraments."[40] To Gillespie, such a view contradicted Scripture. First, seeking to establish the perpetuity of Word and sacrament administration in general, Gillespie appealed to the special tasks given to the apostles, and later to other teachers, in both the Great Commission (Matt. 28) and Ephesians 4:11–13.[41] The Great Commission emphasizes the duration of teaching and baptizing—till Christ returns.[42] Ephesians 4:13 stresses the same truth but with respect to the recipients of preaching. The work of the church is to continue "till we all come in the unity of the

---

38. *MPWA*, 2:229 (Oct. 27, 1643; Sess. 83).

39. For this entire debate, see *MPWA*, 2:229–32 (Oct. 27, 1643; Sess. 83).

40. G. Gillespie, *A Treatise of Miscellany Questions* (Edinburgh, 1649), 1:24–25. Gillespie is allowed to speak here, but if other divines stood in for him they would make the same complaints and argue similar conclusions. See E. Reynolds, *The Pastoral Office* (London, 1663), 11–19.

41. Gillespie, *Miscellany Questions*, 2.

42. Thomas Goodwin understands the text in the same way. See Goodwin, *Of the Constitution*, 11:361.

faith, and of the knowledge of the Son of God, unto a perfect man, unto the measure of the stature of the fulness of Christ."[43] Since Christ has not returned and the saints are far from perfect, teaching and baptizing must still continue.

Second, Gillespie pointed out the importance of preaching in particular: "The preaching of the Gospell is the meane[s] and way ordained of God to save them that beleeve."[44] For this he appealed to Romans 10:14, where the apostle Paul asks his readers, "How then shall they call on him in whom they have not believed? and how shall they believe in him of whom they have not heard? and how shall they hear without a preacher? and how shall they preach, except they be sent?"

Third, the Scot made several qualifications. He was not equating ordination with the rite presbyterians use in ordination: the laying on of hands. Luther and Calvin distinguish between ordination and the laying on of hands, Gillespie admitted, and so did he.[45] Nor was he advocating the necessity of ordination in extraordinary cases, such as in persecuted France.[46] But Gillespie argued that even if sheep have to take the part of a shepherd for a while, there is no need to continue with extraordinary practices ordinarily.[47] He also made clear that he was not suggesting that ordination is necessary for private Christian fellowship and was not arguing that "expectants or probationers" needed to be ordained before preaching.[48] He held that since the latter were occasional preachers who were (in the Scottish system at least) approved and licensed, they had a probational calling and approval.[49]

What Gillespie did want to establish, in the final analysis, is that preachers are normally set apart. The final question in the series of questions posed by the apostle Paul in Romans 10 pertains to the setting apart of the preacher, for, he asked, "how shall they preach, except they be sent?" Preachers are given a special call and a special office. They serve as ambassadors. They are sent. Sending, for Gillespie, denoted a sender, and therefore the text implies, or at least the Scot inferred, a king and an ambassador. For Gillespie, the metaphor of ambassador was important as it is not possible for every Christian

---

43. William Bridge derives an identical lesson from the same text. See his *A Vindication of Ordinances* (London: Peter Cole, 1653), 6–7; and *The Works of William Bridge* (1845; Morgan, Pa.: Soli Deo Gloria, 1989), 4:135. Anthony Burgess concludes similarly in *Spiritual Refining, or, a Treatise of Grace and Assurance Part I* (London, 1658), 495.
44. Gillespie, *Miscellany Questions*, 2.
45. Gillespie, *Miscellany Questions*, 33–34.
46. Gillespie, *Miscellany Questions*, 34–35.
47. Gillespie, *Miscellany Questions*, 55, 61.
48. Gillespie, *Miscellany Questions*, 35.
49. Gillespie, *Miscellany Questions*, 43.

to be an ambassador in Christ's kingdom without total chaos[50] (and it goes without saying that chaos, for Presbyterians, is problematic).

It is the metaphor of ambassador that seemed chiefly to inform the thinking of the divines when they considered preaching and preachers. In a sermon on Jeremiah 23:22, Burgess paused to remind his hearers that ministers are to preach the Word of God as ambassadors.[51] While the divines were able to find references to ambassadors in the book of Jeremiah, they more readily turned to 2 Corinthians 5:20. There the apostle Paul says, "Now then we are ambassadors for Christ, as though God did beseech you by us: we pray you in Christ's stead, be ye reconciled to God." The divines took note of the you/us contrast in the text and assumed that God's ambassadors were given a unique and prominent role. William Gouge, reflecting on this passage, wrote, "Preaching is a clear revelation of the mystery of salvation by a lawful minister." Such a minister is one set apart by God "according to the rule of Gods Word, to be a Minister of the Gospel, doth himself understand the mysteries thereof, and is enabled to make them known to others; he also standeth in Gods room, and in Gods Name makes offer of salvation, 2 Cor. 5:20. This moves men to beleeve and to be saved. This is the ordinary way appointed of God for attaining salvation."[52]

If this is the case, he concluded, ministers ought to preach earnestly, and neglectful ministers ought to fear God.[53] Indeed, Featley urged, "Albeit thy preacher bee a man of no very extraordinary gifts, yet in regard he is an Ambassadour sent from God unto thee if he faithfully (though perhaps not so eloquently) deliver his message unto thee thou oughtst to heare it; and honour him for his Masters sake. His feete cannot but seeme beautifull to thee if they be shod with the Preparation of the Gospell of Peace."[54]

Cambridge student Robert Legard recalled Anthony Tuckney preaching something similar about ambassadors and peace, but rather than emphasizing the duty in the face of pastoral weakness, as did Featley, Tuckney urged the importance of preaching by considering the joy it brought in the place of fear: "The mayne errand of the ambassadour of the gospel, is that sinners would be converted to God; the guilty sinner that knowes he deserves nothing but wrath, when he heares of an ambassador, he expects to heare something from an angry God…[but] the gospel is called the gospel of peace."[55]

---

50. Gillespie, *Miscellany Questions*, 36–38.
51. Burgess, *Spiritual Refining*, 495.
52. Gouge, *Hebrewes*, part 2, p. 132 (sect. 23).
53. Gouge, *Hebrewes*, part 2, p. 132 (sect. 23).
54. D. Featley, *Ancilla Pietatis: or, the Hand-Maid to Private Devotion Presenting a Manuell to Furnish Her with Necessary Principles of Faith* (London, 1626), 65.
55. FSL Add. MS 517, fos. 36v-37r.

Of course, the divines were not limited to 2 Corinthians 5:20 in their argument for a divine warrant for ordination, nor to the image of an ambassador.[56] Turning to 2 Timothy 2, for example, Gillespie noted the commands for Timothy to teach, to take care in teaching, and to appoint successors in teaching, and then noted the obvious: "Teachers are distinguished from those who are taught: Every man may not be a Teacher…it is no part of the general calling of Christians."[57] This was a pivotal point for Gillespie, and he dwelt on it: "The Apostle sayeth not, 'the things that thou heard of me, the same I will that faithfull and able men, who ever shall be willing to the work, teach others also'[;] faithfulnesse, and fitnesse, or ability cannot make a significant calling, but qualifie a man for that which he shall be called unto. Aptitude is one thing: to be cloathed with a calling, power and authority is another thing."[58]

Members of the church have a legitimate reason for skepticism about self-styled ministries. "Without a clear calling, and lawfull Ordination, how shall people receave the word from the mouths of ministers, as Gods word, or as those who are sent from God[?]"[59] Gillespie also noted that Paul expressly instructs the church to supply the preachers with all their needs (1 Cor. 9:13–14). If this instruction is not setting apart a particular class of preachers—that is, lawful ones—then, he jested, "its like enough that People shall have good store of Preachers, and their purses shall pay well for it."[60]

Although the Scots wrote more about the preacher's special commission than most presbyterians, other presbyterians did speak on the topic. In expounding Romans 10:13–35, John Arrowsmith tightly tied the effectiveness of preaching to a proper commissioning and sending.[61] And Burgess emphasized that, like the apostle Paul, ministers are made ministers by the

---

56. Oliver Bowles relies on a similar variety of Scripture texts in defense of ordination. See *De Pastore Evangelico Tractatus*, 1–3.

57. Gillespie, *Miscellany Questions*, 52. Citing Galatians 6:6, Gillespie almost lets the text speak for itself: "Let him that is taught in the word communicate unto him that teacheth in all good things." His comment is simply that "some are Teachers, some are taught," and he adds, "in the Word."

58. Gillespie, *Miscellany Questions*, 53.

59. Gillespie, *Miscellany Questions*, 54.

60. Gillespie, *Miscellany Questions*, 54–55.

61. J. Arrowsmith, *Tactica Sacra, sive de Milite Spirituali Pugnante, Vincente, & Triumphante Dissertatio, Tribus Libris Comprehensa* (Cambridge, 1657), 2.2.6 (p. 114). "*Ubi necessaria statuitur ad salutem Dei invocatio, ad Dei invocationem fides, ad fidem verbi auditio, ad verbi auditionem praedicatio, & ad praedicationem missio; in via scilicet ordinaria. Alias enim extra ordinem fieri potest, ut cum fructu praedicet qui non est missus; sicut interdum ex providentia singulari surdus creadit absque auditu.*"

will of God. That means that "the Ministry is not an humane[62] invention; neither do we plead our own interest, or act in our name, but its Christs interest, we are his Embassadours, we come in his name to you. It is he that giveth us our commission to preach and baptize." That also means "that all the affronts, contempts and rebellions that our Ministry meets with, for its sake it redounds upon Christ himself; and what is done against us, coming in his name is taken by the Lord Christ, as done against himself." Burgess then quoted Luke 10:16: "He that heareth you heareth me; and he that despiseth you despiseth me; and he that despiseth me despiseth him that sent me."[63] Burgess explained that "the learned do from Scripture find a two-fold Kingdome attributed unto Christ": as He is God over the whole world and as He is mediator over His church. "All Church-power is radically...seated in him. So that the power to make Church-officers, doth not arise originally from the people, as (they say) civil power doth," but from Jesus Christ. Thus "Officers in the Church are properly servants to Christ, and receive their power and commission from him." Thus "the Church indeed may apply the person to the office, but Christ institutes and applieth the office to the person."[64]

The assembly's dispute with both lay preachers and Erastians was on this point: Is the ministry an office of Christ's churchly kingdom, bestowed by the Mediator Himself? Gillespie debates an anonymous Erastian who was an opponent of ordination in this sense.[65] It is unlikely that the opponent is Thomas Coleman, a fellow divine with whom Gillespie was forever sparring and who had a distinct method of argumentation. Further, Coleman was not against ordination, though he held that it pertained only to the teaching function of the minister.[66] But Coleman did not see all church power radically seated in Christ. Likewise, Lightfoot, the assembly's only other clearly identifiable Erastian divine, stated that since the time of the apostles there has been a "peculiar order and function for the ministry of the gospel,"[67] but while allowing that the preacher has a special role in the church, he did not see the power to make church officers residing in Christ alone.

The assembly's majority carried on a different argument with the assembly's congregationalists. Presbyterians complained that the congregationalists

---

62. *Humane*: human.
63. Burgess, *Expository Comment*, 28–29.
64. Burgess, *Expository Comment*, 29; see the larger discussion in pp. 28–37.
65. Gillespie, *Miscellany Questions*, 36. Gillespie reports that the work he is referring to throughout was published at Franeker (p. 1).
66. T. Coleman, *Male Dicis Maledicis. Or a Brief Reply to Nihil Respondens* (London, 1646), 10. "For ordination of Ministers, I say it is within the commission of teaching, and so appertains to the doctrinal part."
67. Lightfoot, *Works*, 2:68.

assigned the preacher a special role but equated ordination with the popular election of a pastor by a particular congregation.[68] What is more, neither the congregationalists nor the assembly's Erastians believed that ordination must or should involve the participation of other ordained ministers, although most agreed that the preacher is set apart for God's service in a way and for a function not common with all believers. When William Greenhill (1597/8–1671), an assembly congregationalist, preached about the watchman in Ezekiel 3:17, he simply stated that "Christ himself is the great Watch-man of the Church, he is the Head, and appoints who shall be in his stead. 2 Cor. 5:20 the Apostles were in his stead; so the Prophet here; so all the faithfull Ministers of the Gospel, who are call'd mediately by the Church according to his will."[69] In his treatise on 2 Corinthians 5:19–20, Jeremiah Burroughs observed that "the ministers of the gospel are embassadors of Christ."[70] For Burroughs, Christ's ministerial ambassadors are a greater privilege for the church than mere messengers or stewards. He noted that ambassadors are not sent on trivial missions, thus indicating the importance of the message. He cautioned that ambassadors are not to go beyond the words of commission that they received, indicating a need to preach the gospel from the Scriptures. And just as the king is represented by his ambassadors, so "there is a kind of a representation even of the person of Christ in them." Burroughs also warned his hearers that "an ambassador must give an account of His Embassage," which means that he reports back to heaven (presumably by means of prayer) on the parishioners' response to his preaching.[71]

Coming of Age

One more personal milestone needed to be reached before godliness and good training could make a man eligible for ordaining: he had to mature. Elizabethan statutes and canon law required that the minimum age for ordination to the diaconate be twenty-three years and for the priesthood, the pastoral ministry of the church, twenty-four years. The assembly's committee drawing up the Directory for Ordination proposed to maintain that standard but met with objections. Certain men might be able to

---

68. Gillespie attributes this position to most sectaries and some congregationalists (Gillespie, *Miscellany Questions*, 25); see also S. Rutherford, *The Due Right of Presbyteries* (London, 1644).

69. William Greenhill, *An Exposition of the Five First Chapters of the Prophet Ezekiel* (London, 1645), ch. 3, v. 17, vol. II, p. 332; Greenhill, *An Exposition of Ezekiel* (Edinburgh: Banner of Truth, 1994), 110.

70. J. Burroughs, *Gospel-Reconciliation: Or, Christ's Trumpet of Peace to the World* (London, 1657), 279.

71. J. Burroughs, *Gospel-Reconciliation*, 283; see pp. 280–83.

minister before that age, some assembly members thought. Interestingly, John Ley, who of all assembly members spent the most time with incoming candidates, thought that exceptions should be permitted. All the congregationalists who spoke to the issue also favored removing the minimum age required by statute.[72]

The net effect of the statute had been that no one could enter the ministry immediately after graduating from university. Many attempted to stay on as Oxford or Cambridge fellows. Others enjoyed a kind of ministerial internship: they sat under the tutelage of a godly minister, living in his home and deepening their understanding of theology—a kind of seminary education popular among the godly.[73] This was especially important given the lack of any formal seminary training in the Church of England. By 1643, nine out of every ten ministers were Oxford or Cambridge graduates, a marked improvement over the previous century. But their master of arts gave them knowledge of Latin and Greek (but not Hebrew), and they studied the classical literature of antiquity, not the Scriptures and Christian theology. Only three percent of the clergy had a bachelor of divinity degree (which followed the MA), and even fewer obtained a doctor of divinity degree. Thus, all theological formation was extracurricular.

Where a mentor could be found for these Oxbridge graduates, they had the opportunity to gain the experience and knowledge that would better fit them for ministry. This typical pattern in the life experience of a future minister would have been known to all of the assembly members, many of whom would have benefited from it themselves. Thus, although reminding the assembly of 1 Timothy 4:12, where the apostle Paul urged Timothy not to let others despise his youth, Charles Herle did not see why a man could not at least wait until "the old yeares of 24." Were "the blossoms of March... better than those of May?" As both congregations and elders know, even with a black-and-white insistence on godliness and training, there is still a gray area when it comes to actual readiness for ministry. Thomas Gataker thought it would be "safer" to make men wait until they had reached those years. Palmer noted that if the age were lowered, it would become the new norm. Jeremiah Whitaker noted that years can add "gravity & ability."[74] In the end the assembly determined that these years were necessary and that only then would a candidate be eligible to receive a call, at which point the assembly could test his gifts in preaching.

---

72. Nye, Bridge, and Burroughs. See *MPWA*, 3:28–29 (April 18, 1644; Sess. 203).
73. See Webster, *Godly Clergy in Early Stuart England*.
74. *MPWA*, 3:27–29 (April 18, 1644; Sess. 203). See also the comments of Burges, Herle, and Palmer.

CHAPTER 9

On Preaching: The Word of God as the Ordinary Means of Grace

In Raysing doctrines from the text, his care ought to be That the matter be the truth of God, & what he speaketh he speaketh as the Oracles of God. 2dly, That it be a truth contained in or grounded on that text, that the hearers may discerne how God teacheth it from thence. 3dly, That he cheefly insist upon those doctrines which are principally intended, & make most for the edification of the hearers.
—"Of the Preaching of the Word," Directory for Public Worship

One plank of the Westminster Assembly's pulpit theology frequently appears in sermons, and addresses hearers rather than preachers, calling them to receive preaching as the Word of God. These calls in turn assumed that ministers needed to be ordained and learned because parishioners were to "receave the word from the mouths of ministers, as Gods word" and not merely as man's word.[1]

Preaching as the Word of God

According to the presbyterian William Gouge, this is the message of Hebrews 13:7, which reads, "Remember them which have the rule over you, who have spoken unto you the word of God." Gouge told his Blackfriars audience, "Though that which is uttered by men as Ministers be properly the sound of a mans voice, yet that which true Ministers of God in exercising their ministeriall Function preach, is the Word of God." Lest his auditors, and later his readers, think he has overstated the point of the text, Gouge asks how the words that "ministers do or ought to speak" can be "styled the word of God." The answer is found in the old distinction between extraordinary and ordinary ministers: "God did immediately inspire extraordinary ministers, and thereby informed them in his will. 'For

---

1. Gillespie, *Miscellany Questions*, 54.

the prophecy came not in old time by the will of man, but holy men of God spake as they were moved by the Holy Ghost,' 2 Pet 1:21. Therefore they were wont to use these prefaces, 'The Word of the Lord,' Hos. 1:1; 'Thus saith the Lord,' Isa 7:7; and an apostle thus, 'I have received of the Lord, that which also I delivered unto you,' 1 Corinthians 11:23."

A similar case obtains "for ordinary ministers" as "they have God's word written and left upon record for their use.... They therefore[,] that ground what they preach upon the Scripture, and deliver nothing but what is agreeable thereunto, preach the word of God." A few lines later Gouge returns to this point again: "So close ought ministers to hold to God's word in their preaching, as not to dare to swerve in anything from it." "The apostle," Gouge says, "denounceth a curse against him, whosoever he be, that shall preach any other word" (Gal. 1:8–9).[2]

The congregationalist Jeremiah Burroughs may have had more to say about preaching the Word of God than any other assemblyman. On November 19, 1643, Burroughs made use of a fragmentary quote from Isaiah 66:2, "and that trembleth at My Word," to cultivate a little reverence among his hearers. His sermon does not tell his hearers to fear God; instead, he paints a verbal picture of a God-fearer and allows his auditors to determine whether they fit that picture. A God-fearing man or woman, he says, does not come "to hear the Word in an ordinary way, merely to spend so much time, or to hear what a man could say." Rather, the Word, "either read or preached," is attended to "with all reverence." Such a one examines the preaching but "dares not cavil against it." Burroughs holds up Moab's King Eglon as an example to be followed by the saints—not, of course, in his "heathenish" ways, nor in his untimely and disgusting death, but as one who rose to receive Ehud as an ambassador with "a message from God" (Judg. 3:20). Burroughs then pushes the knife in a little deeper, questioning whether their "hearts...swell against" preaching, asking them what they really think about preaching, and pointing out the irony of those who think they have escaped the world but still show the worst pride in rebelling against the Word.[3]

Underlying this discussion of irreverence and pride is the assumption, obvious for Burroughs, that the faithful preaching of the Scriptures is the Word of God. Because preaching is the Word of God, irreverence and pride are scandalous. This doctrine of preaching as the Word of God lies under Burroughs's entire first sermon and surfaces in various places, such as his discussion of the power of the Word. Reflecting on the Great Commission,

---

2. Gouge, *Hebrewes*, part 4, p. 76 (Sec. 98).
3. J. Burroughs, *Gospel-Fear: or the Heart Trembling at the Word of God* (London, 1674), 6–9.

Burroughs asks about the relevance of Christ's assertion: "All power in heaven and earth is given unto me." "What followes?" Burroughs asks. "'Go therefore and preach'; What may we observe from the connexion? As who should say, 'Know that all the power in heaven and earth that is given to me, shall go along with you while you are preaching my Word, to make good that Word of mine that you preach.'" The power of God in preaching is so great that "every sermon I come to hear, I must expect to be nearer heaven, or nearer hell."[4]

Whether people did respond to preaching and preachers with such attention must have varied in the experience of the preacher. Oliver Bowles recalled that "to us, not to the angels, God has entrusted that power of the keys by which heaven is opened or closed. The treasure of the gospel, into which angels long to look, Christ has deposited with us as its guardians." Thus, "among men we are angels; among those who serve the King of Kings, ambassadors."[5] Perhaps Bowles had a particularly encouraging pastorate. Jeremiah Burroughs, by contrast, was either wont to complain or did not receive such a warm welcome on the part of his own parishioners: "When they come to hear the Word, they come with carnal and vain hearts," Burroughs complained. Nonetheless, the Word is powerful and surprises them: "When they have found that the Word comes to ransack them, and gets into them and grapples with them, and meets with all the inward and secret distemper of their spirits, they are made to fall down before this Word and say, 'Verily, God is in this Word.'"[6]

Famously, theologian Karl Barth argued that in identifying the preaching of the Word of God as the Word of God, "The Word of God is the event itself in which proclamation becomes real proclamation."[7] Preaching for Barth is an important existential moment because it is incarnational. It remains a human event, but God is speaking. This is true in spite of the weakness of human speech, true even in spite of its failings.[8] In an extensive footnote in his *Church Dogmatics*, Barth insisted that his understanding of preaching was shared by his Reformed forefathers.[9] But there are key points of discontinuity that Barth misses. First, in his discussion of the

---

4. Burroughs, *Gospel-Fear*, 14–15, 20.

5. Bowles, *De Pastore Evangelico Tractatus*, Epistle Dedicatory. Text from David Noe's translation (in progress) of Bowles's work, and is one part of a four-volume translation and editing project being led by Dr. Noe and the author, including works by John Arrowsmith, Samuel Rutherford, and Anthony Tuckney.

6. Burroughs, *Gospel-Fear*, 22.

7. K. Barth, *The Doctrine of the Word of God*, vol. 1 in *Church Dogmatics*, trans. G. W. Bromiley, ed. G. W. Bromiley, and T. F. Torrance (Edinburgh: T&T Clark, 2004), I/1, 93.

8. Barth, *Doctrine of the Word of God*, I/1, 93–95.

9. Barth, *Doctrine of the Word of God*, I/1, 95–99.

preached Word, Barth uses the same kind of language and the same kinds of qualifiers for the Word preached that classical theologians reserved for the Word inscripturated; Barth reminds readers that preaching is still free and fully human; preaching is not mechanically dictated, and yet it is God's Word. But older theologians, including the divines of the Westminster Assembly, never made such qualifiers about preaching, because their view of preaching was never open to the same pretensions. Second, noting Barth's reflection on the divine and the human, it is worth observing that Reformers and puritans did not espouse an incarnational analogy for the preaching of the Word, and used it only in a qualified sense even for the written Word. Third, Barth may also be using the incarnational analogy to explain how even defective preaching can still be God's Word, thus assuming a Christological anthropology that assumes that Christ took on fallen flesh.

Finally, and most obviously, older theologians believed that the preached Word was the Word of God only derivatively and only when it faithfully expounded the inscripturated Word. For godly seventeenth-century theologians as well as for their predecessors in the previous century, not every sermon is to be viewed as God's Word, and the Reformation rule for testing sermons is Scripture. Samuel Rutherford was emphatic that following the Spirit of God did not require a Christian to "believe what ever a godly preacher saith."[10] Burroughs encourages hearers to compare what is heard from the preacher with the Bible in their homes, but he gives a caution: When you hear preaching, "do not slightly cast it off." If you hope that what you hear "out of the Word is not the Word," you are coming to sermons with an unwilling, unyielding, unprayerful heart.[11] He ends his sermon by pleading, "When you come to sermons to hear the Word of God, O labor to keep your hearts in a constant trembling frame, and the Word that you do now tremble at will forever hereafter comfort your heart."[12]

Burroughs's exegetical work supporting such exhortations is evidenced in a sermon series on Leviticus 10:3 and in particular his three sermons titled "Of Sanctifying the Name of God in the Hearing of the Word." The passage that Burroughs uses to support his high view of preaching comes from 1 Thessalonians 2:13: "For this cause also thank we God without ceasing, because, when ye received the word of God which ye heard of us, ye received it not as the word of men, but as it is in truth, the word of God, which effectually worketh also in you that believe." Noting that the Thessalonians were

---

10. S. Rutherford, *A Free Disputation against Pretended Liberty of Conscience* (London, 1649), 119.
11. Burroughs, *Gospel-Fear*, 27–28.
12. Burroughs, *Gospel-Fear*, 29.

commended on this point, Burroughs notes that the apostle's sermon "came effectually to work, because they [the Thessalonians] received it as the Word of God."[13] This same principle that worked for the apostle is at work when a minister preaches from the Bible: "Many times you will say, 'Come, let us go hear such a man preach.' Oh no, let us go hear Christ preach, for as it doth concern the ministers of God that they preach not themselves, but that Christ should preach in them, so it concerns you that hear, not to come to hear this man or that man, but to come to hear Jesus Christ."

Burroughs then quotes 2 Corinthians 5:20 and reminds his hearers again that ministers are ambassadors of Christ.[14] In his treatise *Gospel-Reconciliation*, Burroughs uses the same two texts but cites 1 Thessalonians 2:13 only in passing, exhaustively discussing 2 Corinthians 5:20.[15] He takes careful note of the fact that the text says "we are ambassadors for Christ, as though God did beseech you by us."[16] The latter text is cited again in another sermon where Burroughs preaches that it is "as certain God speaks thus by his ministers, as if you heard God speaking by himself."[17] Thus the metaphor of the ambassador implies not only commissioning but also the authority, even the identity of the preacher. Though relying on different portions of the Bible, it is clear that both presbyterians and congregationalists at the assembly believed that God's words, if they were delivered faithfully by God's ambassadors, remained God's words. And thus they concluded that the preaching of the Word of God is in a very real and proper sense the Word of God.

It is obvious that this understanding of preaching has far-reaching consequences in a pulpit theology. It certainly adds to the gravity of the task and helps to explain why the divines held that someone should not preach God's Word unless he was God's ambassador—called, gifted, and trained for the task of preaching. It also helps to explain why the divines considered preaching to be a powerful means of grace.

---

13. J. Burroughs, *Gospel-Worship: Or, the Right Manner of Sanctifying the Name of God in Generall* (London, 1648), 166. In commenting on this passage Lightfoot sees a connection to Scripture but does not mention preaching (Lightfoot, *Works*, 6:56).

14. Burroughs, *Gospel-Worship*, 166. Thus William Bridge can say, "Christ teacheth by the public ministry of the Word." See his *A Vindication of Ordinances*, 17 (and in Bridge, *Works*, 4:144).

15. For the reference to 1 Thessalonians 2:13, see Burroughs, *Gospel-Reconciliation*, 286. For the full treatment of 2 Corinthians 5:20, see pp. 278–317.

16. Burroughs, *Gospel-Reconciliation*, 278.

17. J. Burroughs, *Gospel-Remission, or, a Treatise Shewing, That True Blessedness Consists in Pardon of Sin* (London, 1674), 217.

The Outward and Ordinary Means of Grace

If the preaching of the Word of God is the Word of God, then what is its place in the Christian life and worship? Unsurprisingly, the divines answer that preaching is the ordinary means of grace for Christians. In his *Praelectiones Theologicae*, Anthony Tuckney argues that the "*Verbum Dei externum est ordinarium medium conversionis ad salutem.*"[18] Tuckney makes clear from the start that by "the external word" he does not simply mean Christ, the one preached, but the means itself, preaching.[19]

Stated differently, people are not only saved by Christ, they are saved by Christ through the means of preaching Christ. This position was commonplace among the preachers at the assembly. Anthony Burgess states that the faithful ministry of the Word is "the sure and ordinary way for conversion of men from their evil waies."[20] He states this more strongly in his exposition of 1 Corinthians 3: "The Ministry is the only ordinary way that God hath appointed, either for the beginnings or encrease of grace." After all, "Faith is said to come by hearing" (Rom. 10:17), and his own text informs the Corinthians that Paul and Apollos were the "ministers by whom ye believed" (1 Cor. 3:5).[21] Burgess goes even further and argues that "because it's the ordinary meanes, therefore it's the necessary meanes to which all are tied. We cannot be without it; if a man enjoy it not, his soul becomes like a barren wilderness, yea like a noisome dunghill."[22]

Always more temperate than his peers, Edward Reynolds also urges the right kind of preaching: "The word of grace thus managed is the ordinary instrument which God useth to santifie us, John 17:17 to form Christ in us, to derive the Spirit upon us, and to turn us to the Lord. And the minister of Christ who duly preacheth it, is his herald, and ambassador." It is his task "to proclaim warr against the rebellious, and to publish remission of sinnes unto those that repent and believe."[23]

---

18. "The outward Word is the ordinary means of conversion to salvation." A. Tuckney, *Prælectiones Theologicae, nec non Determinationes Quaestionum Variarum Insignium in Scholis Academicis Cantabrigiensibus Habitae* (Amsterdam, 1679), part 2, p. 258; see pp. 258–64.

19. Tuckney, *Prælectiones Theologicae*, 258. Tuckney guards himself against the charge of "enthusiasmis" because he says conversion is possible without preaching (p. 259). Post-Reformation authors also distinguished between the internal and the external Word, by which they meant the Spirit's testimony to the authority of the Scriptures, and the inspiration and authority of the Word itself. See *PRRD*, 2:202–4.

20. Burgess, *Spiritual Refining*, 500; see also p. 494.

21. Burgess, *Scripture Directory*, 69.

22. *Dunghill*: a stinking manure pile. Burgess, *Scripture Directory*, 69.

23. Reynolds, *Pastoral Office*, 24.

Again, the congregationalists at the assembly were equally vocal in their advocacy of preaching as the primary means of grace. Burroughs once said that "the great standing ordinance in the church of God is the ministry of the Gospel,"[24] and he esteemed preaching as a "great gift," even a "glorious gift" of Christ.[25] Thomas Goodwin notes that whenever churches were founded in the book of Acts, it was done by preaching. He draws attention to the fact that the preaching of the gospel in 1 Corinthians 2:4 is called a "demonstration of the Spirit" and in 2 Corinthians 3:8 a "ministration of the Spirit."[26]

In 1649, William Greenhill dedicated a preface to a portion of his Ezekiel commentary to a defense of preaching's primacy. In a prophetic tone, his commentary announces that "where the Word of God is not expounded, preached, and applied to the several conditions of the people, there they perish." Again, "lay aside preaching and expounding the Scriptures, the people will be scattred, run into errors, wander up and downe as sheep without a Shepheard." He appeals, of course, to the Bible in order to stress the need for preaching. He also appeals to history and cites in length Archbishop Edmund Grindal's letter of protest to Queen Elizabeth after the monarch "was instigated…to abridge the number of preachers."[27] (Greenhill was unwilling to consider that the monarch could have come to such opinions herself.)

Greenhill was well aware of the fact that not everyone agreed with his lofty view of preaching, and he was disappointed that "some there be that thrust hard at it, and endeavour to throw it down." One contemporary objection to Greenhill's view of preaching rested on the fallibility of the preacher. Were not the apostles, unlike seventeenth-century preachers, infallible? Could they then legitimately stress preaching in a way that England's preachers could not? In response to this, Greenhill readily admits the difference but points out that the apostles and prophets did, at times, fail (a point that Burroughs had bypassed in his discussion of a similar theme). When it comes to preaching, the reliability of the apostles rested not in their infallibility but in the Spirit: "That which was needful to be the

---

24. Burroughs, *Gospel-Reconciliation*, 260.
25. Burroughs, *Gospel-Remission*, 76; see also J. Burroughs, *The Saints' Happiness* (James Nichols, 1867), 254–55, 260.
26. Goodwin, *Of the Constitution*, 11:360–61.
27. Greenhill, *Exposition Continued*, Epistle Dedicatory. In the same missive he also notes that "the infinite and only wise God hath annexed to the ministry conversion, Acts 26:18; regeneration, 1 Corinthians 4:15; the addition of sinners to the church and to himself, Acts 2:41, 47; 11:24; faith, Romans 10:14; 1 Corinthians 3:5; the perfecting of the saints, and edification of the body of Christ, Ephesians 4:12; collation of the Spirit, Galatians 3:2; Acts 10:44; yea, salvation, Acts 11:14; 1 Corinthians 1:21; 1 Timothy 4:16."

rule and standard, was given out by an infallible Spirit." Greenhill moves easily from this doctrine to the importance of preaching more broadly: "The Spirit of truth took of Christ's, showed it to them, and led them in all truth." "And," he says in the strongest terms used by any divine, "while the ministers now do bring that truth to you, they are infallible."[28]

---

28. Greenhill, *Exposition Continued*, Epistle Dedicatory.

CHAPTER 10

On Preaching: Audible and Visible Words

The diligent Bee gathereth hony out of Thime, one of the driest herbs that is; and certainly if thou bee not a drone thy selfe, thou mayest sucke from the mouth of the barrenest and (as thou callest him) the dryest Preacher, Doctrine sweeter then the hony or the hony combe.

—Daniel Featley

In placing a high importance on the preaching of the Word, members of the Westminster Assembly knew that many of their contemporaries saw a kind of competition between the audible Word and the visible Word, the latter being visible both in the sacraments and on the printed page. Theologically, each of these means of grace was compatible, and the use of them could together best build up a Christian man or woman. Nonetheless, these means of grace were sometimes perceived as rivals by contemporaries of the assembly, a fact that is routinely flagged by historians of the period.

Preaching and the Visible Word

This "rivalry" between sermons and sacraments was especially evident at the parish level, for at times baptism and the Lord's Supper received more reverence from parishioners than did preaching or preachers. Jeremiah Burroughs was both chagrined and perturbed as he commented on how people treat the sacraments so seriously but give preaching short shrift: "It is an easier matter to convince men and women, that they are bound to sanctifie the name of God when they come to receive the holy communion, than for the hearing of the Word."[1]

Of course, as John Jackson (1600–1648) would point out, the Lord's Supper is itself a kind of "word"—a "visible word, sermoning and preaching

---
1. Burroughs, *Gospel-Worship*, 195.

Christ crucified, yea Christ crucifying unto the eyes."[2] Thomas Coleman so stressed the similarity of the Supper and the sermon that he concluded that excommunication should cut a person off from both means of grace, lest it "debase" preaching; analogous arguments were made about the access of excommunicated persons to corporate prayer. Stephen Marshall offered that an excommunicated person could only rightly be admitted to one of the ordinances "as a meanes to bring him to repentance" and that "If any of those ordinances could reach him with as good effect in his absence, then he ought not to be present." This was an argument for the presence of everyone at the preaching of the Word, but not its prayers. The church's prayers, for example, could do a person good if they were present or absent. Preaching, on the other hand, required a person's presence in order to receive a personal benefit.[3] It seems to have been a given for Marshall that the Lord's Supper was not a converting ordinance.

Preaching and the Printed Word

When it came to ranking the usefulness of various means of grace, it was a foregone conclusion for most divines that preaching would win out over the sacraments since the preached Word could be used for both the conversion and the strengthening of the Christian, the sacraments only for the latter. As has already been seen, the assembly's catechisms openly granted preaching an edge over the reading of the Word when it came to its persuasive effects.[4] Indeed, an emphasis on the importance of preaching can even be detected in some exhortations for *reading* the Scriptures! In 1662 Matthew Newcomen (d. 1669) offered a passionate plea for the reading of the Scriptures, encouraging his congregation to see the efficacy of the read Word for its saving and sanctifying effects. He was employing a line from Paul's farewell sermon to the Ephesians in Acts 20:32, "I commend you to God, and the word of his grace, which is able to build you up," and his point was that even without Paul's preaching, the people of Ephesus could grow as Christians. And yet it is significant that the occasion for this exhortation to read the Scriptures was a farewell sermon. Newcomen felt compelled to deliver his thoughts on reading precisely because he himself would no longer be preaching. Finding himself conscience-bound under the compromising terms of Restoration conformity to leave his pulpit, he was headed

---

2. J. Jackson, *The Communicants Alphabet* in *The Key of Knowledge* (London, 1640), letter "T."

3. For Coleman's speech and responses by Marshall, Temple, and Carter, see *MPWA*, 3:505, 508–9 (Jan. 9–10, 1645; Sess. 357–358).

4. WSC, 89; WLC, 155.

to the Netherlands and could not vouch for the capacities and orthodoxy of his successor in Dedham.[5]

Under normal circumstances, as most members saw it, the reading of the Word aloud could never be a proper substitute for sermons for at least three reasons. First, people are dull and would miss things that the trained reader should not. Second, Ephesians 4:8 teaches that Jesus Christ ascended to give gifts to men. Thomas Goodwin argues that since, in his experience, many people could read, it would be "a derogation from Christ to make a faculty of bare reading to be one of the utmost fruits of his ascension."[6] And third, it is not the letter but the "spiritual meaning of it, as revealed and expounded" that "ordinally [sic] doth convert." Even the devil can quote Scripture. It often takes a preacher to bring out the sense of a passage.[7] He ends by reminding his hearers that Christ died to give gifts to the church, and among those gifts are preachers. Christ emptied Himself so the Christian might be filled.[8]

Other treatments of the subject highlight different reasons for the importance of preaching. Anthony Burgess's explanation of the necessity of preaching is threefold. First, sermons recast the Word and present old things in new ways, making difficult truths digestible and allowing key doctrines to be more clearly settled. Second, there are old things in God's Word that are new to His people and need to be brought out in sermons. And third, preaching is necessary for the pointed and "powerfull application of necessary truths, to the hearts and consciences of men."[9] William Gouge draws a parallel conclusion from a different starting point when he asks how a person can understand the Bible. His answer is that one must read it, meditate on it, but also be sure to "attend to the Preaching of Gods word."[10] Commenting on Mark 2:1–5, Gouge commends the sick man and his friends for their extraordinary effort in trying to reach the ordinary means of grace.[11] Commenting on his experience in London, Edmund Calamy appeared to approve of those who "will not come" to worship

---

5. M. Newcomen, *Ultimum Vale, or, The Last Farewell of a Minister of the Gospel to a Beloved People* (London, 1663), 46; see also 40–46.
6. Goodwin, *Of the Constitution*, 11:363–64.
7. Goodwin, *Of the Constitution*, 11:364.
8. Goodwin, *Of the Constitution*, 11:368.
9. Burgess, *Scripture Directory*, 140.
10. W. Gouge, *Whole Armour* in *The Workes of William Gouge: In Two Volumes* (London, 1627), 156.
11. W. Gouge, *An Exposition on the Whole Fifth Chapter of S. Johns Gospell* (London, 1631), part 1, p. 143. Gouge's conclusion is an odd one since it seems that the men were coming for miraculous healing, not preaching. Healing, in Gouge's own view, is hardly an ordinary means of grace.

"except expounding [will be] joyned with reading."[12] Elsewhere William Greenhill points out that the eunuch of Acts 8 could read the Bible but did not understand it until it was expounded. Ezra and others read the law and gave its sense (Neh. 8:8),[13] and Paul told Timothy to divide the Word aright (2 Tim. 2:15).[14]

In the assembly, Thomas Temple had not argued against the importance of preaching, but he did think that the line penciled between reading and preaching needed to be drawn lightly. When reflecting on the role of an ambassador, Temple promoted the idea that since reading a royal proclamation was as much the task of the ambassador as was the exposition of a proclamation, "he that doth read the scripture doth preach the scripture."[15] Temple, readers may recall, expressed his views during a debate over the office of pastor and had (initially) suggested not that preaching was pitched too high by some of his fellow divines but reading too low. Since Romans 10 states that faith comes through preaching and since he knew people who were saved by reading the Bible, Temple could only conclude that "reading is preaching."[16] His point was that reading was an important part of the pastor's office. But women and children could be saved by reading the Bible, Marshall rejoined. Did Temple think they were preachers too? This was unfair. Temple had by this point clarified his views sufficiently: he was contending that reading belonged to the pastor's office *and* he was arguing that persons could be saved by means other than preaching.[17]

Debate over the elevation of preaching would continue throughout the years that the assembly met. In the spring of 1647, Thomas Wilson, William Rayner, and Joshua Hoyle asked that the questions in the Larger Catechism on the efficacy of the Word of God be limited only to the efficacy of the Word preached.[18] But also in the spring of 1647, in an afternoon Communion sermon far away in southwest Scotland, Samuel Rutherford told his auditors that the "Word's working and the Spirit's working is not tied to the hour of the sand-glass, neither is the Spirit tied to a pulpit, and

---

12. *MPWA*, 2:266 (Nov. 2, 1643; Sess. 87).

13. The exegesis of this text was contested in the assembly. See *MPWA*, 2:265–68 (Nov. 2, 1643; Sess. 87).

14. Greenhill sees Ezra preaching, not translating, as some argue. But it would matter little to his argument, as he brings translation in: "If we may not expound the word because we are fallible, then why should we translate the word out of the original tongue into others, seeing they are fallible, and may, yea have, mistakes therein, as well as others in expounding and preaching." See Greenhill, *Exposition Continued*, Epistle Dedicatory.

15. *MPWA*, 2:265 (Nov. 2, 1643; Sess. 87).

16. *MPWA*, 2:266 (Nov. 2, 1643; Sess. 87).

17. *MPWA*, 2:266 (Nov. 2, 1643; Sess. 87).

18. WLC, 31.

a gown, and a minister's tongue."[19] High as his view was of the usefulness of the Scriptures, his understanding of the variety of means employed by the Holy Spirit was even broader. But Rutherford did not intend to devalue preaching; he warns explicitly that "this doctrine should be right understood, for it warrants not the conventicles and unwarrantable meetings of Separatists and Brownists, who despise public meetings."[20]

The Bible, according to the majority of assemblymen, assumed that God's people needed preaching. However, there were other evidences for the importance of preaching—evidences more loosely tied to the biblical text. Departing from exegetical arguments for the primacy of preaching, John Arrowsmith suggests that since Eve was deceived through hearing false words, it is appropriate that we should be saved by hearing true words, and then says, "We by hearing of the ministry of the Gospel, are brought home to God. As Calvin saith, sweetly, That we who were deceived by the subtlety of the Serpent might be saved by the foolishness of God" (1 Cor. 1:21).[21]

On another level, as Thomas Gataker suggests in a prefatory epistle to a printed sermon, the difference between the preaching and reading of the Word is connected to the mode of communicating: the "vivacitie and efficacie" of the "lifelesse letter…cometh farre short of the living voice."[22] And in a letter to his parishioners at Blackfriars, Gouge writes that he values preaching on the one hand simply because of "Christ's charge, Goe Preach the Gospell." In his mind, "This is that Ordinance wherein and whereby God doth ordinarily, and most especially manifest his owne power, and bestow his blessing." He also notes that "preaching is of power especially to worke upon the affections." "Printing," because it can be read multiple times, "may be one especiall meanes to inform the judgements."[23] (Gataker would likely have concurred with this opinion since he mentions in another preface that he included notations and scholarly references in his printed sermons that would never be appropriate when preaching in the pulpit.)[24]

---

19. S. Rutherford, *Quaint Sermons of Samuel Rutherford Hitherto Unpublished* (London: Hodder and Stoughton, 1885), 167.

20. Rutherford, *Quaint Sermons*, 125.

21. Arrowsmith, *Theanthropos*, 108.

22. T. Gataker, "An Anniversarie Memoriall of England's Delivery from the Spanish," in *Certaine Sermons, First Preached, and Afterwards Published* (London, 1637), part 2, p. 28.

23. Gouge, "To…my beloved Parishioners," in *Workes*. Sedgwick also brings up the enduring aspect of print when he tells his readers that "this [book] may Preach to you when I cannot" in *The Fountain Opened, and the Water of Life Flowing Forth* (London, 1657), Epistle Dedicatory.

24. T. Gataker, *A Just Defence of Certain Passages in a Former Treatise concerning the Nature and Use of Lots* (London, 1626), iv.

Preaching and the Reading of Sermons

The assembly opposed the reading of the Word in church in lieu of preaching, and its members disdained preachers who read sermons written by others in place of preparing their own. But what would they say to parishioners who chose to read a sermon at home rather than listen to one in person?

Popular literacy levels in early modern England are notoriously difficult to estimate, as Heidi Brayman Hackel's subtle essay on the subject contends. At the very least, the percentage of the population able to read may be much higher, especially among men, than other recent studies have suggested. She notes that by the outbreak of civil war in 1642 there were four books printed for every five people in England and that studies of English villages reveal book ownership among 40 percent of men and 25 percent of women—books substantial enough to bother mentioning in a will, suggesting that there may have been volumes of lesser worth lying around the home. Nonetheless, there has been no combined study of signatures, of wills, of parish libraries, of varying abilities to read different kinds of type, and of the literacy levels of women versus men.[25]

All estimates remain hypothetical except for the reading levels of gentry, which hovered around 100 percent. Nonetheless, for a sufficient portion of the population, the decision to read a sermon rather than listen to one was by no means a hypothetical question: "You will say," Burroughs wrote (in one of his printed sermons), "'Cannot we sit at home and read a sermon?'" No. "The great ordinance is the preaching of the Word. Faith comes by hearing, the Scriptures say, and never by reading."[26] He softened this somewhat when he later admitted that his readers "may think that this or the other means may do the deed as well," but he expects that "because God hath appointed this to be his ordinance, therefore, in obedience to him… [they] will attend upon this means rather than upon the other means."[27]

Arguments for coming to church usually included the importance of preaching. Obadiah Sedgwick was concerned not only about those who stayed at home "imployed in worldly business or carnal sports" but also about those who "proudly conjecture that they can receive as much good at home, by reading of a good Book, as they shall by coming to hear the Word publickly taught them." Sedgwick fired a battery of reasons for attending corporate worship, insisting that "private performances must…make

---

25. See H. B. Hackel, "Popular Literacy and Society," in *Cheap Print in Britain and Ireland to 1660*, ed. J. Raymond (Oxford: Oxford University Press, 2011), 88–100.
26. Burroughs, *Gospel-Worship*, 167.
27. Burroughs, *Gospel-Worship*, 202.

way for and give way unto publick ordinances."[28] Among those reasons, he noted that people needed the sacraments and also "ministerial instructions." Indeed, "If God should send a famine of the Word" through public calamity or personal sickness, Christian people would find themselves to be "like the fish out of the water."[29]

There could be little objection to reading sermons; they were put into print for a reason, and assembly members knew their value. The narrower issue was reading as a substitute for preaching and church attendance.[30] In addressing those who would rather stay home, Goodwin suggests that good books and conversations are helpful, particularly in times of spiritual drought, but a steady use of these in the absence of preaching is akin to a reliance on "watering-pots" in the place of rain.[31] Goodwin may have the illiterate in mind when he suggests that God chose preaching so that rich and poor could both be called into the kingdom.[32] He might have been less persuasive to his contemporaries when he preached that the "reading…[of the Word] alone by ourselves" is inappropriate since "our first parents took their infidelity in by the ear, and therefore God thought good to let faith in the same way."[33]

Daniel Featley came to a similar conclusion and offered what may be the most comprehensive, and certainly the most creative, case for hearing sermons "live" rather than reading them at home. Examining the epochal events of redemptive history, he reports that "the holy Ghost in the day of Pentecost came with the *sound*. Where the *sound* is of the Word Preached there goeth the Spirit ordinarily."[34] What for Goodwin was a passing thought is extended by Featley into full-blown polemic: "God in his infinite wisedome hath so disposed the meanes of our salvation, that the soveraigne Antidote against sinne, & death is conveyed into the soule through the same passage, whereby the deadly poyson first entered. Death stole in at the eare by suggestion of the evil spirit, and now life in the hearing of the word passeth in at the same gate of the soule."

Featley worried about people who seem to have an ear for "poison" but not for "the oyle of grace, the most pretious balsame of Gods word instilled by preaching." The "sheepe of Christ who belongest to his fold,

---

28. O. Sedgwick, *Shepherd of Israel, or, God's Pastoral Care over His People* (London, 1658), 340–41; for the whole discussion of church attendance, see pp. 339–44.
29. Sedgwick, *Shepherd of Israel*, 342.
30. Arnold Hunt points to Robert Harris's assertion that sometimes God directs people "to some special book or treatise which fits their case." Hunt, *Art of Hearing*, 165.
31. Goodwin, *Of the Constitution*, 11:360.
32. Goodwin, *Of the Constitution*, 11:363.
33. Goodwin, *Of the Constitution*, 11:363.
34. Featley, *Ancilla Pietatis*, 63.

shew his eare-marke: My sheepe heare my voyce." Featley found hearing a fitting remedy for sin and the brand of a true sheep. He also argued that it indicated good stewardship of time: By listening, the hearer "shalt get that with much ease which cost another man much paines. That which a divine Orator, and heavenly Preacher hath beene many weekes (perhaps yeeres) in laying together, hee scattereth abroad in an hower."[35]

Probably revealing more about his parishioners than about the population at large, Featley's weightiest arguments are leveled not against the lazy, who couldn't be bothered to go to church, but against the learned, who thought they could do better. Featley knew his intended audience well enough to recognize that they would enjoy the irony of *reading* his arguments for *hearing*: Why should someone "well stored" at home with "heauenly provision, and foode of Angels" come to hear a sermon? If "thy library is like a rich Granarie…maist thou not then as well or better spend thy time, in perusing such writings then repairing to the Church perhaps a good way from thy house, to heare a man of meaner gifts then those were or are, whose works thou hast in the last and best editions"? His imaginary interlocutor "hast heard much against hearing" and is thus urged to "heare now a little for it."[36]

Featley first argues that properly employed, different ways of receiving the Word should not be in conflict: "As a great Master of the Law was wont to say, that Courts of justice must not Clash one against another: so it is most certaine that duties of piety ought not Clash, justle, or any way crosse one the other." In other words, "Private reading and publike hearing must both have their places, seasons, and turnes." If for some reason someone is "so straightned in time, or overlaid with businesse that thou canst not allow a fit time for both, let the private, voluntary alwaies give place to the publike necessary duty."[37] This perspective illustrates a common alignment of priorities among the godly and is consonant with the advice given by the Westminster Assembly as a whole. The assembly, for example, had recommended that "if any through necessity bee hindered from being present at the beginning [of a service of worship], they ought not, when they come in to the Congregation, to betake themselves to their private devotions, but reverently to compose themselves to joyne with the assembly in that ordinance of God which is then in hand."[38]

Featley's real case for preaching lies in the half dozen arguments following these opening comments. For instance, he argues that the calling

---

35. Read "hour." Featley, *Ancilla Pietatis*, 59–61.
36. Featley, *Ancilla Pietatis*, 61–62.
37. Featley, *Ancilla Pietatis*, 62.
38. *MPWA*, 5:95 (Doc. 36).

of the pastor and the bond between the parishioner and his pastor should keep hearers coming to church: "If thy Pastor be so strictly charged to preach unto thee, certainly thou art necessarily bound to heare him. For these duties are linked together." This is a capacious argument for sermon attendance, turning every command to preach into a command to hear. And (in a now familiar line of questioning) he asks if "private reading" can offer "the like promises to publike hearing the Word? Or is it of like force and efficacie?" Unlike some godly preachers, Featley thought it peevish to deny that people have come to faith through reading. But he was sure that "where thou canst name one that hath beene wonne to the Christian faith and true godlinesse by bare reading wee can produce many thousands that have beene added to the Church by publike Sermons: yea sometimes at one Sermon." Indeed, he was willing to acknowledge "that men in private reading the Scriptures and other holy books may & do feele some soft and sweet blasts of the holy spirit." But what is that when set beside preaching? "In the publike Ministry of the Word, the Spirit commeth downe like a mighty rushing winde filling the whole roome, wee receive then grace in a fuller measure."[39]

One weakness with printed sermons has to do with delivery. "Sermons preached are compared to raine and deaw, but printed to snow; which though it lye longer on the ground, yet it is much colder, and doth not in like sort pierce, moysten, and fatten the ground as the other." These printed sermons simply cannot have the same penetrating impact as heard sermons, which arrive like rain in due season. Featley even wants his hearers to treasure their notes from the last week's sermon more than the printed sermons on the side table, which can be picked up and read any time. After all, "those things that have passed the presse lye by us; wee may at any time have, and use them: but the notes of a Sermon preached are like the Manna that fell on the Saturday which (if it was not presently gathered) was utterly lost," and thus by implication must be read and studied more diligently. Preaching saturates, preaching is fresh. Good sermons were also personal, and a good preacher, like a physician and pharmacist combined, would prescribe and provide the right remedy. There is a big difference between do-it-yourself medicine derived from books and "a speciall potion or Electuary made by a trusty Apothecary, according to the direction of a Learned Physician, and particularly applyed to thy peculiare disease. Every man hath not the skill of the Apothecary to make the confection, and fewer have the judgement of an experienced physician to direct where and how it ought to bee given."[40]

---

39. Featley, *Ancilla Pietatis*, 62–63.
40. Featley, *Ancilla Pietatis*, 63–65.

Godly preachers were strongly convinced that their sermons had personal relevance to their hearers. Were they not sometimes assaulted for preaching *at* their parishioners? Was it not the case that men and women could be incensed by pointed sermon applications, when in reality (or so the preacher protested) the minister had not even noticed the person's presence in the assembled congregation?[41] Of course, such protestations of a preacher's innocence had the unintended effect of undermining assertions of personal connections between the man behind the pulpit and the people in the pews. But defensive comments on the part of a preacher were hardly determinative of a puritan pastor's sense of the penetrating, personal impact that a sermon could have on those who heard it. One need only recall the oft-told story of Thomas Goodwin who, after hearing John Rogers preach, joined the people of Dedham "deluged with their own tears," and "when he got out" from the service "and was to take horse again to be gone" found himself instead hanging "a quarter of an hour upon the neck of his horse weeping, before he had power to mount, so strange an impression was there upon him, and generally upon the people."[42]

While strong preachers were irreplaceable, stand-alone sermons brought into print had to overcome obstacles if they were to be noticed by the reading public. In the 1640s, godly sermons were not collected with others of their kind and printed in serviceable cloth editions as they were by Nichols in the nineteenth century or the Banner of Truth Trust in the twentieth century. Sermons in the seventeenth century usually appeared in public as thin, unbound quartos, thus in the same style and about the same price as weekly newsbooks (or as the scurrilous pamphlets that proliferated throughout the civil wars and interregnum). What is more, as James Rigney observes, they were sometimes printed with advertisements for other books, the latest legislation, or throat lozenges guaranteed to cure everything from the common cold to the plague. Sometimes printers and authors would take steps to improve a sermon as it came to print. Rigney notes Thomas Valentine's (1586–1665) peace-promoting sermon to the House of Commons, where the printer took the additional (bold) step of incorporating "a version of the royal arms in its decorative initial." And Simeon Ashe (c. 1596, d. 1662) includes an autopsy report in his published funeral sermon for Jeremiah Whitaker, an interesting feature that would not have been appropriate in the church or at a graveside.[43]

---

41. J. Spurr, *English Puritanism, 1603–1689* (New York: Palgrave Macmillan, 1988), 174.
42. R. Halley, "Memoir of Thomas Goodwin," in T. Goodwin, *Works*, 2:xviii.
43. J. Rigney, "'To lye upon a stationers' stall, like a piece of coarse flesh in a shambles,' The Sermon, Print and the English Civil War," in *The English Sermon Revised: Religion,*

Nonetheless, while some sermons struggled in the marketplace, many books were considered more compelling than the local clergyman. There could be problems, as Featly admitted, when "thy preacher bee a man of no very extraordinary gifts." It was for practical reasons as well as for theoretical concerns that preachers were often diffident, even reticent, to see their sermons in print.[44] It led them to make excuses, such as what Charles Herle called "that commonly pretended midwife of the presse, the importunity of friends."[45] Uncertainty about the use of print for sermons could also lead divines to make arguments that actually subverted the puritan emphasis on preaching over reading. Gataker was sufficiently committed to the uniqueness of preaching that he offered a "lengthy apology for publication" of sermons. But he was not so radically committed to its uniqueness that he could resist a creative excuse for sermon publication in his suggestion that writing was a form of speech.[46] An admiring friend of assembly member Samuel Bolton (1605/6–1654) went one step further in describing a collection of his friend's posthumously printed sermons: "Yes. Turn these pages (Reader)—thou wilt see, His every line breathes immortality."[47]

Featley's arguments in favor of substandard preached sermons over superior printed sermons, although creatively stated, are representative of the standard responses among the godly: honor the local preacher. "The diligent Bee gathereth hony out of Thime, one of the driest herbs that is; and certainly if thou bee not a drone thy selfe, thou mayest sucke from the mouth of the barrenest and (as thou callest him) the dryest Preacher, Doctrine sweeter then the hony or the hony combe." Of course, "the truth findeth easy entrance into the soule when she commeth armed, not onely with her owne strength but also with the best aide, wit, or art can afford." Nonetheless, Christians must "affirme with Saint Paul that faith standeth not in the entising words of mans wisedome, but in the demonstration of the Spirit, and the power of God." Mary Morrissey observes that Reformed preachers, while committed to using the tools of rhetoric, did not reduce preaching to a form or branch of rhetoric. A sermon was something else, occupying its own sphere. Thus, while the arts of speech "may move affection," Featley argues that it remains the case that "nothing but Gods Word and the grace of the Spirit can remove corruption. Humane wit and learning may tickle the eare…but never pierce the heart: that is the singular

---

Literature and History 1600–1750, ed. L. Ferrell and P. McCulloch (Manchester: Manchester University Press, 2000), 191–93.

44. Hunt, *Art of Hearing*, 119–24.
45. C. Herle, *Contemplations and Devotions on the Severall Passages of Our Blessed Saviour's Death* (London, 1631), "The Epistle Dedicatorie," cited in Hunt, *Art of Hearing*, 127.
46. Hunt, *Art of Hearing*, 127, 129.
47. Ferdinard Archer's lines in Rigney, "'To Lye upon a Stationers Stall,'" 190.

prerogative of the Word of God." We ask, "What are Rams-hornes in comparison of silver Trumpets? Yet when God commands and appoints, the harsh sound of them, shall demolish those strong holds of Satan which the sweeter and shriller sound of silver Trumpets shall not doe." For Featley, the commute from the home library to the local church is a matter of obedience. "Bee thou obedient to him who is set over thee in the Lord, and must give an account of thy soule. Desire not to have thy eares tickled, but thy heart pricked." Featley pledges that this kind of diligence will always be rewarded: "Make then no doubt but that God will blesse his ordinance and thy obedience; and supply to thee by his Spirit what may bee deficient in the Preachers learning or language"—if, that is, one comes "prepared to the hearing of the Word," and so he begins his directions for proper hearing.[48]

Preaching and Private Conversation

If printed exhortations are inferior to preached ones, so too, private ones were of lower priority than public ones. Returning to a familiar text and metaphor, 2 Corinthians 5:20 and ministers as ambassadors, Gouge argued that there is one "maine difference between [the exposition] of a minister and a private man. A Private ma[n] may have great knowledge of the mystery of the Gospell, and be able to open and declare the sense and meaning of it, but a Minister by vertue of his office hath this prerogative and preheminence above others, that in God's steede [stead] he declareth reconciliation."

This holds a lesson for the man or woman in the pew: "When a Minister preacheth and applieth the promises of the Gospell, he doth not onely declare and make knowne Gods mercy and goodnesse to poor sinners, but also is an especiall meanes to move those sinners to believe those Promiscs, and to imbrace reconciliation with God."[49] There is something special about public preaching.

Rutherford, preaching around the time that complaints were received about disruptive prayer meetings and Bible studies in the army, also pointed out the difference between private and ministerial expositions of Scripture. "There is a very great difference," he says, "between private exhortation and private preaching; even as a common sojour [soldier] gives warning to the army that the enemy is coming on them, and he who is appointed watchman, he gives also warning of the same." Ignoring either is foolish, but to

---

48. Featley, *Ancilla Pietatis*, 65–67; M. Morrissey, "Scripture, Style and Persuasion in Seventeenth-Century English Theories of Preaching," *Journal of Ecclesiastical History* 53, no. 4 (2002): 686–90.

49. Gouge, *Whole Armour*, 262.

ignore the watchman is a double sin. So, too, there is a difference "between a master, who is clad with public authority for teaching scholars, and one of the condisciples [who] teaches another on the same lesson that he teaches." Rutherford, who favored such Bible studies and defended them at the 1640 General Assembly of the Scottish Church, maintained that "none" will say "that either the one usurps the watchman's place or the other the master's charge; but the one does what he does by a special designation for that effect, and the other as he is a member of that body." In Rutherford's view, "A private Christian he ought to help others in the way to heaven; but he ought not to make that his study—to study divinity for that effect."[50]

In practice, public and private piety did not need to be in conflict. After all, the Westminster Assembly itself called people to "meditate" on "and confer" about preaching as a communal exercise, discussing the sermon in groups or families on a Sabbath afternoon: "What time is vacant betweene or after the solemne meetings of the congregation in Publique be spent in Reading, meditation, Repetitions of sermons, especially by calling their families to an account of what they have heard & Catechiseing of them."[51] Even when not sitting under the sermon, it can still be of benefit to build Christians up in private.

But what if preaching is not building up the Christian? What if people are not benefiting from the sermons? The divines were well aware of this problem. Alexander Henderson once admitted in a sermon, "I know many of you who has said, when ye came out from the preaching…that your souls has been nothing bettered by it" (a comment suggesting somewhat more candor in his congregation than in most churches today).[52] One question that assembly members were sure to ask when this complaint was made was whether the person came with a believing heart, ready to hear God's Word. After all, the preached Word is not automatically effective; it must be received by faith. That was the essence of Henderson's response to his own people's complaints. The other question that godly ministers would ask when the problem arose was put to the preachers: Were they preaching Christ?[53]

---

50. Rutherford, *Quaint Sermons*, 167–68.
51. WLC, 160; *MPWA*, 5:122 (Doc. 43).
52. A. Henderson, *Sermons, Prayers, and Pulpit Addresses*, ed. C. M. McMahon and T. B. McMahon (1867; Coconut Creek, Fla.: Puritan Publications, 2012), 38.
53. E.g., Burroughs, *Gospel-Remission*, 77. He tells the ministers that if they lack the esteem and honor of the people, they had better "take pains" to preach Christ.

CHAPTER 11

On Preaching: Christ-Centered Sermons

It's the main end and scope of the Scriptures only to exalt Christ, and the end of the Ministry should be the same with the end of the Scripture.
—Anthony Burgess

Your labours in preaching, will come to little, perhaps to nothing, if it not be Christ, or some thing in reference to Christ, on which you so laboriously insist in preaching.
—Obadiah Sedgwick

The members of the Westminster Assembly were keen to communicate the importance of preaching the whole council of God from the Scriptures only. Thus, when he read about Ezekiel's practice of proclaiming all that the Lord had shown him, William Greenhill had little difficulty transferring the prophet's example into an imperative for ministers: they are to preach only and preach all that they learn at Christ's school (Ezek. 11:25).[1]

The Whole Word

An insistence that ministers preach the whole counsel of God was hardly unique to Greenhill. Anthony Burgess put forth the same standard when he wrote that preachers "must dresse every Sermon at the glasse [mirror] of the Word; they must preach as they read in Scripture."[2] He gave three reasons why the preacher is to preach only (and all of) what the Bible has to

---

1. W. Greenhill, *An Exposition of the Five First Chapters of the Prophet Ezekiel* (London, 1645), 473; Stephen Marshall, according to his biographer, found "most content" or satisfaction in "preaching of Christ" but was sure that "bookes…never taught him to preach Christ." See G. Firmin's preface in S. Marshall, *The Power of the Civil Magistrate* (London, 1657).

2. Burgess, *Scripture Directory*, 141.

say, each building on the apostle Paul's exhortation in 1 Corinthians 3:10 that ministers take care how they lay their foundations.³

The first motivation to take care in preaching is for God's sake. It is His Word that ministers are purporting to preach; His honor is at stake, and He does not approve of man's thoughts being substituted for His. Faithful preaching calls for much humility, prayer, and, of course, study on the part of the preacher, as he must be careful to speak biblical thoughts only.⁴ The second reason to take care in preaching is for man's sake. If God's words are not preached, the sermon loses its promised power. At best it is hay and stubble—useless for spiritual nourishment, certainly not life-giving; at worst parishioners come to drink at the fountain and are given poison. "Foolish and unwarrantable opinions and doctrines of men" are not "able to produce…gracious effects."⁵ The third motive for care in preaching is closest to home: the minister must preach the whole Bible for his own sake. Burgess points out that the preacher is given a ministry, not a "magistery." God, and not the preacher, can best determine what Christians need. The minister "may not be a Master to dictate and affirm what he pleaseth." Rather, he must imitate Paul and deliver to the people what he receives from the Lord (1 Cor. 11:23). If not, Burgess says, we "endanger our own selves" and others.⁶ This, he says, would make the preacher "a snare to, or a murderer of other mens souls" and "the blood of the soul will cry more terribly, than the blood of the body."⁷

Christ the Center

These kinds of commitments are, of course, mere commonplaces among post-Reformation Reformed ministers, exemplified in the counsel of William Perkins (1558–1602) and uttered at the conclusion of his preacher's classic, *The Art of Prophesying*: "Preach one Christ, by Christ, to the praise of Christ."⁸ Certainly all of the Westminster Assembly's theologians were completely convinced of the truth of what Greenhill and Burgess were teaching: the minister must preach only and all of what God has said in His written Word. But they would never have considered such instruction *sufficient* for the preacher. After arguing that "the matter of our preaching

---

3. The context of the apostle's extended metaphor makes it clear that he has preaching ministries in view.

4. Burgess, *Scripture Directory*, 142. Burgess is equally careful in noting that the preacher is not to subtract from God's Word.

5. Burgess, *Scripture Directory*, 143, 142–43.

6. Burgess, *Scripture Directory*, 143.

7. Burgess, *Scripture Directory*, 144.

8. W. Perkins, *The Art of Prophesying* (Edinburgh: Banner of Truth, 1996), 79.

is in general the whole counsel of God," Edward Reynolds went on to say that "More particularly, the matter of our preaching is Christ crucified, and the glad tydings of remission and salvation through him."[9]

For the assembly members, preaching the Bible and preaching Jesus Christ were never mutually exclusive. Quite to the contrary. After all, Christ cannot be preached from anything but the Bible. As Thomas Ford (1598–1674) once commented, "I am not able to apprehend, how Gods works of creation, as sun, moon, and stars, etc. did preach Christ" to people.[10] Scripture, not the created world, was the textbook for preaching Christ—by which Ford and others meant Christ as mediator in His redemptive work. And what is more, the focal point of the Bible itself is the Messiah, and therefore proper exegesis demanded a Christ-focused hermeneutic, which in turn required Christ-centered preaching. Thus Burgess argues that "it's the main end and scope of the Scriptures only to exalt Christ, and the end of the Ministry should be the same with the end of the Scripture."[11]

Richard Muller argues that by the "scope" of Scripture, Reformation and post-Reformation divines were speaking about the focal point or bull's-eye of Scripture, not the breadth or sweep of the Scriptures. The purpose and aim are in view, not the range and the intention.[12] Thus, if the scope of Scripture is Christ, it is not necessary to think that every passage in every biblical book points to Christ but rather that the sum total of the Scriptures points to Christ. This does not seem to have been the understanding of most assembly members. More typical is Burgess, who argued that across the whole sweep of Scripture Christ is to be found: "All the Prophets before Christ, they witnessed of the Messiah.... Abraham, though [he lived] so long before Christ's Incarnation, yet it's said, 'He saw Christ's day.'" The same was true in the Mosaic administration of the covenant: "All those Rammes, those Bullocks, those Goats, they all did typifie a Christ."[13]

Consistent with this emphasis, and following his exhortations to preach the whole Word of God, Burgess expounded the next verse in 1 Corinthians 3 in a Christological fashion, "For other foundation can no man lay, than that is laid, which is Jesus Christ."[14] Burgess had much to say about preaching Christ, the church's one foundation. Christ is the "only

---

9. Reynolds, *Pastoral Office*, 26, 27.
10. T. Ford, *Autokatakritos, or, the Sinner Condemned of Himself* (London, 1668), 41.
11. Burgess, *Scripture Directory*, 150.
12. *PRRD*, 2:209.
13. Burgess, *Scripture Directory*, 150. For the Old Testament ceremonial law preaching Christ, see also J. Lightfoot, *The Works of the Reverend and Learned John Lightfoot* (London, 1684), 1:520; George Walker understood that Christ was to be preached in synagogues, *The Doctrine of the Sabbath* (Amsterdam, 1638), 125–26.
14. Burgess, *Scripture Directory*, 145–56.

foundation, in respect of knowledge and instruction."[15] Moving from epistemology to ethics he argued that "we must preach Christ the foundation of all strength and power, from whom we receive all ability to do any thing that is good."[16] The same applies for ecclesiology and kingdom theology, as Christ is "head of the Church," and "governeth all things."[17] Furthermore, "Christ is to be set up [as] the only foundation, in respect of mediation and intercession with God."[18] Our "persons and duties" are accepted only through Him. No inheritance or blessing comes without His "imputed righteousnesse."[19] Burgess was only beginning. "Christ is to be preached as the foundation of all fulnesse, for all our necessities and spiritual wants."[20] Christ is "the Fountain of all the happiness, joy and spiritual content the godly hearer can have. We are to preach Christ as the centre in whom all the lines of your hope, love, and desire are to meet. Thus Paul himself, 'I determined to know nothing but Christ crucified'" (1 Cor. 2:2).[21] Christ is the one whom we are to expect to meet in the sacraments, prayer, and the preaching of the Word.[22] And "lastly, We are to preach Christ, not only as the foundation of our approaches to God, but of all Gods gracious actions and visitations to us." By that Burgess means that "we are not only to come to God in Christs name, but to expect that God will come to us through Christ." For "God is in Christ, reconciling the world to himself" (2 Cor. 5:19).[23] Of course, some might like to qualify just how Christ was reconciling the "world," when not everyone would be saved. The gospel offer needed to be extended with appropriate sensitivity to biblical Reformed theology and scriptural teaching on the extent of the atonement. Nonetheless, preaching also needed to reflect the encouraging "tenour of the gospel."[24]

Echoing similar sentiments, Obadiah Sedgwick (1599/1600–1658) states that it is "but labour lost to set up anything but Christ." Ministers are "to bee much in preaching Christ." Again, "your labours in preaching, will come to little, perhaps to nothing, if it not be Christ, or some thing in reference to Christ, on which you so laboriously insist in preaching; 'My

---

15. Burgess, *Scripture Directory*, 145.
16. Burgess, *Scripture Directory*, 146.
17. Burgess, *Scripture Directory*, 146.
18. Burgess, *Scripture Directory*, 147.
19. Burgess, *Scripture Directory*, 147.
20. Burgess, *Scripture Directory*, 148.
21. Burgess, *Scripture Directory*, 149.
22. Burgess, *Scripture Directory*, 149–50.
23. Burgess, *Scripture Directory*, 150. The text is erroneously cited as 2 Corinthians 1:19.
24. Ford, *Autokatakritos*, 52–53.

Kingdom,' said Christ, 'is not of this world,' John 18:36. So your business is not the business of the world; Go then and preach the Kingdom of God."[25]

The preaching of Christ, Sedgwick outlines, is the preacher's proper work, sufficient and full work, honorable work, excellent work, and true comfort. The parish preacher must be able to know on the judgment day that he has preached Christ.[26] The missionary preacher also has the weight of this responsibility on his conscience, Thomas Thorowgood (c. 1595–1669) would add. And the task of the hearers—Thorowgood had in mind Native American hearers—was to enlarge their hearts to receive those who endeavor "to preach Christ."[27] Of course, those needing sermons for their salvation were not only in faraway lands. Lost Scottish and English congregations also needed to hear Christ preached, for even unbelievers "needed to be under a pastor's care till they be first converted."[28]

A sense of obligation to preach Jesus Christ in every sermon varied among assembly members, as it appears to have varied among other puritans as well. Philippé Delmé's (d. 1653) textbook on preaching mentions Christ only in passing,[29] Oliver Bowles (c. 1577–1644) gives the subject a chapter,[30] and Edward Reynolds, a treatise.[31] In fact, Reynolds pursues the necessity of preaching Christ from every angle. The origin of his book is an extended sermon on Paul's comment to the Corinthians that he and his fellow preachers "preach not ourselves, but Christ Jesus the Lord; and ourselves your servants for Jesus' sake" (2 Cor. 4:5). In tune with his text, Reynolds explains in some detail that ministers are not to preach themselves, providing examples of how preachers often do make themselves the focus of their sermons.[32] He then goes on to argue that Christ is "the author, the object, and the end of all" preaching. As the author, Christ is the one who sends a preacher on his mission, calling him internally and externally to the pulpit ministry. Christ separates the preacher from other Christian persons, consecrating them for the work they are given. As the king, He gives His ambassadors instructions, chiefly the task to be agents of reconciliation in Christ's place. As the object, Christ is the matter and

---

25. Sedgwick, *Fountain Opened*, 371.
26. Sedgwick, *Fountain Opened*, 371–72.
27. Thorowgood, *Digitus Dei*, To the Reader.
28. Rutherford, *Due Right*, 254. Congregationalists argued that unbelievers must hear the Word from preachers but that the preacher has pastoral obligations only to those who are already converted. Presbyterians responded by asking the congregationalists to consider the case of baptized members who had not yet professed faith and may not yet be converted (e.g., Rutherford, *Due Right*, 256).
29. P. Delmé, *The Method of Good Preaching* (London, 1701), 19–20, 42–44, 49, 52.
30. O. Bowles, *De Pastore Evangelico Tractatus*, Lib. 2, Cap. 13; pp. 79–85.
31. E. Reynolds, *Preaching of Christ* (London, 1662).
32. Reynolds, *Preaching of Christ*, 1–24, esp. 19–24.

message of all our preaching. The law drives us to Christ. The gospel itself resides in Christ, as can be seen in every article of the Apostles' Creed—we believe in the Father of Christ; we believe in the Holy Spirit of Christ; we believe in the holy, catholic bride of Christ; we believe in communion with the subjects of the King, Christ Jesus; and, of course, we preach remission of sins through Christ alone, through His resurrection. Just as the law and gospel find their focus and substance in Christ, so too do all prayers and both sacraments. And as the end of all preaching, the preacher does all that he can to advance the interests and plans of Christ, the people of Christ, and ultimately the glory of Christ.[33]

The law and the gospel were important but delicate topics at and around the time of the assembly. Antinomians (none of whom would appreciate the label and not all of whom deserved it) were said to be announcing that Christians had no need of the Mosaic law; a few held that there was no place even for a moral law. In the midst of the debates over preaching, the entire assembly ground to a halt when it considered the preaching committee's overzealous suggestion that sermon applications should at once challenge antinomians who care too little about evidences of grace in their lives and, at the same time, avoid "the disheartening of weak Christians" who may be insecure about evidences of grace in their lives—a direction particularly targeted at indiscreet ministers.[34] Comments by Jeremiah Burroughs (bap. 1601? d. 1646) indicate that, in his opinion at least, the worry about "indiscrete ministers" was well founded. On more than one occasion he indicates that preaching in his day was getting moralistic in tone. A mere preaching "against the vanities and profits of this world" is really not "the main thing, nor the right method of preaching."[35] Elsewhere he complains that it is common now to "preach morallity." Of course, morality is within the sphere of that which should be preached, but it is not a replacement for the gospel: "The great point that al ministers ought to aim at is the great point of reconciliation, and that is to be preacht."[36]

From a different generation, and from a different text, William Gouge preached the same message: Ephesians 6:19 records the apostle Paul asking the saints to pray "that utterance may be given unto me, that I may open my mouth boldly, to make known the mystery of the gospel." Gouge deduced from the apostle's example that "the Gospell is the proper object of

---

33. Reynolds, *Preaching of Christ*, 24–39. For similar assertions that Christ is the "matter and the author of the gospel," the "sermon, and the preacher, and the power," see Reynolds, *An Explication of the Hundreth and Tenth Psalme* (London, 1632), 249–50.

34. Lightfoot, *Journal*, 280 (June 6, 1644). The motion was sent back to the committee for further work.

35. Burroughs, *Gospel-Remission*, 77.

36. Burroughs, *Gospel-Reconciliation*, 270–71.

preaching." He tells his hearers that the Great Commission was a commission to preach the gospel. And he appeals to the letter to the Romans and notes that those who are called beautiful are the ones who preach the gospel (Rom. 10:15), and he quotes Romans 1:16, which states that "the Gospell is the power of God unto Salvation."[37] Thomas Goodwin concurred. Alluding to Romans 10:15, he submits that preachers would "add more beauty to their own feet" if they would increase their gospel preaching and decrease their discussions of "truths of less moment."[38] And Cornelius Burges would note, just before the restoration of Charles II to his throne, that bishops might add some credibility to their "Pomp" and "perpetual state of honour and dignity above their brethren" if they would occasionally "preach Christ to his flock."[39] "Quenching all zeale in preaching Christ," Thomas Wilson told a gathering of the House of Commons, is as great a sin in England as it was in the days of "the High-priest and his complices" who opposed Jesus and His disciples.[40] Nothing is more important than preaching Christ, and, for Stephen Marshall, all "divisions and subdivisions in other matters of religion" are secondary in comparison. For "as long as each form [of government] carries people to the Word, houlds out Christ in his Word, Christ in preaching, Christ in the sacraments, there is food for souls."[41] Really, only demons should be excluded from preaching Christ, as the example of the Savior demonstrates in Mark 1:34.[42]

In the end, the reason for all the emphasis on Jesus Christ rested on the fact that preachers are His ambassadors and not another's. Christ came into the world saying, "I am the way, the truth and the life." He said He was the "bread of life" that "came down from heaven." He preached Himself as good news to the world. His ambassadors are given the same commission. These were the key notes that Burgess struck in his discussion of the subject. And this was no new thing. "All the Prophets were Prophets of Christ," Burgess writes, and "all the Officers in the New Testament, are the Officers of Christ."[43] Burroughs also highlights the fact that it is not only the main task of the preacher to preach "gospel reconciliation" but that "it is their commission to preach that especially."[44] It is little wonder, then, that after studying John 1:6–9, John Arrowsmith found his ideal model in John the

---

37. Gouge, *Whole Armour*, 255.
38. Goodwin, *Of the Constitution*, 11:228.
39. C. Burges, *No Sacrilege nor Sin to Alienate or Purchase Cathedral Lands* (London, 1660), 11.
40. T. Wilson, *Davids Zeale for Zion* (London, 1641), 19.
41. Marshall, "The Life of Christ," 57.
42. Lightfoot, citing the opinion of unnamed divines in *Works* (1684), 1:642.
43. Burgess, *Scripture Directory*, 145.
44. Burroughs, *Gospel-Reconciliation*, 246.

Baptist, the last prophet of the old era whom the apostle John commends as one who bore witness to the Light, always emphasizing that Christ must increase while he must decrease.[45] True ministers, Arrowsmith writes, "set up Christ in their ministry; they are content themselves to stand in the crowd, and to lift up Christ upon their shoulders; content, not to be seen themselves, so Christ be exalted."[46]

Richard Muller concluded that among the Reformers and the post-Reformation orthodox, "the generalized 'scope' of all Scripture or of the Gospel...is usually identified as Christ or as the revelation of God's mercy and goodness."[47] For most assembly members the concept of preaching "Christ" appears to be interchangeable with the idea of preaching the "Gospel," the good news about Christ. This meant on the one hand that if a Westminster divine was preaching Christ, he would usually preach Christ as savior and mediator. And it meant on the other hand that if he was preaching the gospel, he would preach a gospel expounding Christ and His benefits—all the treasures and blessings and privileges that accompany a saving union or relationship with Jesus Christ.

---

45. Arrowsmith, *Theanthropos*, 103. A quotation from John 3:30.
46. Arrowsmith, *Theanthropos*, 104; see also 112–13. See also E. Reynolds, *A Sermon Preached Before the King* (London, 1669), 35–36; and Reynolds, *Preaching of Christ*, 24–33.
47. PRRD, 2:207.

CHAPTER 12

On Preaching: Christ-Centered Exegesis

When we preach of faith, of repentance, of a godly life, these are but the ladders (as it were) to tread upon, that you may lay hold on Christ.
—Anthony Burgess

That mans ransome and ruine might hold yet a more thorough proportion, both are in a Garden, that as in a Garden man had played the wanton with Gods bounty, so in a Garden too, this more then man might play the Champion with Gods fury; it was in a Garden, that God sought man sold to the devill for an apple, Adam where art thou? and 'tis here in the Garden too, that men seeke God sold by a devill, for as very a trifle: whom seeke ye? Jesus of Nazareth.
—Charles Herle

Just how did the divines at the Westminster Assembly think that Christ or the gospel was to be preached? After all, there are vast parts of the Bible that do not mention Christ by name or the gospel by subject. The answer, in essence, appears to be that the Westminster divines had two approaches to Christ-centered preaching.

Theological Preaching

The approach taken by many assembly members was to preach Christ in a manner that was theologically or dogmatically driven. For students of puritanism, this should not be surprising. The dominant method of preaching among the godly, laid out by William Perkins, was of the exegesis of a biblical text, followed by the identification of the text's major doctrine (often more than one), the uses of the doctrine, and then a further application of those doctrines. The resulting sermon structure and content was more theological than textual in its focus; a sermon on Romans 9 would be more about the doctrine of election than the manner in which that doctrine was presented in that chapter of the Bible.

Nonetheless, it is important to recognize that there is considerable variety in the execution of the doctrinal sermon, as Philippé Delmé argues in his work on the subject.[1] The simplest form that this doctrinal preaching took was "Lutheran," where timeless principles of "law" and "gospel" were pitted against each other. With this approach, the preacher would first identify one or more laws (or precepts or godly character traits) in a biblical text, then carefully convince the congregation that they fall short of that perfect standard, and finally show how Christ is the solution to the problem as the gracious savior of sinners. This type of hermeneutic was an application of a principle. It was an approach to exegesis reflecting on a basic Reformation distinction between the law and the gospel. Certainly the hermeneutic and the principle should be distinguished. A large number of divines accepted a law/gospel *hermeneutic* and applied it in their preaching; virtually *all* divines (Lutheran and Reformed) accepted a law/gospel *principle* and would commonly speak of the law "as a preparative unto the Gospell," where the law is a "schoole-master to bring us unto Christ" (Gal. 3:24).[2]

Nonetheless, for the Reformed ministers at Westminster, this preparatory use of the law by no means excluded other uses of the law. That is to say, when applied by the Reformed orthodox, this law/gospel principle did not result in the denigration of the law as a call to Christian obedience. Biblical commandments were still needed in the Christian life. Anthony Burgess's overgenerous assessment was that there is "scarce any Heretique ever so besotted as to preach Christ" irrespective of repentance and obedience. Indeed, he continued, "if I be Calvinist, Arminian, or any other way, I cannot have any quietnesse, or look for any comfort till I and my sins are divided."[3] In his estimation, "to preach Christ, or faith, or grace, or the benefit of the Sacraments so, as that a godly, exact and diligent walking and workiug [working] is excluded, is to preach another Christ, another gospel then we have received."[4]

Burgess himself willingly employed a law/gospel hermeneutic at times and would preach law/gospel sermons, but he consciously attempted to

---

1. Delmé, *Method of Good Preaching*, 1–7.
2. Gouge, *Whole Armour*, 254. Perhaps Richard Vines was trying to communicate the same idea when he reflected on the time "when Paul was required by Felix to preach to him the faith of Christ." Vines finds it interesting that the Scriptures record the apostle preaching of "righteousness, temperance, and judgement to come, whereat Felix trembled" (Acts 24:25). See R. Vines, *Gods Drawing and Mans Coming to Christ* (London, 1662), 181. But it is also possible that Vines so wanted to elevate the law that he was contesting the maxim that only the gospel converts sinners.
3. A. Burgess, *CXLV Expository Sermons upon the Whole 17th Chapter of the Gospel according to John* (London, 1656), 243.
4. Burgess, *CXLV Expository Sermons*, 127.

develop a well-rounded form of preaching that, in spite of his protests to the contrary, can probably be best labeled "doctrinal preaching." Stephen Casselli judges that Burgess normally preached sermons employing a Perkinsian sermon structure. Such a structure most easily lends itself to doctrinal approaches to preaching Christ. Nonetheless, the more narrow focus of our inquiry is on how Burgess preached the gospel within any structure that he may have employed.[5]

Particularly relevant to a taxonomy of Burgess's own preaching styles is his sermon on 2 Corinthians 1:19 titled "Christ the Alpha and Omega of All Preaching." There Burgess explained to his hearers that there were different understandings of "preaching Christ." By the phrase some "understand the doctrine [or teaching] of Christ," some "Christ and the doctrine of Christ," and some, including Burgess, believe that "Christ onely is to be the subject of all our preaching."[6]

As Burgess saw it, "The subject of the whole Scripture is Christ: The whole Word of God tends to the exalting of Christ." And "when we preach of faith, of repentance, of a godly life, these are but the ladders (as it were) to tread upon, that you may lay hold on Christ."[7] Here Burgess is probably trying to distance himself from those who preach on doctrines like faith and repentance, or perhaps on the Sermon on the Mount or the Lord's Prayer, but somehow manage not to present Jesus Christ as the way of salvation in their sermons. Yet even as he measured out the distance between preaching Christ and preaching about faith or repentance, Burgess effectively argued the case for preaching Christ in Scripture *by means of doctrines* associated with Christ. Stated differently, if one listens to Burgess's discussion, or to his actual sermons, the accent of his preaching falls on biblical doctrine and not on biblical typology.

This is usefully illustrated by Burgess in his enumeration of four ways of preaching Christ.[8] Three of the four links that Burgess finds between the text of Scripture and the Jesus he preached are in fact systematic-theological connections. In the first and easiest approach, one preaches Christ when the historical "Jesus of Nazareth," the fulfiller of prophecy "who was crucified at Jerusalem," is preached. Here preaching Christ is almost foolproof. A direct prophecy in the Old Testament or a reference to Jesus in the New Testament speaks of Christ, and in explaining the prophecy and fulfillment, Christ is thereby preached. Here the content of the

---

5. S. Casselli, *Divine Rule Maintained: Anthony Burgess, Covenant Theology, and the Place of Law in Reformed Scholasticism* (Grand Rapids: Reformation Heritage Books, 2016), 38.
6. Burgess, *Expository Comment*, 556–57.
7. Burgess, *Expository Comment*, 557.
8. The text numbers these four ways as five.

sermon is more textual than doctrinal. But it is textual only to the degree that a prophecy is quoted or echoed in the New Testament passage. Furthermore, it does not answer the question of how Christ can be preached from a New Testament passage of Scripture that has no prophetic echoes, or in an Old Testament passage that is not on the face of it prophetic. For that reason, Burgess employs three additional ways of preaching Christ.

The second way of preaching Christ is to preach Christology, the "God and man" in "both his natures." Here, and only here, does Burgess appear to open the door to the possibility of preaching an ontological Christ without a discussion of the economic Christ—preaching His person apart from His work. And yet in the particular example he supplies, Burgess explains Christology much as Anselm of Canterbury does, even asking *"Cur Deus sit homo"* (Why the God man?) and then linking his discussion of the doctrine of the incarnation with the doctrine of the atonement. In this second approach to preaching Christ, texts of Scripture are employed by the preacher, but Christ is preached by means of posing and answering logical theological questions.

In his third way of preaching Christ, Burgess recommends focusing on Christ in His person and threefold office, explaining His two natures and His work as prophet, priest, and king. Here there is an inevitable blending of doctrinal preaching and what could be called textual preaching. After all, "the man" Jesus, and priests and prophets and kings, are not merely doctrinal terms; they are also biblical types and figures. Thus, doctrinal connections to Christ of this third type often mingle with the type of Christ-centered preaching discussed below.

The fourth way to preach Christ, according to Burgess, is to set Him up "as the King and Lord of his Church, to whose lawes and commands we are wholly to submit" lest we meet Him one day as an angry judge. Burgess defends this method as necessary in the face of antinomian errors about the law and misinterpretations of Scripture. And so "the law is preached, hell and damnation are preached, that so Christ may be the more welcome, that so the grace of the gospel may be the more conspicuous." This final way of preaching Christ is identical to the "Lutheran" law/gospel method discussed above.[9]

With these four ways of preaching Christ, Burgess presents a nuanced form of theological connectivity to Christ that can be effected from any passage of Scripture. It seems similar to that advocated by Obadiah Sedgwick, who was content to remind his readers that "labours in preaching, will come to little, perhaps to nothing, if it not be Christ, or *some thing in*

---

9. Burgess, *Expository Comment*, 557–60, 690–91.

reference to Christ" that is preached.[10] Anthony Burgess's four ways were probably dominant among the assembly's divines, and although the sermon structures of assembly members still await careful bibliographical research and nuanced description, it is likely that all of the assembly's preachers sometimes preached systematic-theological sermons as illustrated in the last three ways Burgess mentions. Certainly Burgess's four ways were used to good effect and, even in printed form, continue to impact Christian readers today.

Textual Preaching

Nonetheless, not everyone at the assembly gravitated toward systematic-theological exegesis and preaching as their primary hermeneutic and sermonic method. As mentioned above, hints of a preference for an alternative method can be seen in the assembly's debates, for some opposed the idea that the Perkinsian form of preaching should be recommended in the assembly's own directory for worship.[11]

That there was more than one understanding of how a preacher should move from the text of Scripture to the Christ of Scripture is also evident from the writings of assembly members. That is to say, there is another stream of Christological interpretation, what might be termed the "textual" or "typological" stream, that feeds into the pool of preachers used as samples for this study. This major approach to preaching Christ focuses, by way of emphasis, on biblical types, themes, and pictures. (To use Burgess's taxonomy of Christ-centered preaching as a reference point, typological preaching expands on Burgess's first way of preaching Christ while not ignoring the minor note struck in Burgess's second way of preaching Christ.)

Perhaps the best way of explaining this kind of exegesis is to provide an example. Although it is a meditation and not a sermon per se, a vivid example of the textual approach to seeing Christ in Scripture is provided in a little book by Charles Herle, prolocutor of the Westminster Assembly after William Twisse. In his study, Herle reflects on Christ's "bloody sweat" in the Garden of Gethsemane, mentioned in Luke 22:44. (This bloody sweat probably meant that sweat was pouring off Christ's body as blood would pour off a wounded man. Two hundred years later Dionysius of Alexandria said that "sweating blood" was still a current expression in his day and referred to "intense pain and distress." He said that people also referred to

---
10. Sedgwick, *Fountain Opened*, 371 (emphasis added).
11. Lightfoot, *Journal*, 273 (June 5, 1644).

weeping "tears of blood" and that it meant the same thing.)[12] Whatever the precise meaning of the term, this was extraordinary suffering. Who would have expected that the Son of God would need angelic help and yet still suffer so terribly? Some early Christians may well have found Luke 22:44 to be embarrassing—they wanted a more courageous savior. This may explain why some ancient manuscripts omit this passage. Herle, on the other hand, had no problems with the text's authenticity. In fact, he finds the passage rich in meaning for Christians.

In "sweat and blood" Herle found "the two best emblemes of labour and passion, of doing and suffering, and so, the best epitomes, or (if you will) journals of our Saviours life and death." This is the case because "both made up the travailes of his soule; the first he wrote in sweat, the other in blood." After all, what was His life other than "a continued sweat of passive action, Hee went about always doing good." And "his death, what, but as incessant a bloodshed of active passion? hee powred out his soule to death." Herle not only could find hints of the doctrines of the active and passive obedience of Christ in this passage, but he also could not "find any two things in nature that may better serve for the indexes, or rather seales, of those his two Testaments" than these two, "sweat and blood." Just think "of the Law, working out in sweat salvation with feare and trembling." Just think "of the Gospell, buying it out with blood in price and value." It was "in these two therefore" that Christ did "beginne his passion, it being to bee the execution of both those Testaments; the complement of the one, and supplement of the other."[13]

But in the wording of the passage Herle found indications of a "further mysterie." If the author's writing style and the printer's italicization and punctuation can be suffered, the reader can follow Herle as he considers that "in these two (Sweat and Blood) begins this our second Adams execution, because in these two (upon the matter) begins the first Adams sentence; the Sweat of his browes, whereby hee must live the life; the blood of mortality, whereby hee must dye the death."[14]

Further significance is found in the two gardens: "that mans ransome and ruine might hold yet a more thorough proportion, both are in a Garden, that as in a Garden man had played the wanton with Gods bounty, so in a Garden too, this more then man might play the Champion with Gods fury; it was in a Garden, that God sought man sold to the devill for an apple,

---

12. Dionysius the Great, *The Works of Dionysius. Exegetical Fragments*, in *Ante-Nicene Fathers* (1886; Peabody, Mass.: Hendrickson, 1994), 6:115.

13. Herle, *Contemplations and Devotions*, 1–3.

14. Herle, *Contemplations and Devotions*, 3.

Adam where art thou? and 'tis here in the Garden too, that men seeke God sold by a devill, for as very a trifle: whom seeke ye? Jesus of Nazareth."

The parallels, and thus the potential types, are not insignificant. "In each Garden wee read of a drawne sword; in that by the Cherubim, in this, by Peter; that flames, but this wounds; that but menaces, but this maimes." In the end, "what was in that Garden but threatend to the first Adam, that was in this Garden suffered by the second; the difference is this, in that first Garden, the sword is still hostily brandished, a flaming sword that turned every way, in this second 'tis peaceably put up, Peter put up thy sword." But "nor shall the difference of these two Gardens bee of lesse comfort then is their concord," for "though in that first Garden of Paradise, the sword still keepes the dispossessed posterity of Adam from ever (here) returning thither"—for we "must first passe under the Angels sword, the stroke of death"—"yet to this latter Garden of redemption on a better Paradise to us, wee have free and safe accesse." There "no sword heere threatens, no Angell keepes the doore." Quite the opposite, for he "who is the Angell of the Covenant, both doore of the Fold, and Keeper of the doore, and that with that irresistible key of David, cryes here, come unto mee all, in a word, as at first in a Garden man was doom'd by God, to earne his bread for life by his sweat, so in a Garden here God earnes for man the bread of life by his Sweat too; nor is it of the browes onely as that, but of the whole body, yea and soule too." And this is a redemption for all types of sinners, "that herein bloody muredrous Caine might have bathed his purple soule as well as idle luxurious Adam his." Yes, "here's for both, both, blood and sweat: and that in the strange abundance of a shoure [i.e., a shower]; nor is it a dewie misty one, but of great drops running downe through his clothes to the ground."[15]

Herle's meditation then turns to a common theme in Christology, asserting that "the least drop of this blood thus dignified by that enriching interest of union: it hath with the God-head, were of price enough, had he so pleased, to have ransomed as many worlds of men, as there bee men in this." Herle was left wondering why Jesus Christ is so "prodigall of his blood thus precious?" Why does Christ invert "that prophesie of all nations flowing unto him, by thus profusely flowing at once to all nations"? The answer is that we have "all of us sinned, and all of us against all the whole Law, in all the whole man: and therefore so full, so proportionate shall bee the satisfaction, that hee who is all in all and for all, will answereably bleed throughout all the whole body." And "nor will this our Eliah thinke, this his selfe-sacrifice once offered for all, compleate enough, unlesse he first

---

15. Herle, *Contemplations and Devotions*, 3–7.

drench it in a floud [i.e., flood] of his owne sweat and blood. But, nor is the cure lesse strange then the Physicke: the Method then the Medicine." Who can understand it? "Ours was the fever, and doth hee bleed? oft times a bleeding in the head (Physitians say) is best stopt by striking a veine in the foot, but here the malady is in the foot, the remedy in the head." We can only conclude that "the spirituall blood of Sin, holds a contrary course to that of the body, it flowes upward against Heaven." Perhaps this adds new significance to God's charge against Cain, that "the voice of thy brothers blood cries up to Heaven." And so "to cure that spiritual bloody Issue of the foot, sinne, must the head thus bleed for it." This deserves qualification of course: "must (I say) not out of any necessity on his side, more then that of his owne decree and promise, all the necessity, at least the need, was ours."[16]

What sets his efforts apart from, say, an Anthony Burgess, is the way in which Charles Herle attempted to draw the reader's attention to the words and phrases of Scripture—in this sense, it was intensely textual. Herle demonstrated that exegesis of a passage can be much enriched by lingering over the inspired text and its language. From this passage and its context he vividly expounded the gospel and creatively touched on justification, the unity of the two testaments, the nature of the atonement, Christology, and the extent of the atonement. His meditation then illustrates his exposition with reference to medicine, implying that Christ as our savior is our physician.[17]

There is a difference, of course, between meditation and preaching. This difference, and the movement from the one to the other, is explicit in Thomas Case's work, which was "first conceived by way of private meditation: afterward digested into certain sermons."[18] The substantial difference between the kind of exegesis displayed by Herle in his meditation and that of a "textual" preacher in his sermon is that the sermon does not usually linger so long in one place. The preacher usually demonstrates how a passage of Scripture relates to Christ and then considers additional points of doctrine and application. Such is commonly the case in the sermons of Daniel Featley, to choose one prominent example. In one sermon (on Psalm 63:9–11) he explains the two levels on which the text is usually read. Patristic authors tended to see it apply to Christ, Reformation-era writers a "literall exposition"

---

16. Herle, *Contemplations and Devotions*, 7–10.

17. For the relevance of this theme in the pastoral literature of the Westminster Assembly's members, see C. B. Van Dixhoorn, "God's Physicians: Models of Pastoral Care and Neglect at the Westminster Assembly, 1643–1653," in *Church Life: Pastors, Congregations, and the Experience of Dissent in Seventeenth-Century England*, ed. M. Davies, A. Dunan-Page, and J. Halcomb (Oxford, forthcoming).

18. T. Case, *Correcion, Instruction: or, a Treatise of Afflictions* (London, 1652). I am grateful to John Bower for pointing out this work to me.

of David's own trials. Featley, characteristically, sees merit in both and cites Calvin's pious observation that we "never read of any blamed for drawing too much water out of the well of life." Featley then argues for line-by-line correspondence between the psalm and the sufferings of Christ.[19] In another Old Testament sermon he sees broad typological correspondences between the failures of Adam and Israel and the meritorious achievements of Christ.[20] These are well-trodden paths, familiar lines of argument and development among textual preachers sensitive to typology.

Nonetheless, a textual preacher could sometimes dwell on the imagery of a text to the point of an extended, sermon-length allegory. Featley's exposition of Exodus 28:15–21 is a case in point. First, the preacher explained in as scientific a manner as possible the historical details of the high priest's breastplate. Then, after issuing appropriate qualifiers, he suggested that emeralds were generated in the Red Sea, and thus "lively set forth the green wounds and bloudy passion of the worlds Redeemer.... The ruby hath a perfect colour of flesh...but with a lustre and resplendency farre above the nature of flesh. What fitter embleme of the rayes of divine majesty shining in the flesh of our Savior?" His exposition of the ruby continued, as did his comments on each of the stones in the priest's breastplate, drawing out parallels between the high priest and the Highest Priest in a manner very similar to that offered by Herle.[21]

It is worth noting that these particular writings are exemplars of a kind of exegesis, not of a particular kind of preaching. Herle's offering draws on contemplations and devotions, and Featley, like many versatile preachers, employs more than one method of linking his text to Christ as mediator—sometimes using more than one approach in a single sermon. His sermon titled "The Royall Priest" begins by connecting Psalm 110:4 to the attributes of God and then to Christ. But thereafter, his exegesis is focused entirely on the text itself, and typological connections are drawn to Christ.[22]

It goes without saying that examples of exegesis such as those just offered will probably evoke a wide range of responses from modern exegetes. The point here is that some exegetes and preachers attempted to communicate the sense of the passage not by extracting a doctrine and then enumerating its uses but by meditating on the vocabulary and phrasing of the biblical text and the use of key words and themes throughout Scripture. To state

---

19. D. Featley, *Clavis Mystica: A Key Opening Divers Difficult and Mysterious Texts of Holy Scripture* (London, 1636), 60–61.
20. Featley, *Clavis Mystica*, 80.
21. Featley, *Clavis Mystica*, 506–7; see also 498–536.
22. Featley, *Clavis Mystica*, 551–69.

it differently, Herle's and Featley's method of communicating these doctrines was not driven so much by the doctrines themselves as by the text of Scripture. And yet, notably, both writers show that typological sensitivity need not lead to an impoverishment of theology; it can perhaps even lead to its enrichment.

Arguably, a stress on Christ-centered preaching was a hallmark of Reformed preaching, and the additional stress on preaching Christ from the Old Testament was almost a Reformed distinctive. Richard Muller argues that it is especially common among advocates of federal theology, a form of covenant theology that reflects extensively on the two Adams of Scripture, both the first Adam and the last.[23] Nonetheless, and in spite of appearances, this present chapter does not attempt to set Christ-centered preaching in its historical context in order to admire members of the assembly. In fact, it is undeniable that Burgess's comment about his own day also reflected on his fellow assembly members: Some preached doctrines—even doctrines relating to Christ, such as His preincarnate existence, christophanies, or the relationship between His two natures and one person—and yet did not preach Christ in the sense that Jesus arguably intended in Luke 24. They could preach Christ as God and not as savior.

Nevertheless, while doctrinal preaching could at times be disconnected from Jesus Christ, equally urgent questions can be posed to Herle: In seeking the significance of words and pictures used or cited or developed in a biblical text, did he know when to stop? What are the controls on the typological method as described? Ministers in the "doctrinal preaching school" who did pay attention to types and symbols tended to be very cautious. They were comfortable with using more obvious types and symbols, especially those actually identified in the New Testament as such. But like John Calvin or Henry Ainsworth they often "deemphasize Christological readings of the Old Testament," or perhaps both Testaments.[24] Richard Muller argues, again controversially, that a "hermeneutic on which rested the Reformers' sense of the unity of Scripture and the identity of all Scripture as the Word fulfilled in Christ was becoming less and less easily maintained as a viable hermeneutic as...Protestantism moved away from the allegorical and typological models of late medieval exegesis toward strictly historical, literal, and grammatical models."[25]

In truth, there was no unassailable method of preaching Christ, and, so far as we can tell, there was limited discussion and critique of alternative ways of preaching Christ this early in the campaign to reform English

---

23. *PRRD*, 2:218–19.
24. For the Old Testament exegesis of these theologians (and others), see *PRRD*, 2:449.
25. *PRRD*, 2:206.

preachers and preaching; certainly it was not a topic over which puritan preachers were likely to divide among themselves. Yet while the craft or art or science of preaching Christ-centered sermons was not deliberately discussed at any length, it does not appear that Christ-centered exegesis and preaching was on the decline among assembly members, including typological exegesis. Most godly preachers would sound, with Edward Reynolds, the insistent note that every minister ought to "preach Christ Jesus," and that pastors should be told to "determine to know nothing among your people but Christ crucified" and to "let his name and grace, his spirit and love triumph in the midst of all your Sermons."[26]

Reynolds simply counseled young preachers to make Christ their "great end…to glorifie him in the [sic] hearts, to render him amiable and precious in the eyes of his people; to lead them to him as a Sanctuary to protect them, a propitiation to reconcile them, a treasure to enrich them, a Physician to heal them, an Advocate to present them and their services unto God." Christ is all things for His people. Christ offers Himself to us "as wisdom to counsel, as righteousnesse to justifie, as sanctification to renue, as redemption to save, as an inexhausted fountain of pardon, grace, comfort, victory, glory." Employing a memorable metaphor, he adds, "Let Christ be the Diamond to shine in the bosom of all your Sermons."[27]

Preaching Christ, for Reynolds, should be done for the sake of those who hear, but it should primarily be done "for Jesus sake, if you love Jesus." This is an argument that Jesus Himself used with Peter in John 21:15–17, which John Chrysostom had noted long ago in his own treatise on pastoral care.[28] According to Reynolds, "If you would have Jesus love you, if you tender his sheep, if you regard his command, if you fear his wrath, if you value his salvation, study the price of souls, snatch souls out of the fire, forewarn souls of the wrath to come, be humble, be faithful, be painful, be pitiful towards the souls of men." In short, "set forth Christs excellency unto the souls of your hearers, that you may be able to say to him at his coming, as he to his Father, Behold me and the children whom thou hast given me. Thus doing, you shall both save your selves and them that hear you."[29]

---

26. Reynolds, *Preaching of Christ*, 46.
27. Reynolds, *Preaching of Christ*, 46.
28. J. Chrysostom, *On the Priesthood*, 2.1, in *Nicene and Post-Nicene Fathers*, Series 1, 9:39.
29. Reynolds, *Preaching of Christ*, 48.

CHAPTER 13

On Study and Style:
"The Spirit's Working"

It is presupposed (according to the Rules of Ordination) that the Minister of Christ is in some good measure guifted for soe weighty a service, by his skill in the originall languages & in such arts & Sciences as are hand maides to Divinity, by his knowledg in the whole body of Theology, but most of all in the holy Scriptures having his senses & hart exercised in them above the common sort of beleevers; & by the illumination of gods Spirit & other guiftes of edification, which (together with reading & studying of the Word) he ought still to seek by prayer, & an humble hart, resolving to admitt & receive any truth not yet attained, when ever God shall make it knowne unto him. All which he is to make use of & improve in his private preparations, before he deliver in publique what he hath provided.

—"Of the Preaching of the Word," Directory for Public Worship

All the learning in the world cannot help us to a sanctified and holy understanding of the Scripture, no, not so much as the true interpretation of it without the Spirit of God: and if learned men cannot do it without Gods Spirit, much less unlearned.

—Anthony Burgess

The kind of studied, deliberate approach to sermon crafting and preaching desired by the Westminster Assembly was not without its critics. Mary Morrissey tells how William Dell, master of Gonville and Caius College, once attacked Sidrach Simpson (c. 1600–1655), master of Pembroke College, for thinking "men now are to get knowledge by studies and humane learning, and not by inspiration." Dell believed that "the Spirit alone is sufficient, both to enable us to know clearly and certainly the things of God, and to publish them unto others."[1] This dispute was in part, no doubt, a Cambridge college rivalry expressed in terms of preaching theory.

---

1. Morrissey, "Scripture, Style and Persuasion," 701, citing W. Dell, *The Stumbling-stone, or, a Discourse Touching That Offence Which the World and Worldly Church Do Take against*

Dell was, after all, a college master, required to inculcate learning in the college's students. And although Simpson did not defend himself in print, there is little reason to doubt that, like all members of the Westminster Assembly and proponents of what Morrissey calls "the English Reformed theory of preaching," Simpson insisted on every sermon's dependence on the Spirit.[2]

Preaching in the Spirit

The insistence on the Holy Spirit and on study was commonplace among English Reformed ministers. Reflecting on the apostle Paul both as a sinner and as a learned man, Anthony Burgess concluded that "all the learning in the world cannot help us to a sanctified and holy understanding of the Scripture, no, not so much as the true interpretation of it without the Spirit of God: and if learned men cannot do it without Gods Spirit, much less unlearned."[3] But it was not an English Reformed theory of preaching only: it was a Reformed theory. "What can preaching of man or angel doe without God," Scottish divine Samuel Rutherford asked; "Is it not God and God only who can open the heart?"[4]

While in one context (as discussed in chapter 9) Reformed preachers argued for the effectiveness of preaching, and thus the need to go to church, they could also, counterintuitively, argue for the indispensability of the Holy Spirit because preaching did not appear to be a sensible means of advancing the gospel.[5] Anthony Burgess stated quite openly that "this instituted means [preaching] is very unlikely for such glorious effects to a carnal eie [eye]."[6] Even in the seventeenth century, preaching was "very despicable and contemptible to human reason." Citing 1 Corinthians 1:21, Burgess highlighted the fact that Paul referred to "the foolishness of preaching." This is not, the divine was quick to say, "that it is so indeed, for it's the wisdome of God to salvation; but the Apostle calls it so according to the principles of human wisdome." This applies both to the "matter" and "manner of preaching"; both are "very unlikely ever to produce such effects: The matter is high, paradoxical, incredible to flesh and blood; The manner of delivering is plain, without the affected wisdom of the world, without either miraculous signes" to please the old world "or scientifical demonstrations"

---

1. Christ Himself. 2. His True Word. 3. His True Worship. 4. His True Church. 5. His True Government. 6. His True Ministry (London, 1653).

    2. For Morrissey's phrase, see Morrissey, "Scripture, Style and Persuasion," 689.
    3. Burgess, *Expository Comment*, 8.
    4. Rutherford, *Free Disputation*, 351.
    5. Burgess, *Scripture Directory*, 69.
    6. Burgess, *Scripture Directory*, 69.

to please the new, "either of which would persuade men."⁷ Certainly it was not without reason that in Burgess's *Treatise of Original Sin* he gives a stern warning to the sophisticated in the audience not to despise preaching, as Augustine once had, prior to his conversion.⁸

The problem with preaching, then, is partly with the matter preached, partly with the plain style of the Word itself. "Preachers of the Word, differ from all the humane Oratours, Greek and Latin," Burgess writes, for orators might "by their eloquence and affections, perswade their Hearers; for it was about Civil and Moral matters, about which men had understandings naturally able to perceive, and wils, naturally able to choose the things perswaded."⁹ Persuasion is readily possible under normal circumstances, but nothing is normal with preaching. "Preaching is about those things, to which man hath no understanding to believe, nor no heart to receive. But God must give the hearing ear, and the seeing eye, else we miscarry." He concludes, drifting into doxology, that "all is of God, both the Word to be heard, and the Ear to hear. Both the Word to be believed, and the heart to believe."¹⁰

If men and women are so unwilling to hear the gospel, and if preaching is ineffectual without God, early modern preachers were willing to ask—at least as a rhetorical device—"What use is there of Preaching? What need of the ministry?"¹¹ The answer always offered was that God has appointed both the ends and the means of salvation. He has determined both the message of the gospel and the method by which it is to be heard. As Burgess wrote, "Though God only gives the encrease, yet it is only in and through the Ministery."¹² Here, as in most points in a theology of preaching, the assembly's presbyterians and congregationalists felt the same tension and gave the same answer. "You will say," Jeremiah Burroughs predicted, "'What need we then so much preaching, and such arguments to work upon our hearts'?" The answer: "We are bound to do what befits creatures to do, and to leave God to do what pleases Him."¹³

But the assembly's theologians pushed the matter further. Why did God appoint means? Why preaching? Two main reasons were supplied, and John Arrowsmith, in his exposition of John 1:6–7, identified both of them. Arrowsmith opened by underlining the fact "that God hath appointed the

---

7. Burgess, *Scripture Directory*, 69.
8. A. Burgess, *A Treatise of Original Sin* (London, 1658), 364–65.
9. Burgess, *Scripture Directory*, 87.
10. Burgess, *Scripture Directory*, 87.
11. Burgess, *Scripture Directory*, 86.
12. Burgess, *Scripture Directory*, 86.
13. Burroughs, *Gospel-Fear*, 91.

ministry of men to be used among men."[14] The first reason for preaching is that humankind is unable to bear the ministry of angels and certainly cannot endure direct contact with God. Manoah and his wife, the prophet Zachariah, even the virgin Mary herself were all quite overcome by the angels that visited them. The people of Israel were completely unable to endure the glorious presence of God at Mount Sinai, begging Moses to speak with God in their place. Thus, out of necessity, Arrowsmith suggested, men are sent to preach to men and women. The second reason Arrowsmith supplied for the necessity of preaching is found in the New Testament. There Paul speaks about preaching in 2 Corinthians 4:7 and says, "We have this treasure in earthen vessels, that the excellency of the power may be of God, and not of us."[15]

Thus the "problem" with preaching is itself the answer. The reliance on God and the work of His Spirit is not a reason to abandon preaching but is the reason for preaching. God deliberately chose a humble means that would amplify His own greatness. Burgess derived an identical lesson from 2 Corinthians 4:7 but also harks back to the picture of 1 Corinthians 3, where Paul reminds his readers that the preacher may sow and water, but God gives the increase.[16] As in the administration of the sacraments, preaching is not automatically effective. The Word, whether visible or audible, needs to be received by Spirit-given faith. And so, although preachers are described as coworkers with God (2 Cor. 6:1),[17] Burgess was quick to say that a minister may be faithful but have no success since "successe is Gods work, not the Ministers duty."[18]

"It is not the means, that works," Burroughs explained, "but God in the means." Again, "Suppose one come and preach the most powerful sermon that ever was, yet except God were pleased to go out with the Word, it would never work savingly to humble your souls."[19] Coming full circle, this does not make the training and study of the minister irrelevant or less important. Burgess wrote, "It's true (indeed) that the Parts and Abilities of one Minister, may be objectively better for Conversion, and more likely for profiting then another: They may propound stronger Arguments to convince the Conscience: They may set those Arguments home with greater life and vigour," but "God only is the efficient Cause of every good and perfect Gift."[20] Thomas Goodwin pointed out that this dependence on God

---

14. Arrowsmith, *Theanthropos*, 96.
15. Arrowsmith, *Theanthropos*, 97–98.
16. Burgess, *Spiritual Refining*, 497, 495.
17. Burgess, *Spiritual Refining*, 495.
18. Burgess, *Spiritual Refining*, 503; see esp. 500–503.
19. Burroughs, *Gospel-Fear*, 91.
20. Burgess, *Scripture Directory*, 87.

gives God all the glory: "He hath chosen preaching of the word, because it is the weakest means of all others, and therefore his power would the more appear unto his glory in it."[21]

God is therefore to receive glory at every point in the preaching of the gospel. He sent His Son, He sends the preachers, His word is spoken, and His power awakens sinners. He is thus glorified in the preaching of Jesus Christ, the savior of the world. "God only giveth the increase," says Burgess, "because of the deep pollution that is in every man, who is not only blind and deaf, but dead."[22] Again, "God only can give the encrease, because he only hath a soveraignty [sic] and power over the heart. Others may speak to the ear, propound Arguments to perswade; but to change the heart, to perswade the heart indeed, that God only can who made the heart.... And so, we Ministers are to look up to God, and you people, that God may be glorified."[23]

To quote Burgess again, "Successe is Gods work."[24] Preaching gives life only "by the operation of the holy Spirit."[25] Or as Rutherford put it, the benefit of the preaching rests in "the Spirit's working."

The need for the Spirit, however, was not a need simply in the moment of preaching but in the preparation and in the person of the preacher, too, for "the Spirit of God is the alone Sanctifier of all gifts and abilities."[26] The preacher's proper dependence on the Holy Spirit is negatively illustrated by the "many" who "have written Comments upon the Bible, that have been very learned men, yet from that sweet flower they have turned all to poison." Thus there "must necessarily be the Spirit of God, besides learning, First, to lead us into all truth. And then secondly, to sanctifie it to our own hearts in an experimental and powerfull manner." It is axiomatic for Burgess that "men may be very Orthodox, and yet know nothing of the work of grace upon their own souls."[27]

---

21. Goodwin, *Of the Constitution*, 11:362.
22. Burgess, *Scripture Directory*, 87.
23. Burgess, *Scripture Directory*, 86–87. Similar sentiments are stated explicitly by other divines. Reynolds, for example, quotes 1 Peter 1:12 as proof that the Holy Spirit is needed for effective preaching (*Works*, 2:148). But often God's help for faithful ministers is not discussed but merely assumed, though not ungratefully. In the preface of a popular work, Gouge mentions that it was difficult for him to find the time to "set down distinctly such points as by Gods assistance were uttered [from] out of the Pulpet." Gouge, *A Guide to Goe to God*, iii.
24. Burgess, *Spiritual Refining*, 502.
25. Featley, *Ancilla Pietatis*, 60.
26. Burgess, *Expository Comment*, 49.
27. Burgess, *Expository Comment*, 9.

Manuscripts, Notes, and Extemporary Preaching

In arguing that the Holy Spirit uses preaching, assembly members accepted that the Spirit is not tied to the use of that means. It was all the more obvious that the Spirit is not tied to one style of preaching. One could preach Christ and His redeeming benefits by dwelling on the text of Scripture or the doctrines of Scripture. One could also use different kinds of methods for preaching the sermon, delivering the message in an extemporary fashion, or with the use of notes, or with a full manuscript.

Extreme proponents of one form of preaching tended to be only on the fringes of the sort of puritans who were at the assembly. Prayer-book episcopalians criticized the godly not only for their extemporary prayers but also for extemporary sermons, although they did not often distinguish between extemporary in the sense of speaking without notes and extemporary in the sense of speaking without prior thought.[28] The godly complained about this kind of criticism and about the assumption that a sermon delivered without notes was delivered without adequate preparation: Alexander Henderson had heard sermons delivered without notes and thought that nowhere was preaching "more spirituall" or with "lesse carnall liberty."[29]

On the other side of the divide, there were those who criticized anyone who used a sermon manuscript: "You read your Sermons out of a Paper; therefore you have not the Spirit." Richard Baxter, a contemporary of the assembly, responded to this remark with his usual candor: "I use notes as much as any man, when I take pains: and as little as any man when I am lazy, or busie, and have not the leisure to prepare. It's easier to us to preach three Sermons without Notes, then one with them."[30]

Arguments against sermon notes were not always so extreme. Popular preaching manuals warned against preaching from full manuscripts, as it could hinder the art of persuasion.[31] And after fighting so hard to get rid of the reading of the church's homilies, some of the godly developed an allergy to reading their own sermons too. As Baxter commented, the creation of a sermon manuscript was time consuming; depending on who was in authority, it could also be dangerous since their enemies could use

---

28. For the distinction: "I know indeed some that preach *without writing;* but their preaching is not therefore *Extempore; extempore* is *unthought,* not *unwritten*" (Joseph Glanville, a contemporary of the assembly, arguing for unwritten sermons in *Seasonable Reflections and Discourses in Order to the Conviction & Cure of the Scoffing, & Infidelity of a Degenerate Age* [London, 1676], 111).

29. A. Henderson, *The Government and Order of the Church of Scotland* ([Edinburgh], 1641), To the Reader.

30. R. Baxter, *One Sheet for the Ministry against the Malignants of All Sorts* (London, 1657), 13–14.

31. Hunt, *Art of Hearing*, 131–34.

sermon notes to incriminate the godly, or the godly could use sermon notes to incriminate others.[32]

Arnold Hunt observes that preachers tended to use more than one method, and a full sermon manuscript was used most often for special occasions.[33] This is no doubt correct. Some preached from notes that ranged from bare sketches to comprehensive outlines, as can be seen with Robert Baillie, Thomas Gataker, William Gouge, and Jeremiah Burroughs, to name a few. Baillie's sermon notes survive in manuscript form. Thomas Gataker, by his own admission, wrote and retained sermon notes substantial enough for him to be able to reconstruct sermons many years after they were first delivered. Gouge's notes are extant, for his "commentary" on Hebrews is a lightly edited edition of his sermon notes. Conversely, Jeremiah Burroughs claims in his expositions of Hosea that he attempted to abbreviate his preached notes for his printed volumes: "You have these Lectures as they were taken from me in preaching, I perused the notes, but I could not bring the style to that succinctnesse that I desired, except I should have wrote all over again, which I had no time to doe:…You have them as I preached them, without any considerable alteration."[34]

Nonetheless, while many used notes, it should not be overlooked that there is surviving evidence that assembly members routinely wrote out their weekly sermons, word for word, as did Cornelius Burges and Herbert Palmer.[35]

All the evidence points to a conviction among the assembly's members that a thoughtful theology of preaching allows for, or even advocates, a happy use of human study by the Holy Spirit. It also suggests that the assembly did not insist that candidates and ministers advocate a particular approach to homiletics. Reform of the pulpit, and the preaching of solid sermons, required a commitment to a prayerful dependence on the Spirit who would, in turn, bless the preacher's work at his writing desk and preaching desk—whatever his method of delivery might be.

---

32. See Anthony Burgess's thinly veiled comments in *Vindiciae Legis: or, A Vindication of the Morall Law and the Covenants* (London, 1647), 78.

33. Hunt, *Art of Hearing*, 134–35. Edward Reynolds insisted in printing a sermon that he sent it to the press "without altering any one line or period of what I then delivered" (*Pastoral Office*, Epistle Dedicatory).

34. For Baillie, see, for example, EUL La iii 109, 543, sermons and papers; and NLS Adv. MS 20.6.4. For Gataker, see his *Marriage Duties Briefely Couched Together* (London, 1620), Epistle Dedicatory; and T. Gataker, *Two Funeral Sermons Much of One and the Same Subject; to Wit, the Benefit of Death* (London, 1620), Epistle Dedicatory. For William Gouge, see Hunt, *Art of Hearing*, 151–54. For J. Burroughs, *An Exposition of the Prophesie of Hosea begun in Divers Lectures upon the First Three Chapters* (London, 1652), To the Reader.

35. For Burges, see, for example, CUL Add.6164 and 6165; Bodl. MS Lat.th.g.2, pp. 87–131; for Palmer, see, for example, CUL Add.3860 and 3861.

CHAPTER 14

Conclusions

If you did delight in the Word of God, you would delight in the Ministers and Ambassadors of the Word lawfully commissioned by Christ: For the great work of the Ministry is to expound and apply the Word; and therefore if you dis-respect the godly learned lawful Ministry of the Word, you take no delight in the Word. They that delight in the Word, will bee at any cost to bring the Word to their congregations, they will part with thousands of gold and silver, rather than with the Word.

—Edmund Calamy

The Westminster Assembly's attempt to reform preaching and preachers in England concluded, or collapsed, in the spring of 1653 with the end of the Long Parliament. Through the remainder of the 1650s, the reforms the assembly had hoped would become mandatory became, at most, voluntary. And yet its members had done a great deal to help facilitate the lawful commissioning or ordination of ministers for what Edmund Calamy, a leading figure at the assembly and a notable preacher in his own day, would call "the great work of the Ministry."[1] What Calamy had in mind was the expounding and applying of the Scriptures. This was the special task of the ambassadors of Jesus Christ, the one the assembly termed the "king and head of his church."[2]

In terms that the Westminster Assembly's own members might appreciate, *God's Ambassadors* has offered a kind of plain-style account of the assembly's own reforming efforts and shared commitments regarding preaching. This volume is still some steps removed from a full reconstruction of a puritan theology of the pulpit, which would need to draw on a wider range of sources than the selections employed here. Hopefully such a work will eventually appear and will draw heavily on surviving manuscript sermons and not merely on print productions. Surely any such study

---

1. Calamy, *Godly Mans Ark*, 70.
2. WCF, 30.1.

should also avoid drawing generalizations about parish preaching from special events such as parliamentary and assize sermons. As deserving as they are of additional study, they are poor samples to determine Sabbath preaching content, as few preachers could resist the opportunities afforded by a bully pulpit.

God's Ambassadors only scratches the surface of the assembly's own work, its debates, and the writings of its members, focusing narrowly on the related topics of preachers and preaching. Yet even within these boundaries we can nonetheless draw some conclusions. One purpose of this study was to outline relevant aspects of the intellectual and ecclesiastical prehistory of the assembly, not only to set the scene for the assembly's own reforms but also to discover historical precedents to the assembly's theology of preaching. Looking back, it appears that the Westminster Assembly evidences a historical reliance on, or at least a historical connection with, previous puritan and Reformed views of the pulpit. This comes as no surprise to historians of seventeenth-century puritanism, even if this continuity in pulpit theory (and in theology) has been somewhat understated by historians of the sixteenth-century Reformation.

In viewing the assembly's statements about preaching in the context of the 1640s in particular, we can posit a shift of focus on the part of most Westminster divines. Prior to the civil war, Archbishop Laud and his alleged popery were enemy number one, in part because of Laud's restrictions on preaching. To be fair, in principle Laud appears to have been opposed to the preaching of lecturers (unbeneficed preachers) only, and for the reason that lecturers ministered outside the bounds of the church and therefore could not be monitored or disciplined (a point that most Reformed churches also would see as a serious problem). Lecturers also had the freedom to lead meetings without reference to the church's liturgy (a point about which most Reformed churches today would express some ambivalence).[3] Nonetheless, the majority of lecturers were Reformed; thus, Laud's ecclesiastical policy against lecturers effectively targeted Reformed preaching in particular—a fact that would hardly have troubled him. Once the war began, however, a myriad of religious fanatics and self-appointed preachers began to feature more prominently in London and elsewhere, and the Westminster Assembly's members diverted their attention to address the problems of sectarian preaching.

The significance of this observation lies in the fact that the rise of the radical lay preachers appears to have only intensified the divines' insistence on trained and ordained men in pulpits, a proper pulpit theology, and the

---

3. Davies, *Caroline Captivity*, ch. 4.

ordinary means of grace. Although the assembly saw varying degrees of antipathy to the sects among its members, and while most congregationalists had a greater tolerance for unconventional means of ministry than did most presbyterians, all parties at the assembly opposed what they saw as the worst excesses of religious radicalism. Here the prominent point to note is that the assembly was aware of the surrounding religious currents but chose to stand against them, only intensifying its vision of the preacher and his preaching.

The reason for this refusal is undoubtedly rooted in the conviction among the divines that the Bible provided a theology of the pulpit. God appointed extraordinary ambassadors in the form of the apostles and continues to appoint ordinary "ambassadors of the Word" in the church in the form of ministers or preachers.[4] These men are set aside, trained, and ordained for a special function. The only setting where an every-member ministry was allowable was at an assembly such as the one in the abbey where, aside from a small bevy of politicians, every member was in fact an ordained minister. Thus, though the radical sects wanted every sheep to be a shepherd,[5] the divines, like their forebears, insisted that God appointed some to be teachers and some to be taught. The divines did not always express this felicitously, as they occasionally divided up the church, without flattering either group, into "ministers and people" or "ministers and Christians."[6] They were, however, always clear that God had given the church preachers, and the church was to be thankful for them.

The backdrop of earlier reform movements and opposition during the 1630s and then the 1640s allows historians to see more concretely the way in which the assembly's members emphasized preaching. It is a truism that puritans highly esteemed their pulpits. This study highlights for the first time the extent to which the assembly went in promoting godly preachers and improved preaching. One needs only to consider the thousands of examinations conducted by the assembly and the fact that it took two days or more for each candidate to sit his examination (or to stand, when it came time for preaching); that each candidate had to be discussed and approved by the full assembly; and that some candidates generated extensive, repeated debates in the assembly's plenary sessions. In addition to working with individual candidates, the assembly spent many weeks refining a process of examination and setting up a new model for assessment and ordination in the Church of England as well as adding directions for preachers in its

---

4. Calamy, *Godly Mans Ark*, 70.
5. See Edmund Calamy's concern about the sects in *MPWA*, 2:242 (Oct. 30, 1643; Sess. 84).
6. See, for example, WLC, answer 54; and Burroughs, *Saints' Happiness*, 260.

Directory for Public Worship. In promoting their model and in involving themselves in the process of quality control, the assembly was also willing to risk internal division in their own debating chamber as well as conflict with the House of Commons. These actions, documents, and exchanges add not only color and texture but also depth to our understanding of the Westminster Assembly and its attempt to reform the English pulpit.

The specifics of the assembly's vision for preaching can be seen in part in its various activities and directories. This study has tried to bring the whole together and then, moving into the realm of the theoretical, has endeavored to identify marks of a pulpit theology shared by assembly members. It has almost become a convention in studies of puritan preaching to emphasize that godly sermons were experimental—passionate, personal, and probing. But while the earnestness, style, and delivery of godly sermons was obvious to contemporaries and is still accessible in surviving sermons, these characteristics of the sermon speak only indirectly to the measure of the minister that the assembly wanted to see in the pulpit and to the kind of sermons that assembly members wanted to hear preached. Here is one of the places where this study finds an opening in the ongoing conversation about preaching and puritanism to insert a point about the theology of preaching drawn from comments on preaching and preachers by the assembly's own members. And what emerges from the writings of the assembly and its members on the subject of preaching is a set of clearly defined essentials, summarized in chapter 7 and in the third part of this book.

If assembly members were not completely unified about how a minister was to become ordained, they at least agreed that the pastoral preaching ministry was a special public calling that needed the recognition of the church and that the only men eligible for such a call needed to be godly, Christlike in their character, and trained students at Christ's school. The preaching of these preachers, it was also decided, must not vary from the Word of God and in one way or another must preach Christ, relying on God's Spirit for a blessing on their labors.

Assembly members were also agreed about how parishioners are to receive the preaching: They are to hear faithful sermons as the Word of God. They are to depend on preaching as the most ordinary and effective means of grace, provided it is heard with faith and blessed by God. Unfortunately, if preaching is so powerful, then in a very real sense the preacher's troubles have just begun. In a special sermon delivered to his fellow divines, Edward Reynolds warned that if they were correct about the preacher's duties, then life would involve hard work. The fact is, there are "noe conditions of life which are not subject to temptations of selfe-seeking." Thus, if there is to be "soe much preaching...we must resolve to live a tedious life. Therfore pray that God would power [pour] out a large spirit of selfe denyall."[7] It was the goal of the assembly not only to find preachers but to find preachers who would deny themselves in order to better serve Christ and His church.

The focus of this book has been on the debates and writings of the Westminster Assembly and its members. Its intention is to describe the reformation that the assembly effected and the pulpit theology of its members. Nonetheless, it seems very likely that this study also offers an entryway into the minds of godly contemporaries. The commitments articulated by the assembly's members and Scottish commissioners resonate with the writings of other Reformers in the mid-seventeenth century, and the members of the gathering were viewed with reverence and respect by godly generations that followed them. This story is part of the larger narrative of puritan history with its seasons of suffering and moments of glory.

The Westminster Assembly is also a chapter in the histories of the churches of England and Scotland, but the assembly's work of pulpit reform was (like a surprising number of the assembly's undertakings) especially focused on the Church of England. The gathering did not examine ministers for the Church of Scotland. During every debate over a preacher for the English church, Scottish divines were silent. They strongly favored a Reformed ministry in England, but we can only guess what the commissioners thought about the frequent interruptions (not always explained in the assembly's minutes) to plenary session debates to affirm the judgment of the examining committee in recommending a man for ministry or to discuss the lot of a parish minister or ministerial candidate whose case presented particular difficulties.

In hindsight, at least with respect to the reform of the English pulpit, the most curious silence in the assembly's minutes was not due to the busyness of the scribes but to the shortsightedness of the assembly as a whole. In its first communication to Parliament, the assembly had declared that the combination of displacements caused by war and ejections initiated by Parliament had "suddenly" created a situation with "such a scarcity of able and faithfull Ministers, that it will be to little purpose to cast out such as are unable, idle or scandalous."[8] In this comment the assembly came as close as it ever would to admitting that as bad as the existing ministry might be in much of the church, it could still in some cases be better than nothing at all.

A "scandalous" man, of course, needed to be ejected (although there are grounds to question whether scandal sometimes subtly elided with political

---

7. *MPWA*, 3:676–77 (Oct. 8, 1645; Sess. 514).
8. *MPWA*, 5:11 (Doc. 1); see also *MPWA*, 5:177 (Doc. 61).

incorrectness—such a failure on the part of an otherwise good minister to reconcile himself to the Solemn League and Covenant). In advocating the dismissal of those who were truly scandalous in life or doctrine, the assembly did well: it would seem that Christians should hold out hope even for ministers in such conditions but that the ministry is not the place for people to work out very basic problems in living and believing.

Nonetheless, if ejection for scandal is defensible, what about other varieties of ministerial defects? It seems possible to envisage an "idle" man becoming more determined to do his work well or an "unable" man be trained to do his work better. It is perhaps in its treatment of the unmotivated and incompetent candidates and ministers that we see the Westminster Assembly's greatest failure. The would-be reformers of previous decades had attempted to retool the reading ministry and make it a preaching ministry, to inspire substandard preachers not only by delivering powerful lectures but also through prophesyings. Their efforts at training their peers and protégés were frequently opposed and then suppressed by the arch-episcopal hierarchy and by unsympathetic monarchs. But those frustrating hindrances were removed even before the start of the first civil war. Under the rule of the Long Parliament there was unprecedented opportunity to resume these activities, and while a study of prophesying during the 1640s is, to my knowledge, still wanting, I suspect that these methods of continuing education experienced something of a revival during the civil wars. Nonetheless, the Westminster Assembly itself made no formal use of prophesyings and never advocated for their use in territory held by Parliament. It goes without saying that in many cases attempts to train ministers would have been rejected or have proved ineffective. Nonetheless, there was a potentially productive route to reforming the Church of England that members of the assembly knew either from their own experience or from godly legend, and they did not take it.

The side effects resulting from this lack of foresight were already evident by 1643 and should have been flagged by the assembly. The gathering could have developed or advocated programs for the rehabilitation of the idle or at least for the training of the unable. Instead they supported Parliament's binary approach to ejection and replacement. The painful payback for this approach, continued throughout the 1640s and 1650s, came at the Restoration in 1660. At that point ministers who had been turned out of their churches turned on those who favored the purge of pulpits in the preceding two decades.

One of the curiosities of John Bunyan's *Pilgrim's Progress* is the lack of development in its cast of characters. With few exceptions, the bad stay bad and the good remain good—an observation that is especially true with respect to those persons cast by Bunyan in the role of teachers and leaders. While members of the assembly did not appear to have a limited perspective on the great good that sovereign grace could do in the lives of their congregants, they seem to have held out insufficient hope for their peers. It is not only, then, a contrast in terms of approach between the assembly and their puritan forebears that is striking. It is also a contrast in terms of hopefulness that is arresting to the student of the assembly's reform. The gathering held out great expectations for the reform of its parishioners through the impact of better preachers. But where were its hopes for the preachers themselves?

Perhaps if the church reforms effected during the civil war had stuck—if the 1660s had not been so very different from the 1640s and 1650s—the assembly may have eventually filled the pulpits of England with a higher caliber of preaching, drawing heavily on recruits from the newly reformed colleges of Oxford and Cambridge. As it was, the Westminster Assembly created a kind of microclimate for godly preachers and preaching for a twenty-year period—a brief thaw in the ecclesiastical ice age that the godly experienced under Whitgift, Laud, and others and that returned with a vengeance with the Restoration of Charles II and the retributive justice of his bishops.

What the assembly did manage to do was to communicate a vision for ministry that was perpetuated, if not in the Church of England as a whole, at least among the dissenting communities in England and in presbyterian and congregationalist communions in Scotland, Ireland, and the North American colonies. It is in those churches that the directories were most warmly received, where the Westminster Assembly's standards for preachers and preaching continued to be respected, and where a continuing reform of the pulpit may still be useful today.

Epilogue

What was true of pulpit theology at the assembly was true for presbyterians and congregationalists for the next two centuries. Preaching held a central place in services of worship and in personal piety, thus providing a unifying principle among English dissenters, Scottish and Irish presbyterians, and colonial puritans. Even during the Evangelical Revival or First Great Awakening, most of the revival preachers of Britain and America, now including evangelical Anglicans, were trained and ordained preachers (with Welsh-born Howell Harris the prominent exception). Preaching was regarded as central to Christian life and worship, and the preaching of God's ambassadors was still seen as the ordinary means that God extraordinarily blessed.

This is what changed with the Second Great Awakening. During this movement Charles Finney introduced new measures and means with his anxious bench, and D. L. Moody, who was admirably gifted as a communicator, saw no need for anyone to train, ordain, or send him. Moody sent himself. Of course, similar things happened during and after the Westminster Assembly. The difference was that during the time of the assembly almost all Protestants considered such measures radical; during the nineteenth century they became mainstream.

If historians can be permitted a few observations on the church of our own day, then I would note that the insistence on the importance and usefulness of preaching in the 1640s and in subsequent centuries may prove to be a useful reference point in current discussions about teaching and gospel communication in which preaching often finds itself on a poor footing. Church members sometimes prefer simply to read their Bibles or find a sermon at home and not trouble with the commute to a corporate worship service. Some people do not like being "preached at." Others, not without good grounds for their complaints, have unhappy memories of rowdy street preachers or unsavory televangelists.

So is it time to change the means used to present the message? Pastors have taken up the challenge and have largely eliminated the second service (and second sermon), opting instead for home Bible studies and community groups. Changing pastoral practice may in fact collate with trends in seminary curricula, as many centers for pastoral training provide courses on gospel content and gospel communication without offering the potential preacher a pulpit theology. This in turn may explain why they are so willing to give up preaching in exchange for other means of teaching and persuasion.

It is often said that a great theme of the Reformation was "semper reformanda," or "always being reformed." Protestant Reformers and their puritan followers held that a healthy church would always be continuously reformed by the Spirit of God through the Word of God. In their historical context, a step forward involved a look backward. While the Reformers were familiar with the medieval church and learned from the Schoolmen when possible, they most frequently harkened back to the sources: the church fathers and, ultimately, to the apostles and prophets.

Maybe the largest step forward that the church could take today would also involve a look backward. From the first generation of Reformers to the Westminster Assembly and, arguably, for two hundred years following the assembly, most Protestants outside the Lutheran and Anglican communions (and many in those communions too!) centered their worship and their lives on the words of God's ambassadors. Whether the ambassadors were extraordinary or ordinary, in any usage of these words, preaching was seen to be the ordinary means of grace for the believer, to be used by God in extraordinary ways.

The same understanding of preaching was held by a one-time scorner of the institution, Augustine of Hippo, who in the opening lines of his *Confessions* echoes the questions of Romans 10: "*sed quis te invocat nesciens. An potius invocaris, ut sciaris? Quomodo autem invocabunt, in quem non crediderunt? Aut quomodo credent sine praedicante?*"[1] It may serve the church well to ask these questions once again: How shall we call on him in whom we have not believed? And how shall we believe in him of whom we have not heard? And how shall we hear without a preacher? And how will they preach, except they be sent? These are not, of course, only Augustine's questions, Calvin's questions, or the assembly's questions. If they were only that, we could dismiss them or say with Herbert Palmer that "if the authority of Mr. Calvin shall make my people believe my word I would rather have had my mouth stoped." But these are the questions of the apostle Paul and, as Palmer rightly assumed, the name of such a man does give authority.

---

1. Augustine, *Confessions*, Book I, section i.

APPENDIX 1

The Duties of a Minister

What follows comprises an excerpt from an early list of votes produced by the assembly on the subject of church government, an urtext for the assembly's eventual Directory for Church Government. In this appendix the original manuscript emendations are not noted as they are in the Oxford edition of the Westminster Assembly's papers.[1]

Ordinary & Perpetuall Officers.

1. Pastor.

> Sess. 87. Nov. 2: Resol.: That there is such an ordinarie & perpetuall Office in the Church as a Pastor. Proved Jer. 3:15, 16, 17 (prophesieing of the time of the Gospel); 1 Pet. 5:2, 3, 4.

> Res.: Eph. 4:11, 12, 13 shall be added to prove that if[2] is such an office & that it is perpetuall.

That which the Pastor is to do from God to the people.

Reading.

> Sess. 88. Nov. 3: Res. N. C.: That the publick reading of the word in the congregation is an holy ordinance in Gods Church.

> Res.: That this shall be added to the former vote, Although there follow no immediat explication of that which is read.

> Sess. 89. Nov. 6. Res.: That the publick reading of the Scripture belongs to the pastors office.

---

1. This text is excerpted from *MPWA*, 5:55–57 (Doc. 19).
2. Read "it."

Sess. 90. Nov. 7: Ord.: 1. That the Priests and Levites in the Jewish Church were trusted with the publick reading of the word, as is proved. Deut. 31:9, 10, 11; Nehem. 8:1, 2, & 13.

Ord.: 2. That the ministers of the Gospell have as ample a charge & commission to dispense the word as well as other ordinances, as the Priests & Levites under the Law. Proved Isai. 66:21; Matt. 23:34 where our Saviour intituleth the officers of the New Testament whom he would send forth by the same names of the Teachers of the old.

Ord.: These propositions shall be brought to prove, That therefor (the Duty being of a morall nature) it followeth by just consequence, that the public reading of the Scriptures belongs to the pastors office.

Preaching.
Sess. 89. Nov. 6: Res.: That it is the office of a Pastor to feed the Flock by preaching of the Word according to which he is to teach, convince, reprove, exhort, & comfort. 1 Tim. 3:2; 2 Tim. 3:16, 17; Tit. 1:9.

Res.: That Catechising, which is a plain laying down of the first principles of the Oracles of God, Heb. 5:12, or of the Doctrine of Christ is a part of preaching pertaining to the Pastors office.

The Dispensation of other Divine Mysteries.
Sess. 91. Nov. 8: Ord.: That it is the office of a Pastor to feed the Flock by the dispensation of other Divine mysteries, proved by 1 Cor. 4:1, 2. The administration of the Sacraments. Matt. 28:19, 20; Mark 16:15, 16; 1 Cor. 11:23, 24, 25, with 1 Cor. 10:16.

Ord.: That he is to bless the people from God, Numb. 6:23, 24, 25, 26, with Rev. 1:4, 5 (where the same blessings and persons from whom they come are expressly mentioned), & Isai. 66:21 where under the names of Priests & Levites to be continued under the Gospell, are meant Evangelicall Pastors who therefore are by office to bless the people. Deut. 10:8; 2 Cor. 13:14; Eph. 1:2.

That which the Pastor is to perform in
the behalf and name of the people to God is

Ord.: To pray for and with his flock as the mouth of the people unto God, proved Act. 6:2, 3, 4; & Acts 20:36, where preaching and praying are joyned as severall parts of the same office. So James 5:14, 15 the office the Elder, that is, the Pastor, is to pray for the sick even in private, to which a blessing is especially promised, much more therefor ought he to performe this in the publick execution of his office as apart thereof, 1 Cor. 14:15, 16.

Ruling.

Sess. 92. Nov. 9: Ord.: That the Pastor hath a ruling power over the Flock as a Pastor. 1 Tim. 5:17; Act. 20:17, 18; 1 Thess. 5:12; Heb. 13:7, 17.

Ord.: That what power the Pastor hath in Discipline & Government, either singlie & alone, or joyntly with others, the assemblie hath thought fit to forbear to set forth at the present untill the particular parts of Discipline & Government come into consideration, so that whatever his power therein is, ought to be saved unto him untill the Discipline it self be debated, and his share therein distinctly set out.

Ord.: That it belongs to the Pastor to take care of the poor. Acts 11:30; 4:34, 35, 36, 37 & 6:2, 3, 4; 1 Cor. 16:1, 2, 3, 4; Gal. 2:9, 10.

Teacher or Doctor.

Sess. 95. Nov. 14: Ord.: That the Scripture doth hold out the name and Title of teacher as well as of the Pastor, 1 Cor. 12:28; Eph. 4:11.

Sess. 96. Nov. 15. Ord.: That Pastors and Teachers are both equall ministers of the word.

Sess. 97. Nov. 16. Ord.: That Pastors and Teachers are both ministers of the Word, & have power of administration of the Sacraments.

Sess. 100. Nov. 21. Ord.: 1. That there be different Gifts & diverse excercises according to those Guifts in the ministers of the word. proved, Rom. 12:6, 7, 8; 1 Cor. 12:4, 5, 6, 7.

Ord.; Res.; Ord.:[3] 2. That Different Guifts may meet in, & accordingly be exercised by one and the same minister, 1 Cor. 14:3; 2 Tim. 4:2; Tit. 1:9.

---

3. Referring to two different parts of the vote and the Scripture proofs.

Ord.; Res.; Res.:[4] 3. Where there be severall ministers in the same Congregation they may be designed to severall Imployments according to the different guifts wherin each of them doth most excell. Rom. 12:6, 7, 8; 1 Pet. 4:10, 11.

Ord.: 4. He that doth more excell in exposition of Scripture, in teaching sound Doctrine, & in convincing gainsayers, then he doth in Application, & is accordingly Imployed therein, may be called a Teacher or Doctor. The places alleged by the notation of the Word, do prove the proposition.

Ord.: 5. A Teacher or Doctor is of most excellent use in Schooles and universities, as of old in the Schools of the Prophets, & at Jerusalem where Gamaliel & others taught as Doctors.

Ord.; Ord.:[5] 6. Where there is but one Minister in a particular Congregation, he is to perform so farr as he is able the whole work of the ministery as appears 2 Tim. 4:2; Tit. 1:9, befor alleged 1 Tim. 6:2.

---

4. Referring to two different parts of the vote and the Scripture proofs.
5. Referring to the vote and the Scripture proofs.

APPENDIX 2

The Directory for Ordination

The directory was first authored in 1644 and went through successive editions before being incorporated into the Directory for Church Government, which itself went through multiple editions. In this appendix the original manuscript emendations are not noted as they are in the Oxford edition of the Westminster Assembly's papers.[1]

> To The Right honourable the Lords & Commons
> assembled in Parliament.
> The humble Advice of the Assembly of Divines
> now sitting at Westminster,
> Concerning the Doctrinal part of Ordination of Ministers

1. No man ought to take upon him the Office of a Minister of the Word without a Lawfull Calling. Joh. 3:27; Rom. 10:14, 15; Jer. 14:14; Heb. 5:4.

2. Ordination is allwaies to bee continued in the Church. Tit. 1:5; 1 Tim. 5:21–22.

3. Ordination is the solemne setting apart of a person to some publique Church Office. Num. 8:10, 11, 14, 19, 22; Act. 6:3, 5, 6.

4. Every Minister of the Word is to bee Ordained by Imposition of hands, and prayer, with fasting, by those Preaching Presbyters to whom it doth belong. 1 Tim. 5:22; Act. 14:23; Act. 13:3.

5. The power of Ordering the whole work of Ordination is in the whole Presbytery. (which when it is over more Congregations than One, whether

---

1. This text is excerpted from *MPWA*, 5:63–69 (Doc. 20).

those Congregations bee fixed or not, in regard of Officers or Members, it is indifferent, as to the point of Ordination.) 1 Tim. 4:14.

6. It is agreeable to the Word, and very expedient, that such as are to bee Ordained Ministers bee designed to some particular Church, or other Ministerial Charg. Act. 14:23; Tit. 1:5; Act. 20:17 & ver. 28.

7. Hee that is to bee Ordained, must bee duely qualified both for life & Ministerial Abilities, according to the Rules of the Apostle in 1 Tim. 3:2, 3, 4, 5, 6; Tit. 1:5, 6, 7, 8, 9.

8. Hee is to bee examined, and approved by them by whom hee is to bee Ordained. 1 Tim. 3:7, 10; 1 Tim. 5:22.

9. No man is to bee Ordained a Minister for a particular Congregacion, if they of that Congregacion can shew just cause of Exception against him. 1 Tim. 3:2; Tit. 1:7.

10. Preaching Presbyters orderly associated, either in Citties, or in neighbouring Villages, are those to whom the Imposition of hands doth appertaine, for those Congregations within their bounds respectively. 1 Tim. 4:14.

11. In Extraordinary Cases something extraordinary may bee done, until a settled Order can bee had: yet keeping as neere as possibly may bee to the Rule. 2 Chron. 29:34, 35, 36; 2 Chron. 30:2, 3, 4, 5.

12. There is at this time (as wee humbly conceave) an extraordinary occasion for a way of Ordination, for the present supply of Ministers.

To the Right honourable the Lords and Commons
assembled in Parliament.
The humble Advice of the Assembly of Divines
now sitting at Westminster,
concerning a Directory for Ordination of Ministers.

It being manifest by the Word of God that no man ought to take upon him the Office of a Minister of the Gospel untill he bee lawfully Called, & Ordained thereunto; and that the Work of Ordination is to bee performed with all due care, wisdom, gravity, & solemnity, Wee humbly tender these Direccions as requisite to bee observed.

1. Hee that is to bee Ordained, beeing either nominated by the people, or otherwise commended to the Presbyterie, for any place, must address himselfe to the Presbytery, & bring with him a Testimonial of his takeing of the Covenant of the 3 Kingdomes, of his dilligence & proficiency in his studies, what Degrees hee hath taken in the University, & what hath been the time of his abode there; and withall, of his age, which is to bee 24 yeares; but especially, of his life and conversation.

2. Which being considered by the Presbytery, they are to proceed to enquire touching the grace of God in him, and whether hee bee of such holyness of Life as is requisite in a Minister of the Gospel, and to Examine him touching his Learning & sufficiency, and touching the Evidence of his Calling to the holy Ministry, and in particular his faire and direct calling to that place.

The Rules for Examination are these.

1. That the Party examined bee dealt with in a Brotherly way, with mildness of spirit, and with special respect to the gravity, modesty, and quality of every one.

2. Hee shalbee examined touching his skill in the Original tongues, and the trial to bee made by reading the Hebrew & Greek Testaments & rendring some portion of them in to Latine. And if hee bee defective in them, enquiry shalbee made the most strictly after his other Learning, and whether hee hath Skill in Logick and Philosophy.

3. What Authors in Divinity he hath read, & is best acquainted with; and trial shalbee made of his Knowledg in the chiefe grounds of Religion, & of his ability to defend the Orthodox Doctrine contained in them against all unsound & erroneous opinions, especially those of the present Age; of his skill in the sense & meaning of such places of Scripture as shalbee proposed unto him in Cases of Conscience, in the Chronology of Scripture, & the Ecclesiastical History.

4. If hee hath not before preached in publique, with approbacion of such as are able to judg, he shall at a competent time assigned him, expound before the Presbytery such a place of Scripture as shalbee given him.

5. Hee shal, with in a competent time also, frame a Discourse in Latine upon such a Common Place, or Controversy in Divinity, as

shalbee assigned him; and exhibite to the Presbytery such Theses as expresse the summe thereof, & maintaine a Dispute upon them.

6. Hee shal preach before the People, the Presbytery, or some and the Ministers of the Word, appointed by them, beeing present.

7. The Proportion of his guifts in relation to the place unto which hee is called, shalbee considered.

8. Besides the trial of his guifts in Preaching, hee shall undergo an Examination in the premisses, two several dayes; and more, if the Presbytery shall judg it necessary.

9. And as for him that hath bin formerly Ordained a Minister, & is to bee removed to another charg, Hee shall bring a Testimonial of his Ordination, & of his Abilities, & Conversation, whereupon his fittnes for that place shalbee tryed by his preaching there, and (if it shalbee judged necessary) by a further examination of him.

3. In all which hee being approved, hee is to bee sent to the Church where he is to serve, there to preach 3 several dayes and to converse with the people, that they may have trial of his guifts for their edification, and may have time and occasion to inquire into, and better know his life & conversation.

4. In the last of those 3 dayes appointed for the trial of his gifts in preaching, there shalbee sent from the Presbytery unto the Congregation, a Publique Intimacion in writeing, which shalbee publiquely read before the People, & after affixed to the church dore, To signify that such a day, a competent number of the members of that Congregation nominated by themselves, shall appear before the Presbytery, to give their consent and approbation to such a man to bee their Minister, or otherwise to putt in, with all Christian discretion & meeknes, what exception they have against him. And if upon the day appointed there bee no just exceptions against him, but the people give their consent, the Presbytery shall proceed to Ordination.

5. Upon the day appointed for Ordination, which is to be performed in that church where he that is to bee Ordained is to serve, a solemn Fast shalbee kept by the Congregacion, that they may more earnestly joyne in prayer for a blessing upon the Ordinance of Christ, & the Labours of his servant for their good. The Presbytery shall come to the place, or at least 3 or 4 Ministers of the Word shalbee sent thither from the Presbytery; of which,

THE DIRECTORY FOR ORDINATION

one appointed by the Presbytery, shal preach to the people concerning the Office & dutie of the Ministers of Christ, and how the people ought to receave & esteem them for the Workes sake.

6. After the Sermon, the Minister who hath preached, shall, in the face of the Congregacion, demand of him who is now to bee Ordained, concerning his Faith in Christ Jesus, & his perswasion of the trueth of the Reformed Religion according to Scripture, his syncere intentions & ends in desireing to enter into this calling, his dilligence in prayer, reading, meditation, preaching, ministering the Sacraments, Discipline, and doing all Ministerial duties towards his Charg; his zeale and faithfulness in maintaineing the trueth of the Gospel, and unity of the Church against error & schism; his care that himself & his family may bee unblameable & examples to the flock; his willingnes in humility & meekenes of spirit, to submitt unto the Admonitions of his Brethren, & Discipline of the Church; and his resolution to continue in his duty against all troubles & persecution.

7. In all which haveing declared himself, prosessed his willingnes, & promised his endeavors, by the help of God, the Minister likewise shall demand of the people concerning their willingnes to receave and acknowledg him as the Minister of Christ, and to obey & submitt unto him as haveing rule over them in the Lord, and to maintaine, encourage & assist him in all the parts of his Office.

8. Which beeing mutually promised by the people, the Presbytery, or the Ministers sent from them for Ordination shall solemnly sett him apart to the Office & work of the Ministry by laying their hands on him, which is to be accompanied with a short prayer, or Blessing, to this effect:

> Thankfully acknowledging the great mercy of God in sending Jesus Christ for the redemption of his people, & for his Ascension to the right hand of God the Father, and thence powring out his spirit, & giveing guifts to men, Apostles, Evangelists, Prophets, Pastors, & Teachers, for the gathering & building up of his Church, and, for fitting & inclining this man to this great Work; to intreat him to fill him with his holy spirit, to give[?] him (whom in his name wer thus sett apart to this holy service) to fullfill the work of his Ministry in all things, that he may both save himself and the people committed to his Charg.

9. This, or the like forme of prayer, or Blessing beeing ended, let the Minister who preached, breifly exhort him to consider the greatnes of his Office

& work, the danger of negligence both to himself & his people, the blessing which will accompany his faithfullnes, in this Life & that to come. And withall, exhort the People to carry themselves to him as to their Minister in the Lord, according to their solemne promise made before: and so, by prayer commending both him & his flock to the grace of God, after the singing of a Psalme, let the Assembly bee dismissed with a Blessing.

10. If a Minister bee designed to a Congregacion, who hath formerly bin Ordained Presbyter, according to the Forme of Ordination which hath bin in the Church of England, which wee hold for substance to bee valide, and not to bee disclaimed by any who have receaved it; then, there beeing a cautious proceeding in matter of Examinacion, let him bee admitted without any New Ordination.

11. And in case any person already Ordained Minister in Scotland, or in any other Reformed Church, bee designed to a Congregation in England, Hee is to bring from that Church to the Presbytery here, within which that Congregacion is, a sufficient Testimonial of his Ordinacion, of his life & conversation while hee lived with them, and of the Causes of his Removeall: and to undergoe such a triall of his fittnes & sufficiency, and to have the same course held with him in other particulars as is sett down in the Rule immediately going before, touching Examination, & Admission.

12. That Records bee carefully kept in the several Presbyteries, of the names of the persons Ordained, with their Testimonials, the time and place of their Ordinacion, of the Presbyters who did impose hands upon them, and of the Charg to which they are appointed.

13. That no mony, or guift of what kind so ever, shall bee receaved from the person to bee Ordained, or from any on his behalf, for Ordination, or ought else belonging to it, by any of the Presbytery, or any appertaineing to any of them upon what pretence so ever.

Thus farre the Ordinary Rules & course of Ordination, in the ordinary way.

That which concernes the Extraordinary way requisite
to bee now practised, followes.

1. In these present Exigencies, while wee cannot have any Presbyteries formed up to their whole power & work and that many Ministers are to bee Ordained for the service of the Armies, & Navy, and to many

Congregacions where there is no Minister at all, and where (by reason of the publique troubles) the people cannot either themselves inquire out, & find one that may bee a faithful Minister for them, or have any with safety sent unto them for such a solemn trial as was before mencioned in the ordinary Rules: especially when there can bee no Presbytery neere unto them, to whom they may addresse themselves, or which may come, or send to them a fitt man to bee Ordained in that Congregacion, & for that people; and yet notwithstanding, it is requisite that Ministers bee Ordained for them by soe who beeing sett apart themselves for the Work of the Ministery, have power to joyne in the setting apart of others who are found fitt and worthy. In these cases, untill by Gods blessing the aforesaid difficulties may bee in some good measure removed, Let some godly Ministers in, or about the City of London, bee designed by Publique Authority, who beeing associated may Ordaine Ministers for the Citty and Vicinity, keeping as neere to the ordinary Rules fore mencioned as possibly they may. And let this Association bee for no other intent or purpose, but only for the Work of Ordination.

2. Let the like Association bee made, by the same Authority, in great Townes & the neighbouring parishes, in the several Counties which are at the present quiet & undisturbed, to do the like for the parts adjacent.

3. Let such as are chosen, or appointed for the service of the Armies, or Navy, bee Ordained as above said by the Associated Ministers of London, or some others in the Counties.

4. Let them do the like, when any man shall duely & Lawfully bee recommended to them for the Ministry of any Congregation, who cannot enjoy liberty to have a trial of his parts & abilities, and desire the help of such Ministers so associated, for the better furnishing of them with such a person as by them shalbee judged fitt for the service of that Church and People.

Cor. Burges Prolocutor pro tempore.
Henry Robrough Scriba.
Adoniram Byfield Scriba.

APPENDIX 3

The Subdirectory for Preaching

This text is one of a number of subdirectories that comprise the Directory for Public Worship, completed in 1645. In this appendix the original manuscript emendations are not noted as they are in the Oxford edition of the assembly's minutes and papers.[1]

Of The Preaching of the Word.

Preaching of the Word, being the power of God to salvation & one of the greatest & most excellent workes belonging to the Mi[ni]stry of the gospell, should be soe performed, that the workeman neede not be ashamed, but may save himselfe & them that heare him.

It is presupposed (according to the Rules of Ordination) that the Minister of Christ is in some good measure guifted for soe weighty a service, by his skill in the originall languages & in such arts & Sciences as are hand maides to Divinity, by his knowledg in the whole body of Theology, but most of all in the holy Scriptures having his senses & hart exercised in them above the common sort of beleevers; & by the illumination of gods Spirit & other guiftes of edification, which (together with reading & studying of the Word) he ought still to seek by prayer, & an humble hart, resolving to admitt & receive any truth not yet attained, when ever God shall make it knowne unto him. All which he is to make use of & improve in his private preparations, before he deliver in publique what he hath provided.

Ordinarily, the subject of his sermon is to be some text of scripture, houlding forth some principle or head of Religion or sutable to some speciall occasion emergent, or he may goe on in some Chapter, Psalme or booke of the holy scripture as he shall se fitt.

---

1. This text is excerpted from *MPWA*, 5:100–103 (Doc. 36).

Lett the introduction to his Text be breefe, & perspicuous, drawne from the text it self, or context, or some parallel place or generall sentence of scripture.

If the text be longe, (as in Histories and parables it some times must be) lett him give a breif summe of it, if short a paraphrase therof, if neede be: in both looking dilligently to the scope of the text, & poynting at the cheife heades & grounds of doctrine which he is to rayse from it.

In analysing & dividing his text he is to regard more the Order of the matter then of wordes; & neither to burden the memorie of the hearers in the begining with too many members of division, nor to trouble their mindes with obscure termes of Art.

In Raysing doctrines from the text, his care ought to be That the matter be the truth of God, & what he speaketh he speaketh as the Oracles of God. 2ly, That it be a truth contained in or grounded on that text, that the hearers may discerne how God teacheth it from thence. 3dly, That he cheefly insist upon those doctrines which are principally intended, & make most for the edification of the hearers.

The Doctrine is to be expressed in plaine termes, or if any thing in it need explication, it is to be opened, & the consequence alsoe from the text cleared. The parallel places of scripture, confirming the doctrine, are rather to be plaine & pertinent then many, (&(if need be) somewhat insisted upon & applied to the purpose in hand). The Arguments or Reasons are to be solid, &, as much as may be, convincing. The illustrations, of what kind soe ever ought to be full of light, & such as may convey the truth in to the hearers hart with spirituall delight.

If any doubt, obvious from scripture, reason, or prejudice of the hearers, seeme to arise, it is very requisite to remove it, by reconciling the seeming differences, answering the reasons, & discovering & taking away the causes of prejudice & mistake. Otherwise it is not fitt to detaine the hearers with propounding or answering vaine or wicked cavilles, which as they are endlesse, soe the propounding & answering of them doth more hinder than promote edification.

He is not to rest in General doctrine, althoughe never soe much cleared & confirmed, but to bring it home to speciall use, by application to his hearers: which, thow[2] all be it it prove a worke of great difficulty to him selfe, requireing much prudence, zeale, & meditation; & to the naturall & corrupt man will be very unpleasant; yet he is to endeavour to performe it in such a manner, that his auditors may feele the word of God to be quicke

---

2. Read "though."

& powerfull, & a discerner of the thoughts & intents of the heart, & that, if any unbeliever or ignorant person be present, he may have the secrets of his hart made manifest, & give glory to God.

In the use of Instruction or Information in the knowledge of some truth which is a consequence from his doctrine, he may (when convenient) confirme it by a few firme arguments from the text in hand, & other places of scripture, or from the nature of that common place in divinity wherof that truth is a branch.

In Confutation of false doctrines, he is neither to rayse an old heresy from the grave, nor to mention a blasphemous opinion unnecessarily. But if the people be in dang[e]r of an error he is to confute it soundly, & endeavour to satisfy their Judgments & consciences against all objections.

In exhorting to duties he is, as he seeth cause, to teach alsoe the means that helpe to the performance of them.

In dehortation, reprehension & publique admonition (which require speciall wisdome) let him, (as there shall be cause) not only discover the nature & greatnes of the sinne, with the misery attending it, but alsoe shew the danger his hearers are in to be overtaken & surprised by it, together with the remedies & best way to avoide it.

In applyinge Comfort whether General against all temtations, or particular against some speciall troubles or terrors, he is carefully to answer such objections, as a troubled heart & afflicted spirit may suggest to the contrary.

It is alsoe some times requisite to give some notes of triall (which is very profitable, especially when performed by able & experienced ministers, with circumspection, & prudence, & the signes cleerly grounded on the holy scripture) wherby the hearers may be able to examine themselves whether they have attained those graces, & performed those duties to which he exhorteth, or be guilty of the sinne reprehended, & in danger of the Judgments threatned, or are such to whom the consolations propounded doe belonge; that accordingly they may be quickened & excited to duty, humbled for their wants & sins, affected with their danger, & strengthened with comfort, as their condition upon examination shall require.

And as he needeth not allwaies to prosecute every doctrine which lies in his text, soe is he wisely to make choyce of such uses as by his residence & conv[e]rsing with his flocke he findeth most needfull & seasonable; & amongst these such as may most draw their soules to Christ, the fountaine of light holines & comfort.

This method is not prescribed as necessary for every man or upon every text; but only recommended, as being found by experience to be very much blessed of God, & very helpefull for the peoples understandings & memories.

But the Servant of Christ, what ever his method bee, is to performe his whole ministry.

1. Painfully, not doeing the worke of the Lord negligently.

2. Plainely, that the meanest may understand, delivering the truth not in the entiseing words of mans wisdome, but in demonstration of the spirit & of power, lesse the crosse of Christ should be made of none effect: abstaineing alsoe from an unprofitable use of unknowne tongues, strange phrayses & cadences of sounds & words, sparingly citing sentences of Ecclesiasticall or other humane writers, ancient or modearne, be they never so elegant.

3. Faithfully, looking at the honor of Christ, the conversion, edification & salvation of the people, not at his owne gaine or glory: keeping noething backe which may promote those holy ends, giving to every one his owne portion & bearing indifferent respect unto all, without neglecting the meanest, or sparing the greatest in their sinns.

4. Wisely, framing all his doctrines, exhortations & specially his reproofes in such a manner as may bee most likely to prevaile, shewing all due respect to each mans person & place & not mixing his owne passion & bitterness.

5. Gravely, as becometh the word of God, shunning all such gesture, voice & expressions, as may occasion the corruptions of men to despise him & his Ministry.

6. With loving affection, that the people may see all coming from his godly zeale & hearty desyre, to doe them good: And

7thly. As taught of God, & persuaded in his owne heart that all that he teacheth is the truth of Christ, & walkeing before his flocke as an example to them in it; earnestly both in private & in Publique recomending his labours to the blessing of God, & wachfully looking to himselfe & the flocke wherof the Lord hath made him overseer. Soe shall the doctrine of truth bee preserved uncorrupt, many soules converted & built up & himselfe receive many fould comforts of his labours even in this life & afterward the Crowne of glory laide up for him in the world to come.

Where there are more ministers in a congregation then one & they of different guifts, each may more especially apply himselfe to Doctrine or Exhortation, according to the guift wherin he most excelleth, & as they shall agree between themselves.

Bibliography

Manuscripts

Bodleian Library, Oxford
MS Lat.th.g.2, Sermons of Cornelius Burges.

British Library, London
Additional MS 15669, Register book of the proceedings of the Committee for Plundered Ministers: sequestrations.

Cambridge University Library
Additional MS 3860, Sermons by Herbert Palmer.
Additional MS 3861, Sermons by Herbert Palmer.
Additional MS 6164, Sermons by Cornelius Burges.
Additional MS 6165, Sermons by Cornelius Burges.
MS Dd XIV.28 (4), Journal of the proceedings of the Westminster Assembly, by John Lightfoot (not in Lightfoot's *Works*). Transcription in C. B. Van Dixhoorn, "Reforming the Reformation: Theological Debate at the Westminster Assembly, 1643–1652" (PhD diss., University of Cambridge, 2004), vol. 2.

Edinburgh University Library
Special Collections, La.iii.109, Sermons by Robert Baillie.
Special Collections, La.iii.543, Sermons by Robert Baillie.

Folger Shakespeare Library, Washington
MS Add. 517, Sermon book by Robert Legard.
MS V.a.432, Sermon book by Robert Legard.

History of Parliament Trust, London
Transcripts of BL Harleian MS 166, Diary of Sir Simonds D'Ewes. Transcribed by A. S. Young.

National Library of Scotland, Edinburgh
Adv. MS 20.6.4, Sermons by Cornelius Burges.

Parliamentary Archives, Westminster
HL/PO/JO/10/1/238, Main Papers of the House of Lords, Aug. 5, 1647—Sept. 7, 1647.

Printed Primary Sources and Editions

The Acts of the Assemblies of the Church of Scotland, from the Year 1638, to the Year 1649, Inclusive. [Edinburgh?], 1682.

Ames, W. *The Marrow of Theology*. Translated by J. D. Eusden. Grand Rapids: Baker, 1997.

Ante-Nicene Fathers. 1886; Peabody, Mass.: Hendrickson, 1994.

Arrowsmith, J. *Tactica Sacra, sive de Milite Spirituali Pugnante, Vincente, & Triumphante Dissertatio, Tribus Libris Comprehensa*. Cambridge, 1657.

———. *Theanthropos, or, God-Man: Being an Exposition upon the First Eighteen Verses of the First Chapter of the Gospel according to John*. London, 1660.

Ashe, S. *Grey hayres crowned with grace*. London, 1655.

Baillie, R. *A Dissuasive from the Errours of the Time*. London, 1645.

———. *Letters and Journals*. Edited by D. Laing. 3 vols. Edinburgh: for Robert Ogle, 1841–42.

Baxter, R. *One Sheet for the Ministry against the Malignants of All Sorts*. London, 1657.

———. *Reliquiae Baxterianae, or, Mr. Richard Baxters Narrative of the Most Memorable Passages of His Life and Times*. London, 1696.

Bower, J., ed. *The Larger Catechism: A Critical Text and Introduction*. Grand Rapids: Reformation Heritage Books, 2010.

Bowles, O. *De Pastore Evangelico Tractatus: in quo Universyn Munus Pastorale; tam quoad Pastoris Vocationem, & Praeparationem; quam Ipsius Muneris Exercitium.* London, 1649.

Bridge, W. *A Vindication of Ordinances.* London: Peter Cole, 1653.

———. *The Works of William Bridge.* 1845; Morgan, Pa.: Soli Deo Gloria, 1989.

Bullinger, H. *The Decades of Henry Bullinger.* Cambridge: Cambridge University Press, 1849–52; reprint, New York: Johnson Reprint, 1968.

Burges, C. *No Sacrilege nor Sin to Alienate or Purchase Cathedral Lands.* London, 1660.

———. *Two Sermons Preached to the Honorable House of Commons Assembled in Parliament at Their Publique Fast.* London, 1641.

Burgess, A. *CXLV Expository Sermons upon the Whole 17th Chapter of the Gospel according to John.* London, 1656.

———. *An Expository Comment, Doctrinal Controversal and Practical upon the Whole First Chapter of the Second Epistle of St Paul to the Corinthians.* London, 1661.

———. *The Scripture Directory, for Church Officers and People.* London, 1659.

———. *Spiritual Refining, or, a Treatise of Grace and Assurance Part I.* London, 1658.

———. *A Treatise of Original Sin.* London, 1658.

———. *Vindiciae Legis: or, a Vindication of the Morall Law and the Covenants.* London, 1647.

Burroughs, J. *An Exposition of the Prophesie of Hosea begun in Divers Lectures upon the First Three Chapters.* London, 1652.

———. *Gospel-Fear: or, the Heart Trembling at the Word of God.* London, 1674.

———. *Gospel-Reconciliation: Or, Christ's Trumpet of Peace to the World.* London, 1657.

———. *Gospel-Remission, or, a Treatise Shewing, That True Blessedness Consists in Pardon of Sin.* London, 1674.

———. *Gospel-Worship: Or, the Right Manner of Sanctifying the Name of God in Generall.* London, 1648.

———. *The Rare Jewel of Christian Contentment.* London, 1648.

———. *The Saints' Happiness.* James Nichols, 1867.

Calamy, E. *The Godly Mans Ark, or, City of Refuge, in the Day of His Distresse.* London, 1657.

———. *Gods Free Mercy to England Presented as a Pretious, and Powerful Motive to Humiliation.* London, 1642.

Calvin, J. *Calvin's Commentaries: The Epistle of Paul the Apostle to the Romans and to the Thessalonians.* Translated by R. Mackenzie. Edited by D. W. Torrance and T. F. Torrance. Grand Rapids: Eerdmans, 1991.

———. *Calvin's Commentaries: A Harmony of the Gospels, Matthew, Mark and Luke.* Translated by T. H. L. Parker. Edited by D. W. Torrance and T. F. Torrance. Grand Rapids: Eerdmans, 1972.

———. *Commentary on the Book of the Prophet Isaiah.* Trans. W. Pringle. Grand Rapids: Baker, 1993.

———. *Institutes of the Christian Religion.* Edited by J. T. McNeill. Translated by F. L. Battles. Philadelphia: The Westminster Press, 1960.

Calvin, J., and J. Sadoleto. *A Reformation Debate.* Edited by J. C. Olin. Grand Rapids: Baker, 1976.

Case, T. *Correcion, Instruction: or, a Treatise of Afflictions.* London, 1652.

Cheynell, F. *Divine Trinunity of the Father, Son, and Holy Spirit.* London, 1650.

Church of England. *Constitutions and Canons Ecclesiastical.* London, 1604.

———. *The Forme and Manner of Making and Consecrating Bishops, Priestes, and Deacons.* London, 1627.

Coleman, T. *Male Dicis Maledicis. Or a Brief Reply to Nihil Respondens.* London, 1646.

Corbet, E. *Gods Providence, a Sermon Preached Before the Honourable House of Commons at Their Late Solemne Fast.* London, 1642.

Dell, W. *The Stumbling-stone, or, a Discourse Touching That Offence Which the World and Worldly Church Do Take against 1. Christ Himself. 2. His True Word. 3. His True Worship. 4. His True Church. 5. His True Government. 6. His True Ministry.* London, 1653.

Delmé, P. *The Method of Good Preaching.* London, 1701.

BIBLIOGRAPHY

A Directory for the Publique Worship of God, throughout the Three Kingdoms of England, Scotland, and Ireland. London, 1644.

Featley, D. *Ancilla Pietatis: or, the Hand-Maid to Private Devotion Presenting a Manuell to Furnish Her with Necessary Principles of Faith.* London, 1626.

———. *Clavis Mystica: A Key Opening Divers Difficult and Mysterious Texts of Holy Scripture.* London, 1636.

———. *A Parallel: Of New-Old Pelgiarminian Error.* London, 1626.

———. *Sacra Nemesis, the Levites Scourge, or, Mercurius Britan.* Oxford, 1644.

———. *A Second Parallel together with a Writ of Error Sued against the Appealer.* London, 1626.

Firth, C. H., and R. S. Rait, eds. *Acts and Ordinances of the Interregnum, 1642–1660.* London: His Majesty's Stationery Office, 1911.

Ford, T. *Autokatakritos, or, the Sinner Condemned of Himself.* London, 1668.

Gataker, T. *Certaine Sermons, First Preached, and Afterwards Published.* London, 1637.

———. *A Just Defence of Certain Passages in a Former Treatise concerning the Nature and Use of Lots.* London, 1626.

———. *Marriage Duties Briefely Couched Together.* London, 1620.

———. *A Sparke toward the Kindling of Sorrow for Sion.* London, 1621.

———. *Two Funeral Sermons Much of One and the Same Subject; to Wit, the Benefit of Death.* London, 1620.

Gillespie, G. *A Treatise of Miscellany Questions.* Edinburgh, 1649.

Glanville, J. *Seasonable Reflections and Discourses in Order to the Conviction & Cure of the Scoffing, & Infidelity of a Degenerate Age.* London, 1676.

Goodwin, T. *The Works of Thomas Goodwin.* 12 vols. Eureka, Calif.: Tanski Publications, 1996.

Gouge, W. *An Exposition on the Whole Fifth Chapter of S. Johns Gospell.* London, 1631.

———. *A Guide to Goe to God.* London, 1636.

———. *A Learned and Very Useful Commentary on the Whole Epistle to the Hebrewes.* London, 1655.

———. *The Sabbaths Sanctification.* London, 1641.

———. *The Workes of William Gouge: In Two Volumes.* London, 1627.

Greenhill, W. *An Exposition Continued upon the Sixt, Seventh, Eighth, Ninth, Tenth, Eleventh, Twelfth, and Thirteenth Chapters of the Prophet Ezekiel.* London, 1649.

———. *An Exposition of the Five First Chapters of the Prophet Ezekiel.* London, 1645.

Harris, R. *The Way to True Happiness.* London, 1653.

Henderson, A. *The Government and Order of the Church of Scotland.* [Edinburgh], 1641.

———. *Sermons, Prayers, and Pulpit Addresses.* Edited by C. M. McMahon and T. B. McMahon (1867; Coconut Creek, Fla.: Puritan Publications, 2012.

Henry, M. *The Complete Works of the Rev. Matthew Henry.* Edinburgh: Fullerton & Co., 1848.

Herle, C. *Contemplations and Devotions on the Severall Passages of Our Blessed Saviour's Death.* London, 1631.

It Is This Day Ordered by the Lords and Commons in Parliament Assembled, That the Meeting of the Assembly of Divines, Together with Some Members of Both Houses of Parliament, Shall Be on Saterday the First of July 1643. London, 1643.

Jackson, J. *The Key of Knowledge.* London, 1640.

Journal of the House of Commons. London: His Majesty's Stationery Office, 1802.

Lightfoot, J. *The Whole Works of the Rev. John Lightfoot.* Edited by J. R. Pitman. 13 vols. London: J. F. Dove, 1823–25.

———. *The Works of the Reverend and Learned John Lightfoot.* 2 vols. London, 1684.

Marshall, S. *A Defence of Infant-Baptism.* London, 1646.

———. *The Power of the Civil Magistrate.* London, 1657.

———. *The Works of Mr Stephen Marshall, Late Minister of the Gospel at Finching-Field in Essex.* London, 1661.

Matthews, A. G., ed. *Calamy Revised: Being a Revision of Edmund Calamy's Account of the Ministers and Others Ejected and Silenced, 1600–1662*. Oxford: Oxford University Press, 1934.

———. *Walker Revised: Being a Revision of John Walker's "Sufferings of the Clergy during the Grand Rebellion, 1642–1660."* Oxford: Oxford University Press, 1948.

The Moderate Publisher of Every Daies Intelligence. Num. 90. (Friday March 18 to Friday March 25, 1652). London, 1652.

Newcomen, M. *Ultimum Vale, or, The Last Farewell of a Minister of the Gospel to a Beloved People*. London, 1663.

Nicene and Post-Nicene Fathers. Edited by Philip Schaff. 14 vols. 1889; Peabody, Mass.: Hendrickson, 1999.

Perkins, W. *The Art of Prophesying*. Edinburgh: Banner of Truth, 1996.

———. *The Workes of That Famous and Worthy Minister of Christ in the University of Cambridge, Mr. William Perkins*. 3 vols. Cambridge, 1617–18.

Price, W. *Ars Concionandi Regulis Perspicuis, & Exemplis Palmariis, & Multifariis, Concinnata & Instructa*. Amsterdam, 1656.

Reynolds, E. *Eugenia's Teares for Great Brittaynes Distractions*. London, 1642.

———. *An Explication of the Hundreth and Tenth Psalme*. London, 1632.

———. *The Pastoral Office*. London, 1663.

———. *Preaching of Christ*. London, 1662.

———. *A Sermon Preached Before the King*. London, 1669.

Rutherford, S. *The Divine Right of Church Government*. London, [1646].

———. *The Due Right of Presbyteries*. London, 1644.

———. *A Free Disputation against Pretended Liberty of Conscience*. London, 1649.

———. *Quaint Sermons of Samuel Rutherford Hitherto Unpublished*. London: Hodder and Stoughton, 1885.

Sedgwick, O. *Christ's Counsell to His Languishing Church of Sardis*. London, 1640.

———. *The Fountain Opened, and the Water of Life Flowing Forth*. London, 1657.

———. *Shepherd of Israel, or, God's Pastoral Care over His People*. London, 1658.

A Solemn League and Covenant, for Reformation, and Defence of Religion. London, 1643.

S[winnock], G. *The Life and Death of Mr. Tho. Wilson, Minister of Maidstone*. [London], 1672.

Thorowgood, T. *Digitus Dei: New Discoveryes; With Sure Arguments to Prove That the Jews (a Nation) or People Lost in the World for the Space of Near 200 Years, Inhabite Now in America*. London, 1652.

Tuckney, A. *Death Disarmed: And the Grave Swallowed Up in Victory*. London, 1654.

———. *Prælectiones Theologicae, nec non Determinationes Quaestionum Variarum Insignium in Scholis Academicis Cantabrigiensibus Habitae*. Amsterdam, 1679.

Twisse, W. *Of the Morality of the Fourth Commandement*. London, 1641.

Ussher, J. *The Whole Works of the Most Rev. James Ussher*. Edited by C. R. Elrington. 17 vols. Dublin: Hodges Smith, and Co., 1864.

Van Dixhoorn, C. B., ed. *The Minutes and Papers of the Westminster Assembly, 1643–1652*. 5 vols. Oxford: Oxford University Press, 2012.

Vines, R. *Gods Drawing and Mans Coming to Christ*. London, 1662.

Walker, G. *The Doctrine of the Sabbath*. Amsterdam, 1638.

White, J. *The First Century of Scandalous, Malignant Priests, Made and Admitted into Benefices by the Prelates*. London, 1643.

Wilson, T. *Davids Zeale for Zion*. London, 1641.

Secondary Sources

Armstrong, R., and T. O'hAnnrachain, eds. *Alternative Establishments in Early Modern Britain and Ireland: Catholic and Protestant*. Manchester: Manchester University Press, 2013.

Barth, K. *The Doctrine of the Word of God*. Vol. 1, *Church Dogmatics*. Translated by G. W. Bromiley. Edited by G. W. Bromiley and T. F. Torrance. Edinburgh: T&T Clark, 2004.

Carruthers, S. W. *The Everyday Work of the Westminster Assembly*. Philadelphia: Presbyterian Historical Society, 1943.

Carson, J. L., and D. W. Hall, eds. *To Glorify and Enjoy God: A Commemoration of the Westminster Assembly*. Edinburgh: Banner of Truth, 1994.

Casselli, S. *Divine Rule Maintained: Anthony Burgess, Covenant Theology, and the Place of Law in Reformed Scholasticism*. Grand Rapids: Reformation Heritage Books, 2016.

Cho, Y. *Anthony Tuckney (1599–1670): Theologian of the Westminster Assembly*. Grand Rapids: Reformation Heritage Books, forthcoming.

Cliffe, J. T. *The Puritan Gentry: The Great Puritan Families of Early Stuart England*. London: Routledge, 1984.

Coffey, J. *Politics, Religion and the British Revolutions: The Mind of Samuel Rutherford*. Cambridge: Cambridge University Press, 1997.

Coffey, J., and P. C. H. Lim, eds. *The Cambridge Companion to Puritanism*. Cambridge: Cambridge University Press, 2008.

Collinson, P. *Archbishop Grindal, 1519–1583*. Berkeley: University of California Press, 1979.

———. *The Elizabethan Puritan Movement*. 1967; Oxford: Clarendon, 1990.

———. "Grindal, Edmund (1516x20–1583)," *Oxford Dictionary of National Biography*. Oxford: Oxford University Press, 2004.

Como, D. R. *Blown by the Spirit: Puritanism and the Emergence of an Antinomian Underground in Pre-Civil-War England*. Stanford: Stanford University Press, 2004.

Cust, R. *Charles I: A Political Life*. Harlow: Pearson, 2005.

Davies, H. *Worship and Theology in England: From Andrewes to Baxter and Fox, 1603–1690*. Princeton: Princeton University Press, 1975.

———. *The Worship of the English Puritans*. Morgan, Pa.: Soli Deo Gloria, 1997.

Davies, J. *The Caroline Captivity of the Church: Charles I and the Remoulding of Anglicanism 1625–1641.* Oxford: Clarendon, 1992.

Davies, M., A. Dunan-Page, and J. Halcomb, eds. *Church Life: Pastors, Congregations, and the Experience of Dissent in Seventeenth-Century England.* Oxford: Oxford University Press, forthcoming.

Dudley, M., ed. *Like a Two-Edged Sword: The Word of God in Liturgy and History.* Norwich: Canterbury Press, 1995.

Eales, J. "Wilson, Thomas (c. 1601–1653)." In *Oxford Dictionary of National Biography.* Oxford: Oxford University Press, 2004.

Ferrell, L., and P. McCulloch, eds. *The English Sermon Revised: Religion, Literature and History 1600–1750.* Manchester: Manchester University Press, 2000.

Fesko, J. V. *The Theology of the Westminster Standards: Historical Context and Theological Insights.* Wheaton, Ill.: Crossway, 2014.

Finlayson, M. G. *Historians, Puritanism, and the English Revolution: The Religious Factor in English Politics before and after the Interregnum.* Toronto: University of Toronto Press, 1983.

Ford, A. *James Ussher: Theology, History, and Politics in Early-Modern Ireland and England.* Oxford: Oxford University Press, 2007.

Gamble, W. G. "'If Christ Fulfilled the Law, We Are Not Bound': The Westminster Assembly against English Antinomian Soteriology, 1643–1647." PhD diss., University of Edinburgh, 2014.

Guy, J., and J. S. Morrill. *The Tudors and Stuarts.* Oxford: Oxford University Press, 1992.

Halcomb, J. A. "A Social History of Congregational Religious Practice during the Puritan Revolution." PhD thesis, University of Cambridge, 2009.

Hamilton, I. *The Erosion of Calvinist Orthodoxy: Seceders and Subscription in Scottish Presbyterianism.* Edinburgh: Rutherford House, 1990.

Hill, C. *The English Bible and the Seventeenth-Century Revolution.* London: Penguin, 1995.

Hillerbrand, H., ed. *Oxford Encyclopedia of the Reformation.* Oxford: Oxford University Press, 1996.

Hughes, A. *Gangraena and the Struggle for the English Revolution.* Oxford: Oxford University Press, 2004.

Hunt, A. *The Art of Hearing: English Preachers and Their Audiences, 1590–1640*. Cambridge: Cambridge University Press, 2010.

———. "The Lord's Supper in Early Modern England." *Past and Present* 161 (1998): 39–83.

Kirby, E. W. "Sermons Before the Commons, 1640–42." *American Historical Review* 44, no. 3 (1939): 528–48.

Lake, P. *The Boxmaker's Revenge: 'Orthodoxy', 'Heterodoxy' and the Politics of the Parish in Early Stuart London*. Stanford: Stanford University Press, 2001.

———. *Moderate Puritans and the Elizabethan Church*. Cambridge: Cambridge University Press, 2004.

Letham, R. *The Westminster Assembly: Reading Its Theology in Historical Context*. Phillipsburg, N.J.: Presbyterian and Reformed, 2009.

Lim, P. C. H. *Mystery Unveiled: The Crisis of the Trinity in Early Modern England*. Oxford: Oxford University Press, 2012.

Lindley, K. *Popular Politics and Religion in Civil War London*. Aldershot: Scolar Press, 1997.

Marchant, R. A. *The Church under the Law: Justice, Administration and Discipline in the Diocese of York, 1560–1640*. Cambridge: Cambridge University Press, 1969.

Merritt, J. F. *Westminster 1640-60: A Royal City in a Time of Revolution*. Manchester: Manchester University Press, 2013.

Milton, A., ed. *The Oxford History of Anglicanism*, vol. 1, *Reformation and Identity c.1520–1662*. Oxford: Oxford University Press, 2017.

Mitchell, A. F. *The Westminster Assembly: Its History and Standards*. London: James Nisbet, 1883.

Morrill, J. S. *The Nature of the English Revolution*. London: Longman, 1993.

———. *Revolt in the Provinces: The People of England and the Tragedies of War, 1630–1648*. London: Longman, 1999.

Morrissey, M. "Scripture, Style and Persuasion in Seventeenth-Century English Theories of Preaching." *Journal of Ecclesiastical History* 53, no. 4 (2002): 686–90.

Muller, R. *Post-Reformation Reformed Dogmatics*. 4 vols. Grand Rapids: Baker, 2003.

Old, H. O. *The Reading and Preaching of the Scriptures in the Worship of the Christian Church.* 7 vols. Grand Rapids: Eerdmans, 1998–2010.

Owen, D. M. *The Records of the Established Church in England Excluding Parochial Records.* London: British Records Association, 1970.

Packer, J. I. *A Quest for Godliness: The Puritan Vision of the Christian Life.* Wheaton, Ill.: Crossway, 1990.

Parker, T. H. L. *Calvin's Preaching.* Louisville: Westminster John Knox Press, 1992.

Paul, R. S. *The Assembly of the Lord: Politics and Religion in the Westminster Assembly and the 'Grand Debate.'* Edinburgh: T&T Clark, 1985.

Pederson, R. *Unity in Diversity: English Puritans and the Puritan Reformation, 1603–1689.* Leiden: Brill, 2014.

Penny, R. L., ed. *The Hope Fulfilled: Essays in Honor of O. Palmer Robertson.* Phillipsburg, N.J.: Presbyterian and Reformed, 2008.

Pipa, J. A. "William Perkins and the Development of Puritan Preaching." PhD diss., Westminster Theological Seminary, 1985.

Powell, H. *The Crisis of British Protestantism: Church Power in the Puritan Revolution, 1638–44.* Manchester: Manchester University Press, 2015.

Powell, H., and E. Vernon, eds. *The Keys of the Kingdom of Heaven: Church Polity in the English Speaking World, c. 1636–1689.* Manchester: Manchester University Press, forthcoming.

Raymond, J., ed. *Cheap Print in Britain and Ireland to 1660.* Oxford: Oxford University Press, 2011.

Richards, T. *A History of the Puritan Movement in Wales from the Inception of the Church at Llanfaches in 1639 to the Expiry of the Propagation Act in 1653.* London: National Eisteddfod Association, 1920.

Richardson, R. C. *Puritanism in North-West England: A Regional Study of the Diocese of Chester to 1642.* Manchester: Manchester University Press, 1972.

Seaver, P. *The Puritan Lectureships: The Politics of Religious Dissent, 1560–1662.* Stanford: Stanford University Press, 1970.

Shapiro, F. R., ed. *The Yale Book of Quotations.* New Haven: Yale University Press, 2006.

Shaw, W. A. *A History of the English Church during the Civil Wars and under the Commonwealth, 1640–1660.* 2 vols. London: Longman, Green, 1900.

Spurr, J. *English Puritanism, 1603–1689.* New York: Palgrave Macmillan, 1998.

Strange, A. D. "Comments on the Centrality of Preaching in the Westminster Standards." *Mid America Journal of Theology* 10 (1999): 185–238.

Surman, C. E., ed. *The Register-Booke of the Fourth Classis in the Province of London, 1646–1659.* London: Dr. Williams's Trust, 1953.

Todd, M. *Christian Humanism and the Puritan Social Order.* Cambridge: Cambridge University Press, 1987.

Trevor-Roper, H. R. *Religion and Reformation and Social Change.* London: Macmillan, 1967.

Van Dixhoorn, C. B. *Confessing the Faith: A Reader's Guide to the Westminster Confession of Faith.* Edinburgh: Banner of Truth, 2014.

———. "Presbyterian Ecclesiologies at the Westminster Assembly." In *The Keys of the Kingdom of Heaven: Church Polity in the English Speaking World, c.1636–1689.* Edited by H. Powell and E. Vernon. Manchester: Manchester University Press, forthcoming.

———. "Reforming the Reformation: Theological Debate at the Westminster Assembly, 1643–1652." 7 vols. PhD diss., University of Cambridge, 2004.

———. "Scottish Influence on the Westminster Assembly: A Study of the Synod's Summoning Ordinance and the Solemn League and Covenant," *The Records of the Scottish Church History Society* 37 (2007): 55–88.

Venema, C. P. "The Doctrine of Preaching in the Reformed Confessions." *Mid-America Journal of Theology* 10 (1999): 135–83.

Webster, T. *Godly Clergy in Early Stuart England: The Caroline Puritan Movement, c. 1620–1643.* Cambridge: Cambridge University Press, 1997.

Wilson, J. F. *Pulpit in Parliament: Puritanism during the English Civil Wars: 1640–1648.* Princeton: Princeton University Press, 1969.

Index

Abbot, George, 26
Ainsworth, Henry, 160
Ames, William, 26
Anabaptists, 34, 36, 54
antinomians, 34–36, 148, 154
archdeacon, 44–48
Arminian theology, 33, 152
Arrowsmith, John, 91, 93, 109, 112, 117, 133, 149–50, 165–66
Ashe, Simeon, 138
atonement, 146, 158
Augustine of Hippo, 112, 165, 180

Baillie, Robert, 34, 92, 98n, 169
Bancroft, Richard, 25–26
baptism, 19, 54, 114–15
Barth, Karl, 123–24
Baxter, Richard, 168–69
benefices, 24–25, 44, 46–47, 84
bible studies, 140–41, 180
bishops, 22, 37, 43–44, 46–49, 74
Bolton, Samuel, 139
Book of Articles of Religion, 44
Book of Common Prayer, 44
Bowles, Oliver, 106, 108, 123, 147
Bradshaw, William, 26
Bridge, William, 64, 69
Bridgeman, John, 53
Brown, John, 31
Bullinger, Heinrich, 19n
Bunyan, John, 176–77
Burges, Cornelius, 30, 34, 66–67, 76, 91, 149, 169
Burgess, Anthony, 105, 110–11, 116–18, 126, 131, 143–46, 149, 151–55, 158, 163–67

Burroughs, Jeremiah, 98–99, 119, 122–27, 129, 148–49, 165, 169
Byfield, Nicholas, 26

Calamy, Edmund, 66n, 70, 112, 131–32, 171
calling, 81, 85, 109, 117
Calvin, John, 18–22, 112, 133, 160, 180
Cambridge college, 45, 163, 177
Cambridge fellowship, 27, 39, 58, 120
Carruthers, S. W., 10
Cartwright, Thomas, 18
Case, Thomas, 158
Casselli, Stephen, 153
cathedral officers, 45–46, 85
Cawdrey, Daniel, 60
Charles I (King), 1, 15, 26, 29, 32–33, 36
Charles II (King), 177
Chester Cathedral, 50
Cheynell, Francis, 15
Christian liberty, 91, 97–98
Christian obedience, 152
Christology, 154, 157–58
church
    governing of, 36–38, 67–70, 75–76
    literacy in, 134
    officers in, 6, 37, 63, 69, 118, 149
    and participation in ordination, 85–87
    patronage of, 24–25
    and practice of discipline, 6, 37–38
Church of England
    induction and institution of clergy, 46–47, 85
    and nomination of ministers, 79
    ordination in, 44–45, 78–79, 173–75
    reforming of, 4–5, 29, 33–35, 101, 176–77

Church of England (*continued*)
　seminary training in, 120
　as the true church, 54–55
Church of Scotland, 74, 89, 91, 175, 177.
　See also Scottish preachers
civil wars (English), 32–35, 38, 49, 61,
　100, 134, 172, 176–77
clergymen. *See* ministers
Coffey, John, 11–12
Coleman, Thomas, 54, 70, 118, 130
Collinson, Patrick, 15, 52
Committee for Plundered Ministers, 101n,
　106–8
community groups, 180
Como, David, 34–36
congregationalists, 13n, 50n, 54–55,
　71, 98n, 118–19, 127, 147n, 173,
　178–79
conversions, 80, 126, 130, 147
covenant of grace, 7
curates, 24–26, 46, 48n

Davenport, William, 32
Davies, Horton, 29
de la Marche, Jean, 66n, 74
deacons, 44–46, 66, 70–75
Dell, William, 163–64
Delmé, Philippé, 147, 152
Directory for Ordination, 77–87, 93, 100,
　112–13, 119
Directory for Public Worship
　subdirectory for preaching, 7–8, 27,
　66n, 89–101, 113, 174
　subdirectory for sanctification of the
　Lord's day, 92–93

Edward VI (King), 22, 33
Edwards, Thomas, 35
Elizabeth (Queen), 18, 22–28, 33, 35, 127
English Revival, 179
episcopacy, 36, 100
episcopalians, 13n, 80, 114, 168
Erastianism, 37
Erastians, 70, 118–19
Evangelical Revival, 80
excommunication, 130

faith, 7, 22, 64, 85, 166
Featley, Daniel, 109, 116, 129, 135–37,
　139–40, 158–59

federal theology, 160
fees, 84–85
Field, John, 18
Finney, Charles, 179
First Great Awakening, 80, 179
Ford, Thomas, 145
French Reformed ministers, 74

Gataker, Thomas, 14, 63–65, 67, 70, 75,
　97, 120, 133, 139, 169
Gibbs, George, 60
Gillespie, George, 66n, 114–15, 117
Godfrey, Robert, 5n, 98n
Goodman, Godfrey, 53
Goodwin, Thomas, 65–66, 72, 74, 108,
　127, 131, 135, 138, 149, 166–67,
　169
Gouge, William, 13, 66n 70, 73, 93,
　97, 116, 121–22, 131, 133, 140,
　148–49, 167n
　grace, 81, 137, 139, 148, 152, 154. *See
　also* covenant of grace; preaching, as
　means of grace
Great Commission, 114, 122–23, 148–49
Great Ejection, 43
Greenhill, William, 119, 127–28, 132, 143
Grindal, Edmund, 22–23, 25, 127

Hackel, Heidi Brayman, 134
Halcomb, Joel, 10, 50n, 101
Hall, Samuel, 60
Harris, Robert, 109
healing, 131n
Heidelberg Catechism, 6n, 98n
Henderson, Alexander, 66n, 113, 141, 168
Henry, Matthew, 41
Henry, Philip, 41
heresy, 24, 95
Herle, Charles, 64, 66n, 70, 120, 139,
　151, 155–58, 160
Heyrick, Richard, 29, 66, 70
Hill, Thomas, 70
Holy Spirit, 8, 19, 21, 110–11, 126–28,
　132–33, 164–67
House of Commons, 3–4, 10, 30, 36–37,
　49n, 76, 101n, 107, 174
House of Lords, 3–4, 44, 60, 107
Hoyle, Joshua, 64, 66, 70, 113, 132
Huguenots, 15
Hunt, Arnold, xvii, 169

INDEX 213

Inns of the Court, 58
Ireland, 58, 63, 89, 177

Jackson, John, 129–30
James I (King), 13, 26, 33, 36
Jerusalem Chamber, xv, 63, 110
Jewel, John, 28
John Chrysostom, 161
Jones, Inga, 10

Kirby, E. W., 90n
Kirk, Ralph, 26

language (foreign)
    requirements for ministers, 56, 73, 81, 83, 93, 108–10, 120, 193
    use in sermons, 92, 111–14, 158, 165
Laud, William, 4, 26, 28–30, 71, 172, 177
Laudians, 59, 64, 69
Launce, William, 60
law/gospel hermeneutic, 152–54
lay preachers, 87, 118, 172–73
laying of hands, 75–76, 86, 115
Legard, Robert, 116
letters of reference, 51–52
Ley, John, 50, 73, 120
Lightfoot, John, 53, 57n, 66n, 70, 76, 90, 92, 108
Lim, Paul, 11–12
Lindley, Keith, 59–61
livings, 24–25, 58. *See also* benefices
Long Parliament, 30, 36, 171, 176
Lord's Supper, 7, 19, 28, 54, 129–30
Lutherans, 152, 154, 180

Marian exiles, 22
Marprelate, Martin, 23
Marshall, Stephen, 17, 29–30, 41, 53–54, 108, 130, 149
ministers
    age requirement of, 119–20
    character of, 93–97, 174
    as divine ambassadors, 114–19, 173
    duties of, 6, 8, 66–70
    education of, 22, 35, 100–101, 108–14, 176–77
    godliness of, 51–52, 81, 94, 105–8
    income of, 24–26, 47–48
    office of, 67–70. *See also* church, officers in
    orthodoxy of, 86–87
    qualifications of, 44–45, 79–80
    removal of, 4–5, 42–43, 100, 175–77. *See also* scandalous ministers
    reputation of, 55–56
    residency of, 24, 47
    scholarship of, 55–56, 79, 81, 93–94
    See also lay preachers; ordination; pastoral care
Mitchell, Alexander, 90
Moody, D. L., 179
moral equity, 69
moral law, 148
Morrill, John, 32, 34
Morrissey, Mary, 139, 163
Mosaic law, 148
Muller, Richard, 145, 150, 160

Newcomen, Matthew, 130–31
Norris, Robert, 9, 90n
Nye, Philip, 54–55, 65

Old, Hughes Oliphant, xvii
ordination, 44–50, 73–87, 114–19, 173–74
Oxford college, 45, 177
Oxford fellowship, 39, 120

Packer, J. I., 97
Palmer, Herbert, 65, 66n, 70, 76, 91, 112–13, 120, 169, 180
Parker, Matthew, 22
Parker, T. H. L., 19
Parliament (English)
    ejection and replacement of ministers, 4–5, 49–50, 175–77
    ministers favored by, 59–61
    and summoning of Westminster Assembly, 3–4, 35–36
    and trials of clergymen, 5
    See also House of Commons; House of Lords; Long Parliament
Parliament (Scottish), 63
pastoral care, 56, 161
patrons, 24–25, 46–48, 57, 84–85
Pentecost, 110
Perkins, William, 26–28, 97, 144–45, 151
Perne, Andrew, 60
pluralism, 24–25, 53–54
poor, 70
prayer, 7–8, 53, 85, 90, 130, 148

prayer meetings, 140–41
preaching
    of another's sermons, 18, 64, 134
    and catechisms, 70–72, 98
    as Christ-centered, 6, 28, 145–61
    as distinguished from reading Word, 63–70, 130–33
    efficacy of, 21–22, 29, 132.
    of extemporary sermons, 168–69
    fallibility of, 127–28
    as gift of Christ, 9, 111, 131
    and hardening hearts, 20
    as hope for spiritually destitute, 6–7
    lack of, 17–22
    and listening to/reading sermons at home, 134–40, 179–80
    as means of grace, 8–9, 21–22, 29, 69, 125–31, 173–74, 180
    obtaining license to, 48–49
    of prefabricated homilies, 22
    in private setting, 140–41
    and salvation, 23–24, 26, 30, 126–27, 132
    structure of, 92, 97–101, 151–55
    as team teaching, 22. *See also* prophesying
    of text-based sermons, 98–99, 155–61
    use of citations in, 112–13
    using manuscripts or notes, 168–69
    of whole Word of God, 9, 19, 23, 143–44
    without ministerial call, 74–75. *See also* lay preachers
    as Word of God, 121–25
    See also puritans, preaching theology of
presbyterianism, 23–24, 36
presbyterians, 13n, 54, 71, 81, 114, 118–19, 147n, 173, 178–79
presbyteries, 49, 50n, 77–87
Price, William, 64, 75, 97n
Prideaux, John, 53
printing press, 32–33
probation periods, 56–57, 70
prophesying, 22–23, 100, 176
propositional sermons, 98–99
puritanism, 18, 23, 32, 35, 80, 151, 174
puritans
    and bare reading of Word, 65
    conversion stories of, 80
    definitions of, 11–16

    and desire for church reform, 22, 32, 36, 38, 43, 87, 100, 107, 173–75, 177, 179–80
    jailing and exile of, 23–24
    network of, 51–52
    preaching theology of, 27–28, 97, 98n, 124, 138–39, 147, 161, 168, 171–74

Rathbone, William, 81
Rayner, William, 70, 74, 132
rectors, 24, 46, 58
Reformation, 34, 69
Reformed churches, 172, 175
Reformed theology, 146, 164
Reformers, 18–19, 29, 35–36, 180
Reynolds, Edward, 34, 126, 147, 161, 167n, 174
rhetoric, 94, 139
Rigney, James, 138
Roborough, Henry, 34
Rogers, John, 138
Roman Catholicism, 33–34, 65, 69
ruling elders, 37
Rutherford, Samuel, 66n, 90–91, 113, 124, 132–33, 140–41, 164

Sabbatarians, 13
sacraments, 6–7, 24, 28–30, 53–54, 74, 114, 129–30, 135, 148
Saint Margaret's Church, 41
salvation, 7, 93, 116, 147, 165. *See also* preaching, and salvation
scandalous ministers, 4–5, 17, 39, 42–43, 58n, 60, 101n, 105, 122, 175–76
Scottish General Assembly, 91n, 141
Scottish preachers, 26
Scripture
    continuities between Old and New testaments, 68–69
    doctrine of, 16
    inspiration and authority of, 126n
    private reading of, 130–33
    proper interpretation of, 9
    public reading of, 63–70, 90n, 92, 130–33
    sovereignty of, 19
    sufficiency of, 8, 70
    textual exegesis of, 155–61
    theological exegesis of, 151–55
Seaman, Lazarus, 66n, 69, 74

INDEX

Seaver, Paul, 28, 30
Second Great Awakening, 179
Sedgwick, Obadiah, 109, 134–35, 143, 146–47, 155
Selden, John, 70
seminaries, 52, 120, 180
sexton, 66
Shaw, William, 10
simony, 47
Simpson, Sidrach, 163–64
sin, 7, 56, 64, 96, 99, 136, 141
Smith, Peter, 66n, 70, 108
Smith, Samuel, 59
Solemn League and Covenant, 60, 63, 75, 79–80, 91, 176
Strange, A. D., 90n
suffering, 56
Synod of Dort, 75

Temple, Thomas, 50, 63–64, 67, 69, 76, 132
testimonials, 79–81. *See also* letters of reference
Thirty-nine Articles, 63, 75, 86
Thorowgood, Thomas, 147
tongues, 111
Trevor-Roper, H. R., 90n
Tuckney, Anthony, 97, 116, 126
Twisse, William, 32, 38, 66n

Ussher, James, 26, 28

Valentine, Henry, 26
Valentine, Thomas, 138
Venema, C. P., 90n

vicars, 24, 46, 58
Vines, Richard, 70, 152n

Wales, 58, 101
Walker, George, 110
Wallington, Nehemiah, 17
Watts, Thomas, 107–8
Webster, Tom, 12, 52
Westminster Assembly
    calling of, 32–35, 38, 41–42
    and debates on biblical exposition, 98–99
    and debates on ministerial training, 110–12, 118–19
    demographic and theological diversity of, 16
    and importance of preaching, 6–9, 69–70, 93, 165–68
    and pulpit reform, xv, 171–75
Westminster Confession of Faith, 27, 86
Westminster Larger Catechism, 5–9, 69, 90n, 98n, 132
Whitaker, Jeremiah, 90, 120, 138
White, John, 3–6
Whitgift, John, 23–25, 177
Wilkenson, Henry Sr., 66n
Williams, John, 53
Wilson, John, 4–5, 97
Wilson, Thomas, 59, 64–68, 70, 74, 113, 132, 149
Woodcock, Francis, 66n

Young, Thomas, 66n, 70